Handbook of European History

Since 1500

HANDBOOK

OF EUROPEAN HISTORY

SINCE 1500

by Sidney A. Burrell

Barnard College, Columbia University

John Wiley & Sons, Inc., New York · London · Sydney

Portions of this book are revised and adapted from
ELEMENTS OF MODERN EUROPEAN HISTORY: MAIN STRANDS OF
DEVELOPMENT SINCE 1500, © 1959 by Howard Chandler,
Publisher.

Library of Congress Catalog Card Number: 65-17856
PRINTED IN UNITED STATES OF AMERICA

PREFACE

**This Preface contains some useful study suggestions.
Be sure to read it before you go on with the book!**

The intention of this book is to give you more than just an outline of historical facts. It also gives you a summary of the major movements and ideas in European civilization into which the facts can be fitted. By giving you this summary and framework it will help you to answer essay questions as well as factual and objective questions in examinations.

To make it easier for you to study, the chapters are divided into sections which make it possible for you to approach the understanding of European civilization one step at a time. If you will proceed with your reading in the following way, you should find it fairly easy to absorb the subject matter as you go along.

First: Read Chapter 1; it gives you the main developments or themes stressed in this book. And also read Chapter 12; it is a summation of what you will find in Chapters 2-11; and much that is in these chapters will make more sense to you as you read them if you have first read Chapters 1 and 12.

Next: Read Chapters 2-11. Notice that each of these chapters has two kinds of reading matter that cover the same historic topics but in different ways. The first kind (The Essential Movement) explains the main movements of a convenient chunk of history. The second kind (Events and Definitions) gives an outline of facts and additional explanatory material for the same chunk of history. If you read these parts in their order, you will avoid the problem of trying to absorb too much unfamiliar historical detail before you know what a chunk of history is all about. You can end with a firm and confident feel of the historical period.

Often: Check your memory for ideas and factual details by referring to the brief chronological chart on the pages that follow this.

Finally: Read Chapter 12; and if you think it may help, read Chapter 1 again.

If you follow this plan carefully, step by step, you will find that you have come to a clear idea of the development of European civilization and to a sound grasp of factual details.

The Periods of History: c. 1000-1789

Period of Time	Political Developments	Social Life and Urbanization	Science and Technology	Intellectual Developments
High Middle Ages. c. 1000-1400	Revival of the imperial idea: Holy Roman Empire founded, 10th century. Rise of medieval papacy: Gregory VII (1073-1085), Innocent III (1198-1216), Boniface VIII (1294-1303). Papal decline began with Great Schism, 1378-1417. Growth of feudal kingship marked beginning of national state. Crusading movements in Palestine (1099-1204), Spain, and the Baltic region.	Growth of medieval towns after 1000; increase in commerce and wealth; towns undermined feudal agrarian society.	Gradual improvement in agricultural techniques; growing commercial and productive specialization; beginning of large-scale textile manufacture in Flanders and Italy.	Renaissance of the 12th century; Anselm, Abelard; spread of Aristotle's writings through western Europe. Founding of Universities: Bologna, Paris, Oxford, Cambridge. Growth of scholasticism: St. Thomas Aquinas (1225-1274).
Renaissance and Reformation. c. 1400-1600	Appearance of new centralized monarchies; decline of feudal nobility; England, France, Spain emerged as strongest states of western Europe. Beginning of great discoveries: da Gama, Columbus, Magellan. Luther began Protestant revolt against medieval church, 1517. Spread of Protestantism: Sweden (1527), England (1534), Denmark (1536), Geneva (under Calvin, 1540), Scotland (1560). Netherlands (revolt against Spain began, 1567). Counter-Reformation:	Rich city civilizations in Italy and Flanders. New business techniques ("rise of the capitalist spirit") stimulated commerce. Appearance of commercial financiers: Medici, Fuggers. Price Revolution increases European cost of living.	Improvements in manufacture: first "industrial revolution," c. 1540-1640. Copernicus's *De Revolutionibus*, 1543. Improvements in navigation and shipbuilding.	Thinkers of the Renaissance (Petrarch, Machiavelli) reacted against scholasticism; growing interest in classical literature; shift in outlook from other worldliness to things of this world (humanism). Protestant leaders reject sacramental views of medieval church; stress faith against works.

The Periods of History since 1789

Period of Time	Political Developments	Social Life and Urbanization	Science and Technology	Intellectual Developments
The French Revolution and the Napoleonic Era, 1789-1815	Threat of bankruptcy brought on French Revolution, 1789; monarchy overthrown, 1792. Reign of Terror, 1793-1794. Napoleon seized power, 1799. France proclaimed an Empire, 1804. High point of Napoleonic conquest, 1810. Napoleon's defeat in Russia, 1812; exile to Elba, 1814; final defeat at Waterloo, 1815. Congress of Vienna resettled Europe, 1814-1815.	French Revolution introduced mass conscription—"nation in arms." Beginning of mass influence in European life.	Technological advances made larger armies and mass warfare possible. British industry decisive in the overthrow of Napoleon.	Beginning of Romantic Reaction to the ideas of the Enlightenment; rise of Kant's philosophy.
The Western World, 1815-1871 (The Conservative System, Triumph of Liberalism, and the Building of Nations)	Prince Metternich and the system of conservative European Congresses, 1815-1830. French July Monarchy, 1830-1848. First British Reform Bill, 1832. Revolutions in Italy and Central Europe, 1848-1849. Unification of Italy, 1859-1870. Unification of Germany, 1864-1871 (Franco-Prussian War, 1870-1871).	Increase of industrialization; growth of cities. Rising demand for social and political reform. Spread of constitutionalism and liberalism.	Increasing use of steam power in industry. Emergence of Britain as leading industrial nation; spread of industrialization to other European states and North America. Triumph of evolution: publication of *Origin of Species*, 1859.	Age of the "Isms": Romanticism, Liberalism, Nationalism, Socialism—Utopian and Marxian. Rise of new philosophical materialism, 1850-1871; beginning of social Darwinism."
The Western World, 1871-1914	Germany emerged as strongest power of continental Europe. Spread of democratic institutions. Intensification of im-	Growth of European population and wealth; rise of real wages in industrial countries, improved standard of mass liv-	Britain's world industrial position challenged by France, Germany, and the United States, 1880-1914. Rise of mass-	Reaction to materialism and scientific rationalism of the mid-19th century; decline of confidence that science had

perial rivalry ("new imperialism"). Beginning of the system of alliances: Triple Alliance (Austria-Hungary, Germany, Italy), 1882; Triple Entente (Britain, France, Russia), 1907. International crises (Morocco and the Balkans), 1911-1914. Assassination of Austrian archduke led to outbreak of First World War, July-August 1914.

ing, 1860-1914. Growing importance of socialist parties; state by means of social legislation became an instrument of social welfare. Urban life predominated in industrial societies.

production techniques in the U.S. after 1890. Petroleum began to supplant coal as an energy fuel. Change in scientific thought ("Revolution in Physics") culminated in Einstein's generalized theory of relativity, 1880-1905.

the answers to all human problems. Rise of antirationalism; growing influence of Freud, *et al.*

The Western World since 1914

The First World War, 1914-1918: Vast movement which quickly resulted in a deadlock among the warring powers. Stalemate broken by intervention of the United States, 1917. Major effects: enormous loss of life and wealth; decline of Europe's political and economic power; rise of the United States. Rise of totalitarianism: (1) Russia: revolution and civil war, 1917-1921; Stalin assumed power, 1924; (2) Italy: Mussolini's Fascists seized power, 1922; (3) Germany: Hitler and the Nazi Party given power, 1933. Aggression of the Axis powers (Germany, Italy, Japan) led to Second World War, 1939-1945: German conquest of Poland, 1939, and France, 1940; entry of Russia and the U.S., 1941. End of war saw Europe further weakened in wealth and manpower. Continued rivalry between U.S. and U.S.S.R. after 1945 ("Cold War"). Awakening of African and Asian nationalism. Organization of the North Atlantic alliance (NATO), 1949. Formation of Eruopean Economic Community ("Common Market"), 1957. Rift between U.S.S.R. and People's Republic of China divides Soviet bloc after 1959.

Urbanization of larger industrial societies. Extensive and rapid world population growth; problem of natural resources. Growing complexity of the problems of the state.

Vast technological expansion of the western world after two world wars. Introduction of atomic energy (atom bomb at Hiroshima, 1945). Industrialization and growth of U.S.S.R. and Asian and African societies. Beginning of space penetration, 1957.

Continued growth of antirationalism and irrationalism; philosophical pessimism of the mid-20th century. Attempts at philosophical reconstruction in the western world; revival of religious interest.

CONTENTS

CHAPTER I

The Position of Europe in 1500

THE ESSENTIAL MOVEMENT

A. The Main Themes of European Civilization

The history of Europe in modern times has been a history of the world's most advanced civilization. Down to about the year 1500 it had not been so, for until that time Europe still lived largely on the intellectual capital of the ancient world, on the ideas, thoughts, and aspirations formulated many centuries earlier by the ancient Hebrews, the Greeks, and the Romans. Even in technology, mathematics, or science—fields in which modern European civilization has been unchallengeably pre-eminent—the European was not an originator or inventor prior to 1500. Here and there, it is true, medieval Europe produced some remarkable original minds, but these—including that greatest of thirteenth-century philosophers, St. Thomas Aquinas, or that fertile genius, Friar Roger Bacon, whose ideas seemed to foretell scientific marvels far ahead of his time—were largely adapters overawed by the wisdom of the ancients and content to draw upon the accumulated learning of men whose achievements seemed much greater than their own. To say this is not to imply that the middle ages lacked either intellectual vitality or inventive genius, for both were present in medieval society. Even so, it must be admitted that western Europe (or Latin Christendom as it is more properly called by historians) was still, for all of its great accomplishments, behind other parts of the world in technical skills and abstract speculation.

Since the year 1500, however, the story has been very different. For

1

almost five centuries the civilization of Europe has demonstrated such vitality and such a capacity for all forms of innovation as to make it preeminent among the civilizations of the earth. Moreover, it has steadily expanded its scope until it has come to include that which we know as western civilization (which comprehends a great deal more than the geographical area of Europe proper) and may, in time, become the first truly worldwide civilization. This is, indeed, an astonishing development and one which would have been impossible to predict a thousand years ago when the nations of Europe were only in their beginnings.

Why the civilization of Europe has thus expanded into globe-girdling prominence during so relatively short a span of historical time has long been an interesting subject of speculation among scholars. Some have argued that the growth was due to an inherent intellectual superiority in the races and peoples of Europe. Others have explained it as the result of peculiarly fortunate climatic and geographic circumstances that have contributed to the vigor of European life. Still others have contended that Europe's civilization is largely a result of chance and that neither special ability nor environment had a great deal to do with it. Perhaps, to some degree, all three of these explanations are correct. They all deal with the indisputable fact that European science and technology as well as certain European political, social, and intellectual traditions have helped to give modern European civilization a position unlike that of any previous civilization.

In order to understand something of how and why the European way of life came to be unique, we must now look backward at some of the historic strands in its development. Since the history of European civilization and that of western civilization are inextricably interwoven, our themes will stress the development of western civilization as a whole. Most sound generalizations and statements about western man are specifically applicable to European man and to his history during the past 500 years. The four most important strands of development or themes in the history of Europe since 1500 are these:

1. Human control over the world of nature (the material environment).
2. Belief in an ordered, purposeful universe and historical progress.
3. The expansion of Europe.
4. The problem of power: the emergence of the mass-oriented state as the political form of western civilization.

1. Human Control over the World of Nature (the Material Environment)

One of the persistent characteristics of western development may be seen in the success with which western man, particularly since about the year 1500, has gradually extended his control over the world of nature or, to put it in another way, over his material environment. This he has accomplished by steadily improving his technological skills, his scientific knowledge, and his capacity for social and political organization.

2. Belief in an Ordered, Purposeful Universe and Historical Progress

In the realm of thought, western man has for long accepted the belief that the universe is both meaningful and purposeful. By this statement we mean that western man has tended to believe that the world in which he lives is not governed solely by chance and that it has a purpose to its existence. It is not a thing of day-to-day survival but a vast system governed by laws and directed toward a specific, if remote, goal. This belief is based in part upon Christian thought and in part upon the theory of secular progress which came to be widely accepted in the 18th and 19th centuries. Whatever its origins, there is no doubt that belief in an ordered, purposeful universe has had a number of important effects. Perhaps the most important of these is the doctrine of progress, that is, the idea that history follows a pattern of change by which man continually betters himself and his environment. The prevalence of this belief has given western man a confidence in himself and his intellectual capacity which in turn has helped him to achieve many of his greatest intellectual, scientific, and technological triumphs.

3. The Expansion of Europe

In the long run the single most important development of modern times is the expansion of Europe overseas which began about the year 1500. Actually, this external or overseas expansion was a later phase of an internal European expansion that began about the year 1000. This earlier expansion was marked by a general quickening of intellectual, economic, and social activity which prepared the way for expansion outside Europe during the later periods of discovery and colonization. As a consequence of this centuries-long process of internal and external expansion, European civilization has been transplanted, adapted, and imitated to a greater extent than any previous civilization in the world's history.

European expansion has five major manifestations which should also be kept in mind as the reader progresses through the book. These are (a) growth of population, (b) rise of towns and cities (increasing urbanization), (c) colonization, first of unsettled areas within Europe, and later of extensive areas overseas, (d) a revolution in the techniques of production and transportation which enormously increased European productive capacities, and (e) a continuous growth of capital wealth (wealth used for productive and gainful purposes) which made possible a relatively steady increase of European economic capacities in modern times.

What was ultimately most significant about Europe's internal expansion, however, was that it prepared the way for the discovery and colonization of vast regions beyond the seas. Without the long gestation of internal expansion from the early middle ages onward there would have been no possibility of Europe's breaking through the cultural isolation that characterized most human societies down to the year 1500. Wealth, technology, and the political organization of the national monarchy all played an important part; and all were developments of medieval origin. While these indirectly made outward expansion possible, Europeans still had to be motivated toward the great effort of discovery and colonization. Undoubtedly, Christian missionary zeal had strong influences, particularly among the Portuguese and Spaniards. So, too, did the more mundane desire for riches. But neither of these was a peculiarly European motivation. Nor did Europeans, at the moment when expansion began, have either skills or wealth beyond those possessed by some other societies. The great Chinese empire, for example, as well as several Islamic societies might also have made the effort. Islam, after all, was scarcely less zealous than Christianity in its desire to convert the heathen. Chinese, Indian, or Arab traders were as anxious for wealth. Why, then, did Europe make the first moves toward creating a world community and civilization? The answer seems to lie in the fact that European motives were not only intense but that European consciousness of the unknown for some mysterious reason stimulated the curiosity and moved Europeans to action as other societies were not so stimulated or moved.

The result of this complex combination of causes was extremely significant for world history. Indeed, it was European expansion that first made all the isolated cultures of the earth conscious not only of themselves but of the world as a whole. Ultimately, the great success of European civilization with its utilization of science and technology, in particular, was to give to all the earth for the first time a true worldwide civilization.

4. The Problem of Power: Emergence of the Mass-Oriented State as the Political Form of Western Civilization

Another important and in many ways unique development of the western world is the modern mass-oriented state. Usually when we think of the modern "mass state" we think of democracies, that is, states where the ultimate political authority remains in the hands of a broad electorate that has complete freedom to choose its own rulers. Many governments, however, are not mass-controlled but are actually more or less totalitarian to the extent that they deny this power of choice to their peoples. Such states, countries like the Soviet Union or its satellites for example, are not untouched by mass influences. Indeed, they contend that they exist solely to serve the ends of the masses. In that sense, though they cannot be called mass-controlled or democratic states as democracy is understood in the West, they are still mass-oriented, or at least profess to be mass-oriented, in their outlook.

The origins of this mass-controlled or mass-oriented state go far back into the European past, farther, indeed, than is sometimes realized. Its beginnings may, in fact, be traced to the early modern national monarchy which began to come into existence at the end of the middle ages. The early monarchical state with its centralized authority, its bureaucracy, and its concern for broader national as opposed to local feudal interests prepared the way for the mass-oriented nation-state of more recent times.

In order to understand at the outset just how European civilization evolved in terms of the above four themes from the 16th through the 20th centuries, it might be wise for the reader to turn first to the last chapter of this book, where each theme's historical development is summarized. By doing so the reader may get a clearer picture of what was transpiring during those centuries which should be helpful to him as he reads through the body of the text.

B. The Concept of Europe

Because Europe has been for so long the core of western civilization and the center of world domination, we often think of it as a separate geographic entity—a continent—distinct from the other great continents of the world. Continent or not, Europe is not a separate geographic unit but a peninsula, a large continental projection, attached to the larger continent of Asia. Indeed, three continents—Africa, Asia, and Europe—are linked together by land connections which have led some geographers to describe the whole Afro-Asian-European land mass as "the great world island."

And yet despite its geographic connections with Africa and Asia, Europe is something distinct from either. Europe is an entity, historically if not geographically, with traditions and a culture peculiarly its own. From time to time throughout history the influences of Africa and Asia have made themselves felt in Europe, but for almost a thousand years these influences have been less important in the shaping of Europe than the environment of Europe itself. In other words, since about the year 1000 the history of Europe has followed a pattern of development which is distinctively its own and which, while not isolated from outside influences, evolved into a civilization with characteristics and attributes not always found in other civilizations. The most important of these characteristics and attributes have already been noticed at the beginning of this chapter, and for that reason we need not deal with them here. What we must understand before we proceed, however, is that "Europe" is a cultural rather than a geographic entity, the creation of many centuries of human effort. In that sense, it can be said that Europe is not a continent but a concept, a state of mind, an awareness of a common sharing of certain beliefs, practices, and ways of looking at the world. To say this is not to say that all Europeans are or have been cast in a common mold. On the contrary, one of the remarkable historical facts about Europe is that while some things are shared in common, there is still within Europe as a whole a great deal of cultural, social, and political diversity.

In more recent times, that is, since about the 18th century, the cultural entity of Europe has been given geographic boundaries, largely for political convenience. Customarily, since that time, Europe has been defined as that body of land with adjacent islands lying between the Ural and Caucasus Mountains in the East and the Atlantic Ocean in the West. Its northern extremities are bounded by the Atlantic and the Arctic Oceans, its southern limits by the Mediterranean and Black Seas. All countries and peoples lying within this region are generally thought of as European, though some ethnic groups, the Turks especially, have for centuries inhabited lands on both sides of the boundary between Europe and Asia.

Historically, however, it was a very long time before this rather arbitrary determination of the frontiers of Europe could be arrived at. Until about a thousand years ago the geographical area of modern Europe was on the fringe of a civilization whose center was the Mediterranean Basin. With the disappearance of the centralized government of the western Roman Empire toward the end of the fifth century, Europe's relations with the Mediterranean world underwent a long slow process of transformation. Down to about the year 1000 the western portions of the Roman Empire were gradually changed under the impact of three major influences: (1) the Germanic invaders who, having made their way into the empire, were unable to preserve its government or civilization and thus gradually created smaller successor states or kingdoms in its place; (2) Latin Christianity (as distinct from Eastern or Orthodox Christianity), whose titular head, the pope, kept alive dreams of restoring the empire and preserved the spiritual authority of Rome over all the Latin West; and (3) the assaults of two later groups of invaders—the followers of Islam (Mohammedans) and the Northmen or Vikings—both of whom from the 8th century onward threatened the existence of Europe until the former were checked and the latter were absorbed into European civilization. By the opening of the 11th century these influences had combined in their various ways to create in rough outline the area we now know as Europe.

Still it was not precisely the Europe that we know today, though many of the traditional European states, England and France for example, already existed in the form of half-feudalized monarchies. Then and throughout the high middle ages (12th through 14th centuries) most Europeans thought of themselves as inhabitants of "Christendom"—an area somewhat vaguely understood to be coterminous with the region which acknowledged the spiritual supremacy of the Roman pontiffs. This included all or parts of modern Italy, France, Spain, Austria, Germany, Hungary, the British Isles, Poland, and Scandinavia. The history of Europe since that period is, in one aspect, the history of the transformation of the idea of Christendom into the idea of Europe, a transformation which was not completed until the 18th century.

With the emergence of this earlier European community about the year 1000, other important developments had their beginning which, over some centuries, were to make Europe the center of a world-wide civilization. Let us now examine the most important of these developments.

C. The Transformation of Europe, 1000-1500

1. The Medieval Church and the Idea of Universality

From the tenth century onward the medieval church, under the impact of a series of internal reform movements, was reorganized and revitalized. During the pontificate of Pope Gregory VII (1073-1085) the papal office was virtually freed from the outside control of the Holy Roman emperors, who had for long tried to nominate papal candidates; the church was thus unhindered in determining its own destiny. As a consequence, the authority of the popes was greatly strengthened, standards of clerical life were improved, and the intellectual life of medieval Europe was stimulated.

With the establishment of papal authority over the whole Latin church and the extension of ecclesiastical reform during the 12th century, the way was prepared for the church's great triumph of the 13th century when the papacy emerged as a strong international institution which claimed both a spiritual and temporal sovereignty over all of western Christendom. The theory that justified this assumption of universal authority was based upon the belief that while the spiritual and temporal powers were distinct and separate, the spiritual, because man's salvation was of greater ultimate concern than his well-being in this world, must take precedence over the temporal whenever a conflict arose between the two. Furthermore, churchmen still held to the hope that the universal dominion of the Roman Empire could be restored and that all Christians would once more become members of a universal commonwealth. To this end the papacy, as early as the year 800, had tried to reconstitute the western Roman empire by crowning Charlemagne, king of the Franks, as emperor of the West. The attempt failed in the long run for two important reasons: first, because conflicts over authority arose between popes and emperors which made it impossible for the two to exercise coequal powers; and, second, because the rising feudal monarchs of western Europe, while they could be brought, sometimes reluctantly, to an acknowledgment of the supreme spiritual authority of the church, refused to bow to the temporal authority of the emperors.

Despite these difficulties, the medieval popes of the 12th and 13th centuries, particularly during the pontificates of Innocent III (1198-1216) and Boniface VIII (1294-1303), were able to assert their authority over western Europe with greater success than any international institution has ever achieved since. At the moment of the papacy's triumph, however, other forces were at work which during the next two centuries, from 1300 to about 1500, were to destroy the edifice the popes had built.

2.　The Rise of National Monarchies and the Decline of the Medieval Church

There were several important reasons for the decline of papal power in the period between 1300 and 1500, but two stand out in general above the rest. One cause was that the vast organization of the medieval church was, like any other great institutional system, continually plagued by breakdown in its own functions and by the incapacity of some of the men responsible for making the system work. A second cause lay in the fact that an institution with such great political and economic power was bound to arouse jealousy and antipathy in local areas or among individuals whose interests on occasion conflicted with those of the church.

Among the most important of the latter were the feudal kings of western Europe. In the scope and exercise of their authority, it must be understood, medieval rulers differed very much from the kings of the 16th through the 18th centuries. A medieval monarch did not possess the financial or military power necessary to make him an absolute ruler. Moreover, he was limited by both the theory and the practice of feudalism. In theory, though he stood at the top of the feudal hierarchy, he was restricted by the terms of the feudal contract that bound the upper echelons of society together. In practice, he was usually only the greatest landlord of his realm; and though according to the feudal ideal all of his vassals held their lands of him and were responsible to him, he was sometimes overshadowed by greater subjects whose landholdings might be more extensive than his own.

The great aim of feudal kings was to overcome these limitations on their power by weakening the nobles and strengthening their own governmental authority. In order to accomplish these purposes, however, the monarchs necessarily had to have support from the church—yet their interests also frequently conflicted with those of the church. The various medieval monarchs thus faced a double problem. If they were to make themselves strong, they had to destroy the local power of their own nobles and simultaneously make the church within their dominions an amenable instrument of government. At the heart of the kings' problems was the matter of finance. Medieval monarchs did not possess the regular forms of modern state revenue such as taxes. They had to get money where they could and they usually depended on their own personal estates for income. Since these were often far from sufficient to support a centralized machinery of government, the kings of the late middle ages strove continually to expand their own personal landholdings and to find sources of revenue apart from the limited and infrequent feudal dues paid them by their vassals.

In their struggle to create an effective system of central government and to find the money to pay for it, some kings of western Europe found support among those of their subjects who were neither great churchmen nor nobles. They were able to do so because to lesser men—townsmen, merchants, small landholders, and others—the authority of the state offered protection and security which the feudal system did not. Kings, for example, frequently guaranteed the freedom of towns against great lords, both spiritual and temporal, gave a large measure of even-handed justice to all their subjects, and provided a more effective military protection against invasion. As a result, the monarchy in countries like England and France was able over many generations to grow and to extend its authority with a certain measure of tacit popular support. The rise of monarchy brought with it a broader conception of nationality. The king stood above all his people, bishops, lords, and commoners, and the king's government comprehended the whole of society. In this power situation the old local loyalties to particular regions or to feudal lords gradually broke down, and in their place appeared a somewhat vague sense of loyalty to the king and to the country which he ruled.

As the power of the monarchs of western Europe waxed, that of the papacy waned. The new-found strength of the national monarchies, however, was not alone responsible for the deline of the church during the 14th and 15th centuries, though it had much to do with it. From the early 14th century onward, when the popes became virtual prisoners of the French crown and took up residence at Avignon (an independent town within the boundaries of France—1305-1376), the various princes of Europe steadily advanced their authority at the expense of the papacy. To add to the church's difficulties, internal conflict between rival candidates for the papal office(Great Schism, 1378-1417) caused a scandal that weakened papal prestige. The schism was finally ended but not without a further struggle. In 1414 a great ecclesiastical council met at the city of Constance in southern Germany and, after deposing all rival claimants, elected a new pope. In so doing the council tried to assert the supremacy of councils over popes (conciliar movement), but with little ultimate success.

Meanwhile, throughout Europe voices were raised in dissent against papal claims to complete authority over all the states of Christendom and also in complaint against clerical abuses. In the unsettled state of the church during the early 15th century, both criticisms began to grow serious. In England John Wycliffe (1320-1384) and in Bohemia John Hus (1374-1415) both preached doctrines which not only called for major reforms within the church but also verged over into heresy. Though the movements headed by these two were finally suppressed, the discontent they voiced was a harbinger of the Protestant revolt that followed more than a century later.

3.   The Social and Intellectual Life of Medieval Europe

Along with the changes taking place in the spheres of religion and politics, a number of important changes in the social and economic life of Europe occurred during the high middle ages. The characteristic forms of medieval economic and social organization had been those generally described under the terms "manorialism" and "feudalism."

"Manorialism" denominates the system by which agriculture, largely for subsistence, was undertaken on a great estate or "manor." The manor was the basic unit of economic and social organization and varied in extent from a few acres to thousands. On the manor lived the vast majority of medieval men, subject to its binding customs and conventions. Few of them were slaves but most of them were "unfree"; that is, they had no right to remove themselves from the land and they were bound by certain obligations to the lord who held the manor. Upward in the social scale were the equally binding customs and conventions of feudalism or the feudal contract, to which the unfree man or serf was not a party.

Feudalism was the method by which the ruling elites of society were bound together. The serf provided subsistence; the lord provided protection. But the lord, in his turn, was obligated to those above him under the feudal contract; for the feudal system, in theory at least, was one in which every man had a superior and no man owned land outright to dispose of as he pleased. The system was held together by the feudal contract, under the terms of which those who held land were obligated to furnish their superiors certain services and certain financial or military aid.

It is important to remember that though the system of landholding which was the basis of feudalism was thus hedged about with customs and restrictions that prevented much ease of social movement, feudalism was not simply an evil oppression as is sometimes thought. Later generations have looked upon it as such because of the centuries-long struggle waged by many Europeans to free themselves from its restrictions and because the privileged position of the landholding nobility came to be resented at a later period. Feudalism must be thought of in its proper historical context. It was a system of government well suited to an agrarian society which lacked a strong central government. The feudal nobility gave, albeit often imperfectly, leadership and direction in a social system which had no other means of providing them. When the society in which it functioned began to change, feudalism slowly disappeared—but not entirely or instantly or in all parts of Europe at the same time. In the countries of central and eastern Europe it lingered until well on into the 19th century. Vestiges of some of its customs and traditions may be found in some parts of Europe even today.

The process that led to the disappearance of feudalism had its beginnings as far back as the 11th century. Though many forces helped to transform feudal society, the major ones were: (1) the rise of towns and cities with an accompanying expansion of trade and manufacture; (2) fluctuations in population, particularly after a great natural disaster like the Black Death of 1348-1349, which often made it possible for those at the bottom of society to win greater economic advantages and a greater measure of social freedom for themselves because of labor scarcity; and (3) the generally expansive nature of medieval economic life, which continually offered opportunities for able and ambitious men to overcome the restrictions and limitations of the feudal social order.

Many historians have regarded the growth of towns and cities as perhaps the most significant of these three forces because urban life had far-reaching effects, both intellectual and social. The very existence of populated centers, which became more numerous after the year 1000, induced the agricultural system to produce a surplus which could be used to feed those elements in the urban population who did not produce food for themselves. As a result, throughout western Europe market areas developed where the rural inhabitants had been impelled by circumstances to change their agricultural techniques to conform to the needs of the towns. In so doing the rural producer also changed the system of feudal-manorial relations. Serfs, as they accumulated money from the sale of surplus food, were

able to transform (commute) their manorial obligations into money payments (rents) to the lord of the manor and were often able to purchase their
freedom from serfdom.

Another important general effect of the rise of towns resulted from the
fact that feudal society was uncongenial to commercial activity. The towns-
man could not be bound to the soil since his commercial activities required
freedom of movement. The normal range of his transactions was not cov-
ered by either the feudal contract or the customary law of the manor. He
also had to have the right of free and outright possession of his goods so that
he could buy and sell easily. In trying to get these things the medieval town
merchant had, of necessity, to alter the very nature of feudal life. His success in so doing greatly broadened the areas of political, economic, and
intellectual freedom. It also gave European society as a whole a great deal
more fluidity by undermining the restrictive system of feudal class relations.

As European expansion became more marked in the 12th and 13th
centuries, a great transformation also took place in medieval intellectual
life. While we often think of the middle ages as a period of intellectual
stagnation, the fact is that medieval men made a number of important con-
tributions to the intellectual development of Europe and the whole western world. The greatest of the medieval philosophers, St. Thomas Aquinas
(1225-1274), recast the writings of the Greek philosopher Aristotle and so
made them an accepted part of Christian theology. The achievement was
important, for though it later made Aristotle's authority a kind of dead
weight in some areas of European intellectual development, it helped to
preserve a major element of classical thought for the western world and had
a major effect on the later development of science. Furthermore, the modern
specialized center of advanced study we now know as the university also
had its beginnings during the middle ages.

After almost three centuries of unparalleled growth and expansion, the
impulse of medieval life was very nearly played out. The century after 1300
was to witness a kind of stagnation in economic activity and intellectual
advance. Europe as a whole was only briefly dormant, however, for a new
time of vitality and expansion was at hand.

CHAPTER 2

Renaissance and Reformation

THE ESSENTIAL MOVEMENT

The terms "Renaissance" and "Reformation" have been used for so long to describe certain definite periods of European history that it is difficult to think of any others to take their places. Yet, to some extent, both are misnomers.

The word "Renaissance" means rebirth and implies that the history of the middle ages was of little relative importance, socially or culturally. Since we know that the medieval period was far more productive and original than was once believed, the period of the Renaissance (14th through 16th centuries) has now come to be thought of not as a sharp break with the medieval past but, rather, as a time when many movements and ideas originating in the middle ages came to fruition. The later period was thus not so much a time of rebirth as of shifting emphasis, a time when the tempo of human activity quickened and men thought more explicitly about things of this world without reference to the hereafter or without allowing themselves to be quite so influenced by the traditional standards of Christian belief as they had been previously.

In somewhat the same way our understanding of the term "Reformation," as used to describe the period of religious struggle in the 16th century, has also changed. When the division between Catholics and Protestants first occurred, the religious leaders who broke away from the medieval church thought of themselves as "reformers" whose purpose was to eliminate the abuses in the church which, as they saw it, had grown up

EVENTS AND DEFINITIONS

A. The Renaissance, c. 1400-1600

1. Economic and Social Change

a. USE OF NEW FINANCIAL TECHNIQUES. Bills of exchange (drafts calling for the payment of sums of money by one merchant in behalf of another), promissory notes, and discounting (deducting of charges for interest in advance from loans), which greatly expanded credit and eased the transfer of wealth, began to be used extensively from the 14th century onward. Earliest public banks created in the early 15th century. Stock and monetary exchanges *(bourses)* established, the most famous of which was that founded at Antwerp, 1531.

b. DEVELOPMENT OF BUSINESS ORGANIZATION. Double-entry system of bookkeeping in use as early as the 14th century. Permanent business partnerships, group organizations to share insurance risks, and, finally, the joint-stock company evolved from the 14th through the 17th centuries.

c. CHANGING ATTITUDES TOWARD TRADE AND FINANCE. Growth of the "capitalist spirit": from the 14th century onward the search for material wealth and the inherent conditions of economic enterprise in a money economy undermined the prohibitions of the church against the taking of interest (usury) and selling at more than a "just price." In part, this was a reflection of the growing interest in things of this world, of a

during the long centuries of papal supremacy. In most cases, they wished not to create something new or to destroy the unity of Christendom by founding numerous sects and denominations but rather to restore the church as it had been founded by Christ and the apostles. For this reason they were driven to appeal to the authority of the Bible as against the authority of the popes and the historical traditions of the church. But because the language of scripture was (and is) in many places ambiguous or even contradictory, they found themselves in disagreement, not only with the medieval church but also among themselves. As a consequence, the great Protestant hope of reforming and preserving a united Christian church was never achieved. The medieval church (thenceforward to be known as the Roman Catholic church) continued to exist side by side with the various new Protestant denominations; and the Reformation, with time, took on the aspects not of a reform movement but of a religious revolution with far-reaching significance.

A. The Renaissance

1. Economic and Social Changes

By the late 14th century the forces of economic expansion, which had begun their work some two or three centuries earlier, had produced a high level of material well-being, particularly in the great European cities. At first this increase in wealth was most noticeable in the Italian peninsula and the Low Countries (now Belgium and Holland), but in time it spread rapidly to other parts of northern and western Europe. As it spread, it created a new, sophisticated, mercantile civilization, outstanding examples of which were the great city-states: Venice, Genoa, Florence, Milan in Italy; Antwerp, Bruges, and Ghent in the Low Countries; and the towns of the Hanseatic League in north central Germany. The most brilliant manifestations of this new civilization were those in Italy, where the continuity of city life from Roman times onward had never been completely broken. In the Italian cities great merchant families made use of their wealth to promote learning and the arts. In so doing, however, they seldom lost sight of the practical side of their affairs; in these Italian merchant communities many of the business skills were developed which were later to be used internationally. For the first time there appeared on the European scene the great financier whose wealth made him the creditor of kings and gave him a power (sometimes exaggerated by later historians) to influence political decisions.

The Renaissance also saw the completion of that process of state de-

desire for well-being in the here and now without awaiting some future life. With the growth of this new spirit and the greater accumulation of commercial and financial wealth, the great merchants and financiers became important figures.

D. NEW MEN OF WEALTH. Three outstanding illustrations of the new financial-mercantile class were: ■ (1) Giovanni dei Medici (1360-1429), merchant and banker of Florence, who founded the powerful Medici family. His descendants later became princes and popes. ■ (2) Jacques Coeur (*c.* 1395-1456), merchant of Bourges in France, possessed the largest fortune ever amassed by a private individual in France down to his time. Friend, confidant, and adviser to French kings. ■ (3) The Fugger family in Germany began to grow in wealth at the end of the 14th century. By the 16th century its members were the wealthiest men in Europe, one of whom supplied the vast sums needed to carry the imperial election of 1519 in favor of Charles of Hapsburg.

2. The Great Discoveries

A. CAUSES. (1) Growth of wealth, which made expensive and risky overseas ventures possible; (2) religious and national zeal; (3) desire for gain; (4) effort of some religious minorities to escape persecution; (5) curiosity and the simple desire to increase knowledge; and, finally, (6) the development of a technology that made long oceanic voyages possible (compass, sternpost rudder, seaworthy construction of ships, improved methods of celestial navigation).

B. CHRONOLOGY OF DISCOVERY AND SETTLEMENT TO 1620. Journeys of Marco Polo to the Far East, 1271-1295. Prince Henry the Navigator of Portugal began to promote voyages of discovery along the African coast, 1418. Discovery of the Azores, 1427-1431, and Cape Verde Islands, 1455-1457. Diaz rounded the Cape of Good Hope, 1487-1488. ■ First voyage of Columbus, 1492. Vasco da Gama sailed to India, 1497-1499. Cabot brothers touched the coast of North America, 1497-1498. Balboa discovered Pacific, 1513. ■ Conquest of Mexico by Cortez, 1519-1521. Magellan's expedition circumnavigated the world, 1519-1522. ■ Conquest of Peru by Pizarro, 1532-1533. First English circumnavigation of the globe by Drake, 1577-1580. Beginning of Dutch trade with the East Indies, 1595-1597. Founding of the English East India Company,

velopment begun by medieval kings. Curiously enough, the areas most affected by this change, namely, England, France, and Spain, were not the first to feel the effects of the quickened economic and intellectual tempo. It was in Italy that the new spirit first appeared, but there the Renaissance was a period of political chaos when city fought city and foreign powers intervened to carve out Italian possessions for themselves. In the three aforementioned states, however, the end of the 15th and the beginning of the 16th century saw the emergence of three strong dynasties (Tudors in England, Valois in France, Hapsburgs in Spain) who greatly increased the power of their respective governments and virtually eliminated the last vestiges of feudal opposition. With the rise of these new states the center of European power shifted to the Atlantic fringe, and a new era—the age of the absolute monarchies—had begun.

2. The Great Discoveries

While the important internal changes were taking place in the 15th and 16th centuries, another series of events decisively altered the relations of Europe with the rest of the world and led ultimately to Europe's becoming the center of a worldwide cultural and economic community. These were the great discoveries beyond the seas. Columbus's famous voyage was but one of many and, in its way, only the most sensational of them. The discoveries, and the colonization movements that followed in their wake, were the further result of a number of medieval and Renaissance developments: (1) the internal expansion of European wealth which made it possible to finance costly voyages and to undertake extensive colonization programs; (2) a rise in the level of shipbuilding techniques; (3) improvement in the methods of economic and political organization— e.g. the joint-stock company, which made possible the sharing of great economic risks, and the strong, centralized state which enabled European rulers to give sanction and support to overseas activities; and (4) the growth and improvement of communications within Europe which stimulated interest in remote territories. The motives which drove Europeans to undertake the risks of discovery and exploration were varied. Many were driven by hope of sudden wealth or by the desire to open new trade routes. Some hoped to Christianize the pagans or, later, to escape from religious persecution at home. Kings were moved by considerations of power and prestige. All, however, were impelled by some form of that

1600; of the Dutch East India Company, 1602. ■ English settlement in North America (Jamestown), 1607. Founding of French Canada (Québec) by Champlain, 1608. Establishment of the English in India, 1609-1614. ■ Voyage of the *Mayflower;* second permanent English settlement in North America, 1620-1621.

3. Literature and Thought

A. IN ITALY. *Divine Comedy,* written between 1300 and 1311, while it reflected the ideals of the 13th century also foreshadowed the future since it was written in the vernacular (Italian rather than Latin). The writings of Petrarch (1304-1374) characterized the change; topics chosen were secular in interest. Publication of Boccaccio's *Decameron,* 1353. Founding of the humanist school at Mantua, 1425. Marsilio Ficino became head of the Platonic Academy (whose members opposed the Aristotelian influences of the medieval schoolmen) at Florence, 1458. Rule of Lorenzo de Medici ("the Magnificent") in Florence, 1469-1492. Appearance of Machiavelli's *The Prince,* 1515.

B. OUTSIDE ITALY. Publication of the first part of Cervantes' *Don Quixote* (Spain), 1505. Erasmus' *In Praise of Folly* (1509) satirized contemporary ills, particularly those of the church. Thomas More's *Utopia,* 1516. Foundation of the Collège de France (1530) which became the center of French humanism. Rabelais' *Gargantua and Pantagruel,* 1532. Andreas Vesalius published *Seven Books on the Structure of the Human Body,* 1543. Appearance of Copernicus's *De revolutionibis orbium coelestium (On the Revolution of Celestial Bodies),* 1543. Shakespeare's first plays appeared, 1590-1594. Publication of the first part of Edmund Spenser's *The Faerie Queene,* 1590.

4. Renaissance Art

A. IN ITALY. Giotto's frescoes at Padua, 1305. Botticelli painted "Birth of Venus," 1485. Leonardo da Vinci's "Last Supper" painted, 1485-1498. Construction began on the basil-

the Church's shortcomings in the early 16th century. Concordat of Bologna between papacy and Francis I of France gave the king virtual control of the French Church; publication of new Greek edition of the New Testament by Erasmus; indulgence mission of Tetzel to Germany, 1516. Reign of the Emperor Charles V, 1519-1556.

1. Lutheranism

Luther's life: born at Eisleben, 1483. Studied at University of Erfurt whose leading theologian, Gabriel Biel (d. 1495), was under the influence of the "nominalist" philosopher William of Ockham (c. 1300-49). Like most Ockhamists, Luther believed in the separation of reason and faith. Entered the order of Augustinian Eremites, 1505; ordained priest, 1507. Visited Rome, 1510-11, and taught at Wittenberg after 1512. Gradually came to conclusion that man is "justified by faith alone," 1512-1517. In reaction to the Tetzel indulgence mission published his 95 Theses, 1517. Excommunicated by Pope Leo X, 1520. Defied Emperor Charles V at Diet of Worms, 1521. Took the side of the princes in suppressing Peasants' Revolt, 1524-25. Later history of Lutheranism: Augsburg Confession (*Confessio Augustana*) set forth principles of Lutheran belief, 1531. National Protestant (Lutheran) church established in Sweden, 1527; in Denmark, 1536. Lutheran-Catholic religious wars (1546-55) culminated in Peace of Augsburg, 1555, which recognized Lutheranism; permitted princes to determine which faith would prevail in their territories ("cujus regio, eius religio").

Calvinism

Translation of the Bible into French, 1523-1530. Calvin converted to Protestantism and fled Paris, 1533. Publication of Calvin's *Institutes of the Christian Religion*, 1536. Founding of theocratic Calvinist state at Geneva, 1541. British exiles carry Calvinist ideas to England (after the accession of Elizabeth I in 1558) and Scotland (John Knox returned in 1559). Scottish parliament severed ties with Rome, 1560. Death of Calvin, 1564. Revolt of the Netherlands begun in part under Calvinist auspices, 1566. Declaration of Dutch independence from Spain, 1581. Religious Wars in France (Catholics against

e and Reformation

restless human vitality and curiosity which has been so marked a characteristic of modern European civilization.

3. Literature and Thought

In the literary movements of the Renaissance two distinctive features emerged. The first of these was the tendency, already evident in Dante's *Divine Comedy* (though, as we have seen, its content was purely medieval), to make use of the native (vernacular) languages rather than medieval Latin as a medium of expression. This change, though it did open the way to a broadening of interests and tastes, was not all gain, for it resulted in the decline of an international language which had helped to unify western Christendom. The second distinctive feature of the new literature was its emphasis on man and man's place in this world (humanism), stimulated by an interest in the writings of classical antiquity. Because many of the leading literary figures of the early Renaissance, men like the poet-scholar Petrarch (1304-1374), wished to return to the grammatical purity of classical Latin which medieval Latin had lost, it later came to be assumed that medieval scholars had known nothing of the great literary works of antiquity and that the Renaissance scholars, by rediscovering them, had truly ushered in an age of "rebirth." The claim was an exaggeration, but it was not entirely without meaning, for Renaissance scholars and thinkers did help to shift both the intellectual and literary interests of the time from Christian to classical or secular subjects. With this shift a great number of thinkers began to concern themselves with man as he is in the world of here and now. Our best illustration of this new tendency is to be found in the writings of that tough-minded realist, Niccolo Machiavelli (1469-1527), whose political writings—the most famous of which was *The Prince*—helped to divorce political theory from Christian morality. At the other extreme, however, was the Dutch humanist scholar Erasmus (1466-1536), whose breadth of knowledge led him to exalt human values but not to separate them from the traditional Christian ethics.

4. Renaissance Art

The art of the Renaissance also reflects the change in emphasis characteristic of its literature and thought. While architecture, as seen in the great Gothic cathedrals had been the highest artistic achievement of

ica of St. Peter's (Rome), 1506. "School of Athens" and "Disputa" painted by Raphael, 1509-1511. Painting of Michelangelo's "Last Judgment," 1534-1541. Death of Titian, 1576.

B. OUTSIDE ITALY. Albrecht Dürer's woodcuts on "The Revelation of St. John" (Germany), 1498. Hans Holbein the Younger settled in England, 1532. Philibert Delorme published French manual of architecture, 1561. Escorial Palace built by Philip II of Spain at Madrid, 1563-1584. Death of El Greco, 1625, greatest Spanish painter of the Renaissance.

B. The Reformation

John Wyclif (1320-84) of England attacked the theology of the medieval church, 1378-80; Wyclif's followers, known as Lollards, suppressed by King Henry IV (1399-1413). Great schism of the church finally healed by Council of Constance; same council also executed the Bohemian John Hus for heresy, 1415. Restoration of papal unity with election of Martin V, 1517. Hussite Wars in Bohemia, 1420-33. Conciliar movement, which threatened papal authority, finally lost out in struggle with papacy when Council of Basel, 1431-49, failed in its attempt to make a representative council the governing body of the Church. Decline of the Renaissance papacy: pontificate of the humanist pope, Nicholas V, 1447-55; Alexander VI (Borgia), 1492-1503. Establishment of the Spanish Inquisition, 1478. Savonarola preached against clerical abuses at Florence, 1494-98. Humanist criticism of clerical abuses: *In Praise of Folly* by Erasmus, 1509; *Utopia* by Sir Thomas More, 1516; *The Letters of Obscure Men* by Rubeanus and Ulrich von Hutten, 1515-17.

Influence of humanism on the Reformation: Although humanist criticism had much to do with preparing the climate of opinion that made the Reformation possible, humanism and Protestantism were separate and distinct movements. Humanist critics, particularly in northern Europe, were not anti-Christian or even opposed to the medieval Church as it was constituted about 1500. Most of them, when the crisis of the Reformation came, remained within the Church. Their writings and attitudes, however, inadvertently made men aware of

medieval man, in contrast, the Renaiss
such individual forms of art as paintin
of a revolution in artistic method, the
subjects with a natural exactness and
lacking in medieval art; and while he
pression, he also chose many that were
naturalism may be traced from its be
paintings through the pictures and
Leonardo da Vinci (1452-1519), Mi
(1477-1576), whose work typifies the
enriched artistic medium.

B. The Reformation

When we look for the general ca
tween Catholics and Protestants, whi
1546) in the first quarter of the 16t
The first type arose from the g
toward the world in which they lived
15th, and 16th centuries. These ch
persons resentful of an authority like
professed to be universal and super
the moral curbs placed on them by th
disfavor and envy on the growing w
cracy of such a powerful organization
tional prohibitions of canon law ag
and against other business practic
and honorable, even though these
ing the late middle ages. Moreove
and the growth of a sense of natio
many Europeans to think of the pa
institution which drew taxes from t
of these growing forces of secular d
of break with papal authority migl
to cause it. Attitudes had changed
more to a rejection of the church's s
The second variety of general
aissance church itself, which gave
to criticize and thus helped to crea
fact was that some of the churchm
majority, had succumbed to the se

discipline and morality had become lax in many places, and, what was worse, some of the Renaissance popes themselves were guilty of flagrant abuses of their high office. Thus a combination of discontents came into existence, some aroused by secular feelings and others by a fear that the church, through certain of its practices, was placing the salvation of thousands of human beings in jeopardy. For men like Martin Luther and John Calvin (1509-1564), who were destined to become the two leading figures of the Protestant movement, the latter issue was by far the most important. Though there were men who would follow their lead for selfish, material reasons, these two acted on the high religious purpose of restoring the church of the apostles.

1. Lutheranism

In 1517, Luther initiated the religious revolt in Germany with a public challenge (Ninety-five Theses) to debate certain propositions which struck at the heart of the prevailing theology of the church and implicitly questioned papal authority. His challenge struck a chord of popular response and within a few years had led to his expulsion from the church. What made it possible for Luther to succeed where earlier religious leaders had failed was the decision on the part of certain territorial princes and nobles to back him in his struggle. This support left the lands of the Holy Roman Empire divided into two armed camps. On one side were the Lutheran nobles and on the other the Emperor Charles V (1519-1556), who remained loyal to the Roman Catholic church. After a period of protracted warfare in which the two sides fought each other to a standstill, the Peace of Augsburg (1555) effected a compromise by allowing local princes to determine what the religions of their territories would be. With this adjustment, Protestantism became a permanent part of the European historical tradition.

2. Calvinism

While Lutheranism spread throughout north Germany and into Scandinavia, elsewhere in Europe a new and equally strong protest movement was also taking shape. In Switzerland, where the religious leader Ulrich Zwingli had begun the revolt of 1524, a new and powerful personality—John Calvin, a French preacher of the new doctrines who had fled to the city of Geneva in 1536—undertook to organize the church which afterwards bore his name. The distinctiveness of the Calvinist church organization lay in the fact that it allowed the laity to participate in church functions as members of the governing body known as the "presbytery." Above the presbytery was a hierarchy of graded courts which undertook the surveil-

the Calvinist Huguenots), 1563-1598: massacre of St. Bartholomew wiped out important French Huguenot leaders, 1572; Henry IV became Catholic convert from Calvinism, 1593, and issued the Edict of Nantes granting toleration to Huguenots, 1598.

3. Anglicanism

Henry VIII (1509-1547) summoned the Reformation Parliament, 1529. Henry divorced Catherine of Aragon and married Anne Boleyn, 1533; Pope Clement VII excommunicated Henry. Henry proclaimed head of the Church of England, 1534. Dissolution of the monasteries, 1536-1539. Protestant reforms pushed under Edward VI (1547-1553); first English Book of Common Prayer published, 1549. Catholism restored during the reign of Queen Mary, 1553-1558. Queen Elizabeth I (1558-1603) established Anglican church: Act of Supremacy recognized queen's control of the church and Act of Uniformity (both in 1559) ordered Englishmen to conform to the new ceremonies. Thirty-nine Articles (1563) defined the theology of the Church of England.

English Puritans began to protest against vestiges of medieval customs in the English Church after 1566. Richard Hooker wrote the *Laws of Ecclesiastical Polity* which defined the theological position of Anglicanism, 1594-1601. James I (1603-25) rejected Puritan demands for reform at Hampton Court Conference, 1604.

lance of public morality with far greater efficiency than any the courts of the medieval church had possessed. From the outset Calvin made it plain that his movement was intended to supplant the medieval church, to become, in other words, the universal, "reformed" church of Christendom. Impelled by this purpose, Calvinism spread rapidly into France, the Low Countries, the Holy Roman Empire, Scotland, and England. Wherever it appeared, the militancy of its adherents frequently led to conflicts with the existing authority and in some countries to bitter wars of religion.

3. Anglicanism

Anglican Protestantism, that branch of the new movement which developed the English state church, differed from Lutheranism and Calvinism in that the original leadership of the revolt did not come from a great religious leader (though many prominent churchmen gave it their support) but from the state. King Henry VIII (1509-1547) broke with papal authority and proclaimed himself head of the Church of England in 1534. His motives were complex—personal, political, dynastic, patriotic, and vaguely reformist. At first, this break took the form of a schism (separation) in which all the forms, ceremonies, and much of the theology of the medieval church were preserved. Gradually, however, as Henry moved to abolish the monasteries and to introduce other changes, the English church became more and more Protestant. In the reign of Edward VI (1547-1553) the Protestantizing of the church was accelerated with such success that the efforts of the Catholic Queen Mary (1553-1558) to restore England to her own faith proved unavailing. With the accession of Elizabeth I (1558-1603) the form of the Anglican church was finally settled by a compromise in which the organization of the medieval church was retained but the theology of continental Protestantism became the basis of doctrinal belief. Unfortunately, though many Englishmen were satisfied with this middle-of-the-road position, others were not, and this discontent sowed the seeds of later trouble. Catholics disliked the Church of England's theology and its denial of papal authority, whereas the Puritans, a new group so known from their wish to "purify" the church, were angry at its retention of certain Catholic elements. In spite of these difficulties, the Anglican church, because it was purposely broad and comprehensive in its doctrines, was able to include in its membership the great body of loyal Englishmen. In this way it became the prototype of the new kind of "national church that sprang up all over Europe in the wake of the Reformation.

4. The Catholic Reformation

Founding of the Theatine (1524) and Capuchin (1525-1528) orders for the purpose of reforming clerical life. Society of Jesus (Jesuits) organized by Ignatius Loyola (1534); recognized by the pope, 1540. The order was intended through its militancy and discipline to win back Protestants and to combat heresy. Council of Trent reaffirmed the doctrinal position of the church and pronounced the various Protestant theologies to be heresies; undertook extensive reforms in clerical life, 1545-1563. Reform of the Roman curia (central governing body of the Catholic Church) by Pope Paul IV, 1555-1559. Index of prohibited books established, 1557.

5. The Historical Significance of Protestantism

(a) Major Religious Divisions of Europe after the Reformation. (E in parentheses denotes established or official state churches.)
(1) Lutheran:
North Germany: Hesse (E), Saxony (E), Brandenburg (Prussia) (E), Württemberg (E).
Scandinavia: Denmark (E), Norway (E), Sweden (E), Finland (E).
(2) Calvinism:
Rhenish Palatinate (E), parts of Hungary and Poland, regions of western and southwestern France, parts of north Germany, the Netherlands (E), Scotland (E), parts of England, northern Ireland, Geneva (E), and parts of Switzerland.
(3) Anglicanism:
England and Wales (E); established church in Ireland though the great majority of the population remained Catholic.

4. The Catholic Reformation

In the face of growing religious unrest which threatened, by the middle of the 16th century, to destroy the medieval church completely, a series of movements was begun within the Catholic church to strengthen its organization and to eliminate some of the things that had brought on the Protestant revolt. Moves to counter the various outbreaks of religious rebellion sometimes took the form of repression. The Inquisition, a special administrative body originally organized in the middle ages for the examination of heretics, was given wide powers, particularly in Spain and Italy, while the support of Catholic kings and nobles was solicited to prevent the further spread of heresy. The greatest successes of the church, however, were achieved as a result of a spiritual rejuvenation in which the Society of Jesus (Jesuits), founded in 1540 by the soldier-saint Ignatius Loyola (1491-1556), took the lead. By stressing discipline, loyalty to the papacy, and a firm adherence to both religious principles and intellectual standards, the Jesuits were able to keep and to win back countless numbers for the church. In the climax a great church council held at Trent in Italy (1545-1563) reaffirmed the doctrinal teachings of the church; and while this orthodox body prevented any final reconciliation with the Protestants, it reformed numerous things that had been complained of and restored the high standards of Catholic clerical life.

5. The Historical Significance of Protestantism

Protestantism has sometimes been looked upon by historians as the source of many such modern developments as capitalism, liberalism, democracy, and nationalism. In the main, this conclusion has derived from the belief that Protestantism, and particularly Calvinism, by its stress on scriptural authority and through its theology, opened the way to a philosophy of individualism which greatly influenced modern economic and political thinking. This view is sound only if we look at certain indirect effects of Protestant thought. Both Luther and Calvin rejected the doctrine implicit in medieval theology that men could win their salvation through any merits (good works) of their own. Men were saved, they held, because God willed that they should be saved and not through any ministrations or sacraments of the church. In other words, salvation was given to men because they had faith in God and not because they did good in the world. The major Protestant theologians stressed this view because they felt that the medieval church had placed too much stress on certain practices which made it seem that men could buy their way into heaven. In thus arguing, however, leading Protestant thinkers had to face up to a dilemma. If men were saved by faith alone, then what incentive was there for human

(4) Roman Catholic:
Poland, most of Hungary, south Germany, Austria, France, Spain, Portugal, the Italian peninsula. Where the Roman Catholic Church survived it was invariably the established church.

(b) Other Religious Movements.

(1) English Puritanism originated c. 1566 as a movement to "purify" the Church of England.

(2) Socinianism, forerunner of later Unitarianism, founded by Laelius (1525-62) and Faustus (1539-1604) Socinus (Sozzini), two 16th-century Italian reformers.

(3) Separatism: term applied to those English Puritan groups after 1588 who wished to "separate" from the Church of England rather than to reform it from within.

(4) Arminianism: movement within Calvinism named for the Dutch theologian Jacobus Arminius (1560-1609) who sought to mitigate the extreme predestinarian theories of orthodox Calvinism.

(5) Jansenism: mainly a French movement within the Roman Catholic Church which, like orthodox Calvinism, tended to stress predestination. Took its name from the Dutch Catholic theologian, Bishop Cornelis Jansen (1585-1638), whose posthumous work *Augustinus* (1643) became the theological basis of the movement.

(6) English-speaking denominationalism: one of the extraordinary characteristics of English Protestantism was its tendency to divide into numerous denominations. Among the more famous of these were: the Independents (Congregationalists), whose leading members were the poet John Milton, Oliver Cromwell, and the New England theologian John Cotton; the General Baptists, believed to have been founded by the English nonconformist clergyman John Smyth in 1611; the Quakers founded by George Fox (1624-91) about 1647.

lance of public morality with far greater efficiency than any the courts of the medieval church had possessed. From the outset Calvin made it plain that his movement was intended to supplant the medieval church, to become, in other words, the universal, "reformed" church of Christendom. Impelled by this purpose, Calvinism spread rapidly into France, the Low Countries, the Holy Roman Empire, Scotland, and England. Wherever it appeared, the militancy of its adherents frequently led to conflicts with the existing authority and in some countries to bitter wars of religion.

3. Anglicanism

Anglican Protestantism, that branch of the new movement which developed the English state church, differed from Lutheranism and Calvinism in that the original leadership of the revolt did not come from a great religious leader (though many prominent churchmen gave it their support) but from the state. King Henry VIII (1509-1547) broke with papal authority and proclaimed himself head of the Church of England in 1534. His motives were complex—personal, political, dynastic, patriotic, and vaguely reformist. At first, this break took the form of a schism (separation) in which all the forms, ceremonies, and much of the theology of the medieval church were preserved. Gradually, however, as Henry moved to abolish the monasteries and to introduce other changes, the English church became more and more Protestant. In the reign of Edward VI (1547-1553) the Protestantizing of the church was accelerated with such success that the efforts of the Catholic Queen Mary (1553-1558) to restore England to her own faith proved unavailing. With the accession of Elizabeth I (1558-1603) the form of the Anglican church was finally settled by a compromise in which the organization of the medieval church was retained but the theology of continental Protestantism became the basis of doctrinal belief. Unfortunately, though many Englishmen were satisfied with this middle-of-the-road position, others were not, and this discontent sowed the seeds of later trouble. Catholics disliked the Church of England's theology and its denial of papal authority, whereas the Puritans, a new group so known from their wish to "purify" the church, were angry at its retention of certain Catholic elements. In spite of these difficulties, the Anglican church, because it was purposely broad and comprehensive in its doctrines, was able to include in its membership the great body of loyal Englishmen. In this way it became the prototype of the new kind of "national church that sprang up all over Europe in the wake of the Reformation.

4. The Catholic Reformation

Founding of the Theatine (1524) and Capuchin (1525-1528) orders for the purpose of reforming clerical life. Society of Jesus (Jesuits) organized by Ignatius Loyola (1534); recognized by the pope, 1540. The order was intended through its militancy and discipline to win back Protestants and to combat heresy. Council of Trent reaffirmed the doctrinal position of the church and pronounced the various Protestant theologies to be heresies; undertook extensive reforms in clerical life, 1545-1563. Reform of the Roman curia (central governing body of the Catholic Church) by Pope Paul IV, 1555-1559. Index of prohibited books established, 1557.

5. The Historical Significance of Protestantism

(a) Major Religious Divisions of Europe after the Reformation. (E in parentheses denotes established or official state churches.)

    (1) Lutheran:

        North Germany: Hesse (E), Saxony (E), Brandenburg (Prussia) (E), Württemberg (E).

        Scandinavia: Denmark (E), Norway (E), Sweden (E), Finland (E).

    (2) Calvinism:

        Rhenish Palatinate (E), parts of Hungary and Poland, regions of western and southwestern France, parts of north Germany, the Netherlands (E), Scotland (E), parts of England, northern Ireland, Geneva (E), and parts of Switzerland.

    (3) Anglicanism:

        England and Wales (E); established church in Ireland though the great majority of the population remained Catholic.

restless human vitality and curiosity which has been so marked a characteristic of modern European civilization.

3. Literature and Thought

In the literary movements of the Renaissance two distinctive features
emerged. The first of these was the tendency, already evident in Dante's
Divine Comedy (though, as we have seen, its content was purely medieval), to make use of the native (vernacular) languages rather than medieval Latin as a medium of expression. This change, though it did open
the way to a broadening of interests and tastes, was not all gain, for it
resulted in the decline of an international language which had helped
to unify western Christendom. The second distinctive feature of the new
literature was its emphasis on man and man's place in this world (humanism), stimulated by an interest in the writings of classical antiquity. Because many of the leading literary figures of the early Renaissance, men like
the poet-scholar Petrarch (1304-1374), wished to return to the grammatical purity of classical Latin which medieval Latin had lost, it later came
to be assumed that medieval scholars had known nothing of the great
literary works of antiquity and that the Renaissance scholars, by rediscovering them, had truly ushered in an age of "rebirth." The claim
was an exaggeration, but it was not entirely without meaning, for Renaissance scholars and thinkers did help to shift both the intellectual and
literary interests of the time from Christian to classical or secular subjects.
With this shift a great number of thinkers began to concern themselves
with man as he is in the world of here and now. Our best illustration of
this new tendency is to be found in the writings of that tough-minded
realist, Niccolo Machiavelli (1469-1527), whose political writings—the most
famous of which was *The Prince*—helped to divorce political theory
from Christian morality. At the other extreme, however, was the Dutch
humanist scholar Erasmus (1466-1536), whose breadth of knowledge
led him to exalt human values but not to separate them from the traditional Christian ethics.

4. Renaissance Art

The art of the Renaissance also reflects the change in emphasis characteristic of its literature and thought. While architecture, as seen in the
great Gothic cathedrals had been the highest artistic achievement of

ica of St. Peter's (Rome), 1506. "School of Athens" and "Disputa" painted by Raphael, 1509-1511. Painting of Michelangelo's "Last Judgment," 1534-1541. Death of Titian, 1576.

B. OUTSIDE ITALY. Albrecht Dürer's woodcuts on "The Revelation of St. John" (Germany), 1498. Hans Holbein the Younger settled in England, 1532. Philibert Delorme published French manual of architecture, 1561. Escorial Palace built by Philip II of Spain at Madrid, 1563-1584. Death of El Greco, 1625, greatest Spanish painter of the Renaissance.

B. The Reformation

John Wyclif (1320-84) of England attacked the theology of the medieval church, 1378-80; Wyclif's followers, known as Lollards, suppressed by King Henry IV (1399-1413). Great schism of the church finally healed by Council of Constance; same council also executed the Bohemian John Hus for heresy, 1415. Restoration of papal unity with election of Martin V, 1517. Hussite Wars in Bohemia, 1420-33. Conciliar movement, which threatened papal authority, finally lost out in struggle with papacy when Council of Basel, 1431-49, failed in its attempt to make a representative council the governing body of the Church. Decline of the Renaissance papacy: pontificate of the humanist pope, Nicholas V, 1447-55; Alexander VI (Borgia), 1492-1503. Establishment of the Spanish Inquisition, 1478. Savonarola preached against clerical abuses at Florence, 1494-98. Humanist criticism of clerical abuses: *In Praise of Folly* by Erasmus, 1509; *Utopia* by Sir Thomas More, 1516; *The Letters of Obscure Men* by Rubeanus and Ulrich von Hutten, 1515-17.

Influence of humanism on the Reformation: Although humanist criticism had much to do with preparing the climate of opinion that made the Reformation possible, humanism and Protestantism were separate and distinct movements. Humanist critics, particularly in northern Europe, were not anti-Christian or even opposed to the medieval Church as it was constituted about 1500. Most of them, when the crisis of the Reformation came, remained within the Church. Their writings and attitudes, however, inadvertently made men aware of

medieval man, in contrast, the Renaissance artist turned his attention to such individual forms of art as painting and sculpture. As a consequence of a revolution in artistic method, the new artist was able to portray his subjects with a natural exactness and a richness of detail that had been lacking in medieval art; and while he still chose religious themes for expression, he also chose many that were nonreligious. The growth of artistic naturalism may be traced from its beginnings in Giotto's (*c.* 1270-1337) paintings through the pictures and sculpture of such great figures as Leonardo da Vinci (1452-1519), Michelangelo (1475-1564), and Titian (1477-1576), whose work typifies the new diversity and variety of a vastly enriched artistic medium.

B. The Reformation

When we look for the general causes of the great religious split between Catholics and Protestants, which began with Martin Luther (1483-1546) in the first quarter of the 16th century, we find two kinds.

The first type arose from the great changes in the attitude of men toward the world in which they lived, that had occurred during the 14th, 15th, and 16th centuries. These changes were bound to make many persons resentful of an authority like that of the medieval church, which professed to be universal and supernational. Kings and nobles disliked the moral curbs placed on them by the church's teachings and looked with disfavor and envy on the growing wealth and the administrative bureaucracy of such a powerful organization. Merchants were restive at the traditional prohibitions of canon law against the taking of interest on loans and against other business practices that are now accepted as normal and honorable, even though these prohibitions had declined in force during the late middle ages. Moreover, with the rise of strong monarchies and the growth of a sense of national distinctiveness, it was difficult for many Europeans to think of the papacy as anything other than an Italian institution which drew taxes from them to serve its own ends. In the face of these growing forces of secular discontent, it is probable that some sort of break with papal authority might have come without a Martin Luther to cause it. Attitudes had changed and the changes led men more and more to a rejection of the church's spiritual teachings.

The second variety of general cause of the Reformation lay in the Renaissance church itself, which gave Luther and other Protestants something to criticize and thus helped to create the upheaval that followed. For the fact was that some of the churchmen, though by no means all or even a majority, had succumbed to the secular influences of the age. Ecclesiastical

the Church's shortcomings in the early 16th century. Concordat of Bologna between papacy and Francis I of France gave the king virtual control of the French Church; publication of new Greek edition of the New Testament by Erasmus; indulgence mission of Tetzel to Germany, 1516. Reign of the Emperor Charles V, 1519-1556.

1. Lutheranism

Luther's life: born at Eisleben, 1483. Studied at University of Erfurt whose leading theologian, Gabriel Biel (d. 1495), was under the influence of the "nominalist" philosopher William of Ockham (c. 1300-49). Like most Ockhamists, Luther believed in the separation of reason and faith. Entered the order of Augustinian Eremites, 1505; ordained priest, 1507. Visited Rome, 1510-11, and taught at Wittenberg after 1512. Gradually came to conclusion that man is "justified by faith alone," 1512-1517. In reaction to the Tetzel indulgence mission published his 95 Theses, 1517. Excommunicated by Pope Leo X, 1520. Defied Emperor Charles V at Diet of Worms, 1521. Took the side of the princes in suppressing Peasants' Revolt, 1524-25. Later history of Lutheranism: Augsburg Confession (*Confessio Augustana*) set forth principles of Lutheran belief, 1531. National Protestant (Lutheran) church established in Sweden, 1527; in Denmark, 1536. Lutheran-Catholic religious wars (1546-55) culminated in Peace of Augsburg, 1555, which recognized Lutheranism; permitted princes to determine which faith would prevail in their territories ("cuius regio, eius religio").

2. Calvinism

Translation of the Bible into French, 1523-1530. Calvin converted to Protestantism and fled Paris, 1533. Publication of Calvin's *Institutes of the Christian Religion*, 1536. Founding of theocratic Calvinist state at Geneva, 1541. British exiles carry Calvinist ideas to England (after the accession of Elizabeth I in 1558) and Scotland (John Knox returned in 1559). Scottish parliament severed ties with Rome, 1560. Death of Calvin, 1564. Revolt of the Netherlands begun in part under Calvinist auspices, 1566. Declaration of Dutch independence from Spain, 1581. Religious Wars in France (Catholics against

beings to live decent, moral lives? This problem Calvin felt he had solved when he argued that those who possessed faith and were truly among the "elect" chosen for salvation could not be immoral. On the contrary, because they were saved, they would "demonstrate their election" by their austerity, self-denial, and personal morality. This theory, some historians have contended, led the Calvinist to an extreme emphasis on individual morality that made him a hard-working, frugal, productive member of society. Because these virtues are conducive to the accumulation of wealth, it has also been argued that Calvinism was a religion peculiarly favorable to the development of modern capitalism. In this sense, there may be an element of truth to the argument, though it does not take into consideration one or two important facts: first, that such virtues are not always peculiar to Protestant or, specifically, Calvinist societies; and second, that in their social thinking and attitudes the Catholics and Protestants of the 16th and 17th centuries shared many views.

In somewhat the same way it has been said that Protestantism was largely responsible for modern liberalism and democracy because it promoted religious toleration, emphasized religious individualism, and among some sects, used the forms of representative government. Again, such arguments may have some validity if we recognize that these results were quite indirect and inadvertent. At their inception many of the larger Protestant denominations were not believers in religious toleration and, in many cases, came round to it only when it was clear that their own churches were not going to supplant all others. Nor were Protestants, over all, believers in democracy, any more than most people in the 16th and 17th centuries. Like most other Europeans of the period, they would have been horrified at the modern democratic state.

In one important area, but again indirectly, Protestantism seems to have had a significant effect, though even this one should not be exaggerated. This was the influence of Protestantism on the rise of modern nationalism. Some, but by no means all, of the Protestant churches, and particularly those which, like the Church of England, became state-supported or established institutions, tended to unite patriotism and denominationalism by coming under the control of the state. In this way, though it was usually not their intention to do so, they helped to destroy the older, organized unity of Christendom which had been one of the major characteristics of medieval civilization.

After all, it should not be forgotten that Protestantism, whatever its social or political effects, was still a religious movement concerned with religious aims and purposes. We should be careful not to read backward into it(or other historical movements for that matter) ideas and attitudes which were completely alien to its point of view.

EVENTS AND DEFINITIONS

Leading European Dynasties, 1500-1800.
(a) England (after 1603 known as Great Britain).
   (1) The Tudors, 1485-1603.
      Henry VII, 1485-1509; Henry VIII, 1509-1547; Edward VI, 1547-1553; Mary, 1553-1558; Elizabeth I, 1558-1603.

CHAPTER 3

The Age of the Absolute Monarchies

THE ESSENTIAL MOVEMENT

The period from the 16th through the 18th centuries was a time when most of the nations of modern Europe took the form in which we know them today. In almost every major western country the power of the king had grown to a point where those other elements in society, viz., the feudal nobility and the church, which had formerly acted as checks on royal authority, were now either completely broken or else absorbed into the royal administration. There were, of course, exceptions to this pattern of development, most notably England, where the power of the crown was drastically curbed by the end of the 17th century, but, in the main, the 300 years lying between 1500 and 1800 saw the monarchs of Europe victorious in the extension of their power and authority. As we have seen, European kings from the middle ages onward had come more and more to symbolize the new, impersonal nation-state. The king's law, the civil administration, the standing army were all instruments of a new kind of statecraft which, while they were employed to serve the interests of the prince, were also intended to serve the society over which the crown had absolute power. This was the ideal of absolute monarchy and in the degree that it approached this ideal it was successful in maintaining itself. Unfortunately, however, this kind of state had several great weaknesses which, in the end, wrought its undoing. First, its efficiency and impartiality depended not only upon a bureaucracy (whose members often entrenched themselves in offices which were bought and sold

(2) The Stuarts, 1603-1714.

James VI (of Scotland) became James I of England, 1603-25; Charles I, 1625-49; Interregnum (rule of the army leaders, most important of whom was Oliver Cromwell, d. 1658), 1649-60; Charles II, 1660-85; James II, 1685-88; William and Mary, 1688-1702; Anne, 1702-14.

(3) The Hanoverians (House of Brunswick).

George I, 1714-27; George II, 1727-60; George III, 1760-1820.

(b) France.

(1) Valois kings.

Charles VIII, 1498-1515; Francis I, 1515-47; Henry II, 1547-59; Francis II, 1559-60; Charles IX, 1560-74; Henry III, 1574-89.

(2) Bourbon kings.

Henry IV, 1589-1610; Louis XIII, 1610-43; Louis XIV, 1643-1715; Louis XV, 1715-74; Louis XVI, 1774-92.

(c) Holy Roman Empire (House of Hapsburg).

Maximilian I, 1493-1519; Charles V, 1519-56; Ferdinand I, 1556-64; Maximilian II, 1564-76; Rudolf II, 1576-1612; Mathias, 1612-19; Ferdinand II, 1619-37; Ferdinand III, 1637-57; Leopold I, 1658-1705; Joseph I, 1705-11; Charles VI, 1711-40; Francis I (of Lorraine), 1745-65, and Maria Theresa, 1740-1780; Joseph II, 1765-90; Leopold II, 1790-92; Francis II (took title of Francis I of Austria after 1806), 1792-1835.

(d) Russia (Romanovs).

Michael, 1613-45; Alexis, 1645-76; Theodore III, 1676-82; Ivan V, 1682-89; Peter I (the Great), 1689-1725; Catherine I, 1725-27; Peter II, 1727-30; Anna, 1730-40; Elizabeth, 1741-62; Peter III, 1762; Catherine II (the Great), 1762-96; Paul I, 1796-1801.

(e) Prussia (Hohenzollerns).

Frederick William (the Great Elector), 1640-88; Frederick I (first Prussian king), 1688-1713; Frederick William I, 1713-40; Frederick II (the Great), 1740-86; Frederick William II, 1786-97; Frederick William III, 1797-1840.

or passed from father to son) but also upon the personal abilities of a sovereign (whose qualities as a ruler, because of the uncertainties of dynastic inheritance, varied greatly from generation to generation). Second, though western European kings were to some extent limited in their absolute freedom to make political decisions, there was nothing short of rebellion or military defeat by a neighboring state which could keep them from carrying out policies that were sometimes dangerous to the welfare of their subjects. And, third, while the absolute monarchy did a great deal to destroy the powers and privileges of the nobility, it did not erase them entirely and, in some cases, actually increased them so long as the nobles were willing to become the servants and supporters of the state. These three weaknesses, coupled with rising costs of government from the 16th century onward, created a number of complex problems with which absolute governments were less and less able to cope successfully.

A. Dynastic Conflicts and Wars of Religion

In the period between 1500 and 1715, the territorial and dynastic ambitions of the various European states led to an almost incessant warfare which gave the ascendancy first to one power or group of powers and then to another. These contests were not simply straightforward struggles for lands and power but were complicated by the religious divisions of the Reformation. Just as there were Catholic and Protestant parties which fought savage civil wars in many countries, so, too, there were Catholic and Protestant nations whose interests divided the whole of Europe into armed camps. In time, however, while religious motives were occasionally strong enough to sway the policies of particular rulers or countries, other considerations, more mundane, came to have an increasing effect on national policies. By the end of the 16th century it was already possible to observe the rather frequent crossing of religious lines in order to form alliances. A generation later, with the coming of the Thirty Years' War, such practices were quite common. Nonetheless, in spite of the decline of religious partisanship as a cause of wars, many conflicts were greatly intensified when religious zeal coincided with other motives. This was one of the major reasons why the wars of the period from 1500 to 1715 were often fought with an unexampled bitterness that did not subside until after the signing of the Peace of Westphalia in 1648.

Let us now look briefly at the role of several of the more important states in the international affairs of this troubled period.

A. Dynastic Conflicts and Wars of Religion

1. Spain

Reign of Ferdinand and Isabella (1479-1516) saw the union of Castile and Aragon, the downfall of the last Moorish state, and the beginning of Spanish overseas expansion. Charles I (of Spain) became king (1516-1556) and Holy Roman Emperor as Charles V, 1519-1556. Hapsburg-Valois rivalry led to wars with France: 1521-1529; 1535-1538; 1542-1545; 1551-1559; which ended with the Treaty of Cateau-Cambrésis—a Spanish triumph that marked the high point of Spanish influence in Europe.

Philip II (1556-1598) committed Spain to the cause of the Catholic Reformation: (1) revolt of the Netherlands, 1568-1609; (2) attempt to invade England—defeat of the Spanish Armada, 1588; (3) intervention in French Wars of Religion, 1589-1598.

Spain entered the Thirty Years' War (1618-1648) on the side of the Austrian Hapsburgs against France. Defeat of the Spanish army by French at Rocroi, 1643, marked the end of Spanish military supremacy in Europe. Treaty of the Pyrenees (1659) signalized the decline of Spain and the rise of France.

Reign of Charles II, 1665-1700, last of the Spanish Hapsburgs. To avoid controversy over succession England, Holland, and France undertook to dispose of Spain and its empire by private agreement, 1698. King Charles, in anger, left his throne to Philip of Anjou, grandson of Louis XIV of France. Austria, England, and Holland formed the Grand Alliance, 1701, to prevent possible union of French and Spanish crowns. War of Spanish Succession, 1701-14.

2. France

Reign of Francis I (1515-1547) marked by the so-called Hapsburg-Valois Wars (see Spain above) and beginning of Protestant movement in France. Treaty of Cateau-Cambrésis (see Spain above), 1559. Wars of Religion, 1563-1598 (see Calvinism, chapter VI). Reign of Henry IV (1589-1610) marked by restoration of strong monarchy and granting of toleration to Huguenots (Edict of Nantes, 1598).

1. Spain

The 16th century was the era of Spain's greatest power. By the year 1500 a number of smaller kingdoms in the Iberian Peninsula had been consolidated under two rulers, Ferdinand and Isabella, who had destroyed the last vestiges of the ancient Islamic power and embarked on an ambitious program of overseas exploration and colonization which was destined to bring wealth and greatness to the newly unified Spanish kingdom. Through intermarriage, the crowns of Spain and the Holy Roman Empire came into the possession of a single dynasty (Hapsburgs), whose leading representative, the Emperor Charles V, was the most powerful ruler of the 16th century. Even so, Charles, a devout Catholic, was not able to check the rise of Lutheranism in Germany. Neither could he entirely eliminate the danger to his family territories arising out of his long rivalry with France. Nevertheless, Charles at his abdication was able to leave to his son, who became Philip II of Spain (1556-1598), a rich inheritance of lands and power. Philip, who was the epitome of the hard-working absolute monarch, at once embarked on a series of projects which were to weaken Spain permanently. All vestiges of religious dissent were ruthlessly suppressed in his dominions. Spanish commerce and industry were rigorously controlled. The military strength of Spain was committed to the cause of the Catholic Reformation and to the weakening of the French monarchy. Philip's most disastrous policies led to a protracted rebellion in the Low Countries, by which Holland finally won its independence, and also to an unsuccessful attempt to conquer England which failed with the defeat of the Spanish armada by the English in 1588. The last years of Philip's life ended in defeat at the hands of the resurgent French monarchy. From these disasters Spain never recovered, though she was to remain a major force in European politics during the first half of the 17th century. By the year 1700 the Spanish kingdom had sunk to the level of a second-rate power.

2. France

The French monarchy, after many vicissitudes which saw it decline from a peak of greatness in the 13th century to the low point of English conquest during the Hundred Years' War (1338-1453), emerged at the end of the 15th century as one of the strong states of Europe. With the accession of Francis I (1515-1547) the long rivalry between the French kings and the Hapsburgs, which was to influence European international relations for more than two centuries, was begun. Despite

LouisXIII (1610-1643) made Cardinal Richelieu (in power from 1624 to 1642) his chief adviser. The latter (1) broke the independent power of the Huguenots, (2) strengthened the monarchy by checking the feudal nobles, and (3) curbed the House of Hapsburg by intervening in the Thirty Years' War on the side of the German Protestants (1635-1648).

Reign of Louis XIV (1643-1715) saw the emergence of France as the leading power of Europe. Treaty of the Pyrenees, 1659 (see Spain above). Colbert as Controller-General of Finances (1662-1683) stimulated French economic growth and created the system of mercantilism in its classic form (see p. 37, text). Wars of Devolution, 1667-1668 (over the Spanish Netherlands); 1672-1678 (against Holland). Revocation of the Edict of Nantes (1685) forced thousands of Huguenots into exile. War of the League of Augsburg (over the Rhenish Palatinate), 1688-1697. War of the Spanish Succession (over uniting the crowns of Spain and France), 1701-1714. Treaties of Utrecht (1713) and Rastadt (1714) provided that Louis XIV's grandson Philip V should remain on the Spanish throne but that France and Spain should never be unified. Death of Louis XIV (1715) left France severely strained in finances and manpower. Louis XV, 1715-74, great-grandson of Louis XIV, succeeded. "Mississippi Bubble," 1718-20, caused by speculation promoted by the financier John Law. France participated in the War of the Polish Succession in alliance with Spain and Sardinia, 1733-38. War of the Austrian Succession in which France allied with Prussia supported the Bavarian elector's claims to the Holy Roman Empire against Maria Theresa, 1740-48. "Diplomatic Revolution" saw France allied with the Hapsburgs for the first time in history in the ensuing Seven Years' War, 1756-63.

3.   England

Reign of Henry VII (1485-1509); order restored after the Wars of the Roses; monarchy strengthened; Court of Star Chamber established, 1487. Reign of Henry VIII (1509-1547) chancellorship of Cardinal Wolsey, 1515-1529; Act of Supremacy made Henry head of the English Church, 1534 (for other changes see Anglicanism, chapter VI).

his incessant wars, Francis strengthened the monarchy and during the period of religious upheaval kept France firmly Catholic although a large segment of the French population was won over to Calvinism. In the reign of his son, Charles IX, a series of civil wars began between Catholics and Huguenots (Protestants) which lasted to the end of the 16th century. These were not terminated until the former Protestant prince, Henry IV (1589-1610), issued the Edict of Nantes (1598) granting religious toleration and a measure of security to the Huguenots.

Under Henry and his successors, Louis XIII (1610-1643) and Louis XIV (1643-1715), both the French state and French society underwent a process of reconstruction after the long period of religious struggle. As a consequence, France emerged during the last half of the 17th century as the leading nation of Europe. The architects of this reconstruction were Cardinal Richelieu (1585-1642) under Louis XIII, and Cardinal Mazarin (1602-1661) under Louis XIV. Through their efforts the royal government was made transcendent over French localism and various elements (Huguenots and nobles) potentially dangerous to the state were deprived of any further power to do harm. Withal, the state did its best to strengthen the economy through the protection of French manufactures and the strict regulation of foreign trade. This policy, known as mercantilism, was fully developed and put into practice by Colbert (1619-1683), the finance minister of Louis XIV. The work of these three men enabled King Louis to embark on that series of expansionist wars at the end of the 17th century which, while they made France feared throughout Europe, disastrously weakened the internal structure of French society and dissipated its laboriously accumulated wealth.

In spite of the unfortunate foreign policy of Louis, the late 17th century was one of the brilliant periods of French history. Cultivated persons everywhere looked to France for cultural inspiration, and the French language became a second tongue for the social and intellectual elites of Europe. This, too, was a great era of French literature which produced such names as Corneille (1606-1684), Molière (1622-1673), and Racine (1639-1699).

3.   England

The history of the English monarchy during the 16th and 17th centuries was, in its conclusion, quite different from that of France or Spain. For more than 150 years, however— from 1485 to 1640—it looked as though England, too, would go the way of most other western European states and become permanently an absolute monarchy. Under the strong Tudor dynasty, whose leading representatives were Henry VII

Reign of Elizabeth I (1558-1603): defeat of the Spanish Armada, 1588; "Golden Age" of English literature.

Reign of James I (1603-1625): conflict with parliament over finances and extension of royal power, 1604-1624.

Reign of Charles I (1625-1649): Petition of Right, 1628; dissolution of parliament and eleven years of personal rule, 1629-1640; Scottish rebellion (1637-1640) forced Charles to call the Long Parliament in 1640; civil wars, 1642-1649; execution of Charles I, 1649.

Commonwealth and Protectorate, 1649-1660: Commonwealth (republic) supplanted the monarchy, 1649-1653; Oliver Cromwell (1599-1658) assumed title of Lord Protector, 1653-1658.

Restoration of the monarchy (1660); reign of Charles II, 1660-1685: Clarendon Code (for the suppression of Protestant dissenters who were not members of the Church of England) formulated, 1661-1665; Charles II and parliament in conflict over the right of his Catholic brother James to succeed to the throne, 1679-1681; Charles attacked the leaders of the Whig party (which favored religious toleration and limited monarchy) and tried to re-establish absolute rule in England, 1681-1685.

Reign of James II (last Catholic king of England), 1685-1688: James attempted to re-establish the Catholic faith and provoked the "Glorious Revolution" of 1688.

Reign of Mary II with William III (of Orange), who had been invited to the English throne, 1689-1702: Bill of Rights, 1689, permanently limited royal power; Act of Settlement, 1701, reserved the English throne for Protestants.

Reign of Anne, 1702-1714: union of England with Scotland, 1707; Peace of Utrecht (1713) saw England's emergence as the leading maritime power of Europe.

Reign of George I (formerly ruler of the small German state of Hanover), 1714-1727: beginning of modern cabinet government under Sir Robert Walpole, first prime minister of England, 1721-1742.

George II, 1727-60, continued Walpole in office. War of Jenkins' Ear with Spain, 1739-48; England participated in the War of the Austrian Succession from 1744-48 as an ally of Austria. Second Jacobite Rebellion, known as "The Forty-five," attempted to place the Stuart pretender, Charles Ed-

(1485-1509), Henry VIII (1509-1547), and Elizabeth I (1558-1603), every tendency pointed in that direction. By reducing the English nobility to obedience, assuming the headship of the church, and reorganizing the machinery of government, these monarchs gave to England a state with all the characteristics of the new kind of monarchy. Though less popular and less able than their Tudor successors, the first two kings of the house of Stuart, James I (1603-1625) and Charles I (1625-1649), tried to carry on with these developments but met disaster in the attempt. In the middle of the 17th century the growth of royal absolutism was suddenly checked by the outbreak of civil war. After a long period of intermittent struggle, which saw the monarchy temporarily replaced by a military dictatorship under Oliver Cromwell (1649-1658), the power of the crown was conclusively curbed by the "Glorious Revolution" of 1688.

Though there are many reasons for England's divergence from the general European pattern of political development, one of the most important was the result of a peculiarly English historical happenstance. England, unlike the continental states, had not only preserved its medieval representative body, the parliament, but had seen that body grow in strength until it had become an integral part of the English system of government. Theoretically, even so late as the 17th century, parliament was not an independent political body representing the will of the people but a dependent institution which the king might merely consult in public matters and which he did not have to call into existence at all if he did not wish to. Because the problem of government finance had become serious by the 17th century, the king was forced to resort to parliament more and more often for financial aid. This aid parliament would give him only at the price of his surrendering some of his powers. When in the end Charles I, in desperation, tried to rule without parliament entirely, his expedient helped to bring on civil war. For Charles, in so doing, challenged a number of discontented groups who were strongly represented in parliament. These were the country gentlemen (gentry), lawyers, merchants, and the various religious groups who were called Puritans. These groups spearheaded the opposition to the crown and, throughout the century, continually tried to hold its power in check.

With the Revolution of 1688, England did not become at once either a democracy or a constitutional monarchy in the modern sense. What it did become was a state in which the final constitutional power was controlled by a rather limited elite of great landholding nobles and gentlemen and a few wealthy merchants who were strong enough to make their influence felt in parliament. Though the English electoral system was to remain thoroughly unrepresentative until drastically re-

ward ("Bonnie Prince Charlie"), on the British throne; rebels decisively defeated at Culloden, 1745-46. Seven Years' War between England and France, 1756-63. Great war ministry of William Pitt the Elder led England to victory, 1757-61. Reign of George III, 1760-1820. Peace of Paris terminated war, 1763.

4.   The Holy Roman Empire

Reign of Charles V (1519-1556): abdication of Charles permanently separated Spain and the Empire under two separate branches of the Hapsburg family.

A. THE THIRTY YEARS' WAR, 1618-1648. Growing religious rivalry within the empire (among Catholics, Lutherans, and Calvinists) led to Thirty Years' War, 1618-1648, which passed through four major phases: (1) the Bohemian period, 1618-1625, when the Bohemians, who had rejected the Emperor Ferdinand II as their ruler and elected Frederick V, a Calvinist and elector of the Rhenish Palatinate, as their king, were defeated by the imperial armies; (2) the Danish period, 1625-1629, when Christian IV of Denmark intervened in the war and was forced to withdraw after defeats by the imperial armies; (3) the Swedish period, 1630-1635, when the Swedish king, Gustavus Adolphus, invaded Germany and was everywhere victorious over the imperialists until his death at the Battle of Lützen in 1632; (4) the Swedish-French period,

formed in the 19th century, the revolution engineered by this small aristocratic oligarchy of Englishmen in 1688 was not without great historical significance. Not only did it become the model which justified later revolutions, including those in America and France, but it helped to preserve the traditions of parliamentary government at a moment when they were rapidly disappearing in other parts of Europe.

In other ways, too, the history of England during the 16th and 17th centuries was marked by developments of importance to the western world. This was a remarkable era of English intellectual and social vitality which had its beginnings in one of the great periods of the world's history, the "Golden Age" of Queen Elizabeth. English seamen, like Drake and Hawkins, pushed into seas previously unknown to England and destroyed the seapower of Spain with their daring. A generation after the defeat of the Spanish armada in 1588 the first English settlements were made in North America. With these events the whole of the western hemisphere came under European colonization and was thus destined to become a part of the larger community of western civilization. In literature, Shakespeare (1564-1616), Spenser (1552?-1599), and Milton (1608-1674) stand out amid a cluster of others that helped to make this one of the major epochs in the history of English writing, for each of these was to have an influence reaching far beyond his native land.

4.   The Holy Roman Empire

By 1500, the Holy Roman Empire, which was originally intended to be the proud successor of the first Roman Empire, had become a loose confederation made up largely of small German-speaking principalities who acknowledged the rule of the Hapsburgs as nominally elected emperors. Unlike France or England, the Empire had never developed a centralized government, and the rise of Lutheranism and Calvinism furthered its disunity by dividing the Catholic emperors from their large body of Protestant subjects. In the first quarter of the 17th century, tension between the two camps finally led to the outbreak of a long and unhappy war. This struggle, known as the Thirty Years' War (1618-1648), was more than just a religious conflict. At stake also was the question of imperial authority. If the emperor could make himself master of a strong, unified empire whose princes were dependent directly upon his rule, then the old Holy Roman Empire might well become the most powerful state in Europe. It was in fear of this eventuality, as well as for religious reasons, that other European states came to be involved in the struggle. Before it was finished, at one time or another, England, the Netherlands,

1635-1648, when Sweden and France in alliance carried on the
war against the Holy Roman Emperor.

B. PEACE OF WESTPHALIA, 1648. After long war which
resulted in serious losses of men and wealth throughout Germany, both sides finally negotiated the Peace of Westphalia,
1648. By its terms the power of the Holy Roman Emperor was
reduced to a shadow; religious toleration was won by the Calvinists; and the independence of the Netherlands was recognized. War left German lands in a state of chaos for almost a
generation. Slow recovery of the empire: imperial forces drove
Turks from Hungary, 1682-1699, but not before the Turks' last
siege of Vienna, 1683.

Death of the last male heir of the Hapsburg line (Charles
VI, 1711-1740), who had tried to secure the rights of his daugh-
ter, Maria Theresa (1740-1780), to the Austrian throne by means
of the Pragmatic Sanction, led to the War of the Austrian Succession, 1740-1748.

"Diplomatic revolution" ended the long rivalry between
France and Austria and brought them into alliance against
Prussia and England during the Seven Years' War, 1756-1763.

Reign of Joseph II (1765-1790) marked the era of "enlightened despotism" in Austria.

5. Holland and Sweden

A. HOLLAND. War of Dutch Independence (two phases:
1568-1609 and 1621-1648) resulted in recognition of Holland's
independence at Peace of Westphalia, 1648: duke of Alva sent
by Spain to suppress Dutch revolt, 1567; declaration of Dutch
independence, 1581; death of William the Silent (prince of Orange), 1584; beginning of Dutch mercantile expansion and overseas settlement, c. 1595; twelve years' truce between Dutch
and Spaniards, 1609-1621; renewal of hostilities, 1621-1648,
ended in formal recognition of Dutch freedom.

B. SWEDEN. Gustavus I (Vasa) led successful rebellion
against Denmark, 1520, and became king, 1523-1560; beginning of Swedish expansion into Baltic region. Sweden accepted
Lutheranism, 1527. Eric XIV, 1560-1568, continued expansion
of Swedish power in Baltic area. Gustavus Adolphus, 1611-
1632, made Sweden the leading Baltic power; intervened successfully in Thirty Years' War (see Holy Roman Empire above).
Reign of Charles XII, 1697-1718, marked the decline of Swed-

Denmark, Spain, Sweden (under its great king, Gustavus Adolphus), and France, had all taken part on one or the other side in the conflict. The war had three significant results in that at its conclusion (Peace of Westphalia, 1648), the hope of uniting all German-speaking lands under a single ruler was virtually ended until the 19th century, Spain was further weakened as a major European power, and France had emerged as the strongest continental state.

5. Holland and Sweden

The 17th century also saw the rise of two lesser states, Holland and Sweden, to brief periods of greatness. Holland, following a long struggle against Spain for her independence, became, after 1600, one of the leading colonial powers of Europe. By developing her seapower and commercial skills, this small country was able to play the role of a great state until the beginning of the 17th century, despite a relatively small population and a scarcity of natural resources. Sweden, on the other hand, while even poorer in resources and population, had the advantage of able leadership and excellent military organization which made it possible for the Swedes to dominate the Baltic regions and parts of northern Europe throughout the 17th century. With the rise of Russia after 1700, Sweden's position rapidly declined to that of a lesser European state.

ish power: Swedes defeated by Russians at Poltava, 1709; treaty of Nystadt, 1721, ended Sweden's dominance of the Baltic.

Hostilities with Russia renewed by Sweden in an effort to regain lost territories, 1741-43. By terms of the Treaty of Abö (1743) Sweden was forced to cede Finland to the Russians. Third Russian war, 1788-90, achieved initial successes; Swedes finally forced to conclude the Treaty of Wereloe which left Russia in possession of Finland and Karelia.

B.   The Shift to Eastern Europe: Prussia and Russia

1.   Prussia (Brandenburg)

Union of Prussia and the electorate of Brandenburg by inheritance, 1618. Reign of Frederick William the Great Elector, 1640-1688, saw the building of a strong army and a centralized government. Frederick III, elector of Brandenburg, assumed title of "King in Prussia," 1701. Frederick William I (1713-1740) created powerful Prussian army. Frederick II (the Great), 1740-1786, conquered Silesia in the War of the Austrian Succession, 1740-1748, and in alliance with England against Austria, France, and Russia successfully fought to keep it during the Seven Years' War, 1756-1763. Prussia remained one of the leading military powers of Europe until the Napoleonic era.

Treaty of Hubertusburg, 1763, guaranteed Prussia's retention of the conquered territory of Silesia. Series of domestic measures undertaken by Frederick II intended to restore Prussia after the war: remission of provincial taxes; establishment of central bank at Berlin (1765); major drainage projects undertaken. For all of these efforts, Prussia remained a not very happy model of 18th-century autocracy.

B. The Shift to Eastern Europe: Prussia and Russia

Until the end of the 17th century the focus of European events was upon the long-established states and kingdoms of western Europe. After 1700 this focus was broadened to include two new states, Prussia and Russia, whose emergence as major powers was to alter permanently the old system of international relationships in Europe. Both of these new monarchies came into existence at a time when absolutism was at its height in the West and were, therefore, able to incorporate into their system of government all the institutions and practices of the new absolutism without at the same time accepting the long-established forms of law and the customary sanctions which tended to limit the powers of western absolute monarchs. As a consequence, the sovereigns of Prussia and Russia were able to construct state systems which were far more efficient in the exercise of power, far more authoritarian, and, in some ways, far more ruthless than any existing in western Europe.

1. Prussia

With small exaggeration, it is possible to say that the kingdom of Prussia was created by a continuous and deliberate act of will on the part of an able line of north German princes whose reigns extended over a period of about 150 years (1640-1786). The territory from which these Hohenzollern rulers first began to expand their power consisted of the old border or march (mark) lands of Brandenburg in north central Germany, an area neither particularly fertile nor unusually endowed with natural resources. By clever manipulation and remarkable foresight, the rulers of Brandenburg (known as "electoral princes" in the 17th century and as "kings in Prussia" after 1701) were able to outmaneuver their neighbors diplomatically and to build up their civil service and army with such effect that by the opening of the 18th century their small state of Prussia had expanded into a formidable European power. With the accession of Frederick the Great (1740-1786), the new kingdom possessed a leader of genius and daring who led his country in successful wars with its far more powerful neighbors and, at one period during the Seven Years' War (1756-1763), actually kept at bay a powerful alliance of Austria, France, and Russia. The great effort required for so small a country to maintain itself as a major power forced the Prussian state to subordinate other forms of social activity to the interests of the military

2. Russia

Reign of Ivan III (the Great), 1462-1505, first Russian national ruler. Ivan IV (1533-1584) formally assumed title of tsar (czar, caesar) and thus laid claim to the pretensions of the Byzantine emperors. Russian patriarchate separate from that of Constantinople established, 1589.

Civil war ("time of troubles") resulted in the calling of the Romanov dynasty to the Russian throne, 1613.

Peter I (the Great), 1689-1725, undertook to "westernize" Russia and to transform it into a significant European power. His aims: (1) to give Russia an outlet to the sea; (2) to make the country strong militarily and economically by introducing West European skills; and (3) to increase the central authority of the state over church and nobles. In the Great Northern War, 1700-21, Peter broke Sweden's power in the north; though first defeated by Charles XII at Narva, 1700, Peter later won a decisive victory over the Swedes at Poltava, 1709. Peter's internal reforms: nobility made to serve the state; industry and trade encouraged; government of the Orthodox Church brought under control of the state. Treaty of Nystadt, 1721, marked Russia's emergence as the leading northern power. Russia emerged as a major European military power by participating in the Seven Years' War, 1756-63, in alliance with Austria and France against Frederick the Great. First Russian university founded in Moscow, 1755. Reign of Catherine the Great, 1762-96, saw an extension of Peter the Great's work of reform; Russian expansion in Turkey and Siberia began; ancient kingdom of Poland partitioned among Russia, Austria, and Prussia in 1772, 1793, and 1795.

C. The World of 18th-Century Europe

Overseas expansion and settlement during the seventeenth century.

The seventeenth century witnessed a less spectacular

establishment and led to the founding of a military caste and a tradition as harsh and demanding in its way as that of Sparta in the ancient world.

2. Russia

Of equal significance to western civilization was the emergence of Russia as a European power during the same period. For centuries the Slavic peoples of the great east European plain had been isolated from the mainstream of west European development. During the early middle ages Latin Christian missionaries had converted the Poles (*c.* 963) and brought the medieval kingdom of Poland into western Christendom, while, at about the same time, German colonists, pushing eastward across the Elbe and Oder rivers, had conquered and Christianized other groups of Slavs. Both movements had stopped short of the area now known as Russia which, as a consequence, came under influences and developed a society and customs somewhat different from those of the west European community of states. There the missionary efforts of the Greek Orthodox Church brought Russian lands within the Greek Christian orbit; then a period of Tartar rule, beginning in the 13th century, kept the peoples of the area in isolation from the West. Not until the 15th century did the modern state begin to expand outward from the principality of Muscovy (Moscow). As it grew, its rulers began to think of themselves as the Caesars (czars or tsars) of the "third Rome" and took on the style and manner of Byzantine autocrats, while their power was greatly enhanced by the unsettled conditions of the Russian frontiers. By the 17th century the Russian state was pressing hard against the older Slavic kingdoms of Poland and Lithuania as it gradually moved its borders westward.

At this juncture there came to the Russian throne the famous "westernizing" Tsar Peter the Great (1689-1725), who deliberately initiated a policy intended to bring Russia up to the western level of military and economic strength. With ruthless energy he made his country a European power for the first time in its history. Though it was for long inferior to the rest of Europe in its economic and technical development, the appearance of such a vast sprawling state with its expansionist tendencies was to change the European balance of power permanently.

C. The World of 18th-Century Europe

By the opening of 18th century, a significant change had taken place in the relations of western Europe with the rest of the world. While Europe's wars were still fought over European objectives—namely, ter-

but more consistent expansion of European holdings over-seas. If there were few major discoveries, colonization and development went on apace so that by the end of the century that worldwide commercial network created by the European imperial system had virtually come into being. In general, European colonization tended to follow three patterns: (1) in regions like Latin America a resident aristocracy of Spaniards and Portuguese ruled a large and long-settled but relatively primitive population who worked for the ruling Europeans as a labor force; to some extent the Europeans intermarried with the native population; (2) elsewhere, in North America for example, where the native population was too sparse to furnish an adequate labor force, Europeans pushed the natives aside and established European communities whose inhab-itants lived by their own labors and in so doing made use of European skills and techniques; (3) in most parts of Africa and Asia the Europeans did not settle in great numbers but sought only to establish trading stations and to develop com-mercial monopolies.

D. The 18th-Century Struggle for Overseas Empire

In the Peace of Utrecht (1713; War of the Spanish Suc-cession) Britain gained from France: Acadia, Hudson's Bay, Newfoundland, and St. Kitts; from Spain, Gibraltar and the right to trade with Spanish colonies for 30 years (the *Asiento*).

The Treaty of Aix-la-Chapelle (1748; War of the Austrian Succession) provided for the mutual restoration of colonial conquests.

In the Treaty of Paris (1763; Seven Years' War) Britain gained from France: Canada and Cape Breton Island, Grenada in the West Indies, and French possessions on the Senegal in Africa; from Spain, Florida. Britain restored Goree in Africa

ritorial rivalries, dynastic ambitions, and power alignments—a new and important element began to play an often decisive part in the diplomatic and military strategy of European states. Heretofore, struggles over colonies or commercial concessions in other parts of the world had been localized affairs which did not always affect the welfare or the position of a particular state in international politics. After 1700, however, victory or defeat in remote areas like India or North America could often determine the outcome of a European war.

The reason for this change is not far to seek. A significant part of Europe's economic well-being now depended upon overseas connections. Great amounts of capital and large numbers of Europeans had migrated to lands outside Europe. Indirectly, of course, the economic power of the new relationship had been making itself felt in Europe for generations. Since the 16th century the gold and silver brought to Spain from the new world had been pumped, in the regular course of commercial exchange, into the European economic system. As a result, the decline in the purchasing power of money, which had been observable in European life from the 15th century onward, became more marked; indeed, it was a "price revolution" which enormously increased the cost of living. The effects of this sudden increase were far-reaching and contributed to the economic hardship not only of individuals but even of governments. The financial difficulties of many European monarchs during the 16th and 17th centuries, which in turn caused political tensions and upheavals, are indirectly traceable to this economic revolution. In this sense, the European economy was already global, and Europe itself was the center of a complex network of relationships reaching outward to all parts of the earth.

D. The 18th-Century Struggle for Overseas Empire

Two nations, England and France, were more directly involved in and affected by this transformation during the 18th century than any others. Holland and Spain both had passed the zenith of their power, and no other continental states were in a position to challenge Anglo-French hegemony outside Europe. As a consequence, these two were the major antagonists in a long series of intermittent struggles for empire which lasted for almost a century and terminated on the eve of the French Revolution. In each of these conflicts, beginning with the War of the Spanish Succession (1702-1713), through the War of the Austrian Succession (1740-1748), the Seven Years' War (1756-1763), and ending with the War of the American Revolution (1778-1783), England was

and Pondichery and Chandernagor in India to France; Cuba
was returned by Britain to Spain. This treaty marked the
height of Britain's colonial power in the 18th century.

In the Treaty of Paris (1783; War of the American Revo-
lution) Britain granted independence to American colonies,
Tobago and Senegal to France, Minorca and Florida to
Spain. This was the only colonial war of the century in which
Britain lost more than she gained.

almost regularly victorious. Only in the War of the American Revolution did she suffer any reversal. It was during this century that England acquired vast territories which historians have come to call the First British Empire, since a great deal of it, including her colonies in North America, was lost in 1783. She did, however, come into possession of Canada and retain it, and she cemented her hold upon large parts of the subcontinent of India.

CHAPTER 4

The Scientific Revolution and the Age of the Enlightenment

THE ESSENTIAL MOVEMENT

During few periods of his history has western man ever really possessed the confidence to believe that by his reasoning alone he could fathom all the questions about himself and his existence. For the greater part of his historic life man has sensed something unknown or mysterious that lies just beyond his powers of rational explanation. Traditionally, he has assigned that unknown to the sphere of religious faith, confessing that the universe in all of its mystery is truly explicable only in terms of the divine. On a few historic occasions, however, the elation of a great and significant intellectual discovery, which seems to push the boundaries of his understanding deep into the unknown, has raised his confidence in his own powers to a point where he believes himself capable, after all, of finally answering the questions that have puzzled him since the beginning of time. One period when men came close to achieving this confidence was during the age of Greek intellectual greatness in the 5th and 4th centuries B.C. Another began with the opening of the 18th century, reached its zenith a few decades later, and carried over, at least in the sphere of scientific thought, into the 19th and 20th centuries. Much of this confidence remains with us, though doubting voices have been raised in our own time to question, once again, the possibility of man's ultimately knowing all that there is to know about himself and his universe.

EVENTS AND DEFINITIONS

A. The Scientific Revolution

Many of the earliest and most significant scientific discoveries of the early modern period were made in the field of
astronomy. Some of the more important of these were: (1)
the formulation of the heliocentric (sun-centered) theory of
the solar system by Copernicus (1473-1543) whose *On the
Revolution of Celestial Bodies* transformed the bases of scientific thought; (2) Johannes Kepler (1571-1630) formulated his
three laws of planetary motion; (3) Galileo Galilei (1564-1642)
perfected telescope (1609) which proved the Copernican theory; Galileo also formulated the laws of "local motion" (mechanics); (4) Isaac Newton (1642-1727) published his conclusions on the laws of celestial mechanics (theory of gravitation)
in *Principia mathematica* (1687); Pierre Simon de Laplace
(1749-1827) completed and developed the Newtonian astronomy in his *Système du Monde* (1796).

Mathematics and Natural Philosophy: Francis Bacon
(1561-1626) set forth his inductive method and prepared the
way for modern experimental method in his *Novum Organ-
um*; René Descartes (1596-1650) wrote *Discourse on Method*
and first applied algebraic method to geometry; Blaise Pascal
(1632-1662) discovered mathematical theory of probability;
Newton and G. W. Leibniz (1646-1716), the German philosopher, independently discovered the Calculus; Joseph Lagrange
(1736-1813) created the calculus of variations and systema-
tized differential equations.

Medicine, Biology, and Chemistry: Theophrastus von
Hohenheim (Paracelsus), c. 1490-1541, broke with the medical tradition of Galen and used chemical drugs in medical
practice; Andreas Vesalius, 1515-1564, published his great
work on anatomy, *Fabrica Humani Corporis* in 1543; William
Harvey, 1578-1657, formulated a general theory of blood circulation in his *On the Motion of the Heart* (1628); Anton van
Leeuwenhoek, 1632-1723, Dutch microscopist, did not invent
the microscope but he did perfect the technique of micro-
scopic observation in scientific experiments; John Ray, 1627-
1705, laid the foundations of modern descriptive and system-
atic biology; Carl Linnaeus (von Linne), 1707-1778, evolved
the first successful system of biological classification (1735);
Georges Cuvier, 1769-1832, founded the modern science of

A. The Scientific Revolution

What gave the 18th century its confidence in the power of man's reason to reduce the unknown was a revolution in thought which had occurred in the century preceding. The 17th century was a "century of genius" in the words of a great modern scientific philosopher, a time when a whole galaxy of outstanding figures suddenly appeared on the intellectual horizon of Europe. Why men like Galileo, Descartes, Newton, or Leibniz should have been born within the brief span of a single century is something no one can explain. In part, their achievements in what we now call the field of science may have been the result of accident. More probably they were the result of a combination of complex social factors that came together at a particular moment and produced the intellectual stimuli needed for such discoveries.

Another part of the explanation must surely lie in the fact that certain underlying ideas or assumptions, many of them reaching back to the Greeks, were shared by all those who speculated in the natural sciences. The most important of these was the assumption that the universe was an ordered and orderly system so regulated that it could be understood by those who had the knowledge, the patience, and the intelligence to do so. The assumption of order in nature was the basis of philosophy and mathematics and had, for centuries, been implicit in the belief that the universe was controlled by fixed and certain natural laws. This faith, however much it may have been modified during the period between the fall of Rome and the high middle ages, had never been entirely lost and was, as we have seen, an important part of the intellectual heritage of the medieval philosophers.

The major difficulty with this assumption that the universe was rational and orderly lay in the fact that much of what men were able to observe empirically, i.e., through their senses, did not always seem to square with the harmony expressed in mathematics and natural law. Fortunately for modern science, thinkers of the later middle ages and the Renaissance were not daunted by this apparent contradiction, which made it seem, for example, that the sun traveled round the earth. As the science of mathematics continued to develop, men continued to make use of it to test, to probe, and to explain all the seemingly disordered phenomena of the world in which they lived. In so doing, they sometimes ran foul of the theories of Aristotle, on which a part of medieval theology was based, and thus came into conflict with ecclesiastical authority. Despite these difficulties, their own intellectual aspirations drove them to continue their efforts until a major break-through had

paleontology; Johann van Helmont, c. 1580-1644, first studied chemical gases; Robert Boyle, 1627-91, sought to make clear the fundamental nature of chemical transformation in his *Sceptical Chymist* (1661); Joseph Priestley, 1733-1804, isolated oxygen; Antoine Lavoisier, 1743-94, proved that while matter may alter its state as a result of chemical reactions it does not alter its amount.

Scientific Academies: one of the ways in which scientific knowledge was accumulated and spread was through the organization of learned bodies or academies. Among the more famous of these were: Accademia Secretorum Naturae (Naples), 1560; Accademia dei Lincei, of which Galileo was a member (Rome), 1603-30; Royal Society of London, 1662; Académie des Sciences (Paris), 1666.

B. The Enlightenment

The Newtonian discoveries appeared to reinforce a method of inquiry first put forward by Descartes (1596-1650) that seemed to promise great possibilities for the study of man and human society. By searching every field of knowledge for basic axioms whose truth could not be doubted when subjected to the most searching analyses, men might hope to erect a "social science" as accurate and valid as the physical sciences. John Locke (1632-1704), English philosopher and political theorist, provided the basis for the later philosophies of the Enlightenment in his *Essay Concerning Human Understanding*

been achieved in the field of astronomy, where many of the great advances in early modern science were made. The man responsible for this discovery was Nicholas Copernicus (1473-1543), who found that by assuming the sun rather than the earth as the center of the system of planets he could explain the movements of the sun, moon, stars, earth, and planets much more clearly and in simpler mathematical terms. It is important to remember here that Copernicus did not have empirical evidence for the heliocentric theory (sun-centered) when he offered it in place of the geocentric theory (earth-centered). For the evidence of the senses indicated to him, as it had to men for centuries, that the sun went around the earth. Copernicus proposed the new hypothesis out of a belief that nature was orderly and that this orderliness was compatible with the simpler mathematical expression that the new theory permitted.

With this discovery, the whole science of mathematics, and with it astronomy, underwent a revolution that had far-reaching effects. Within a hundred and fifty years the search for ever more precise mathematical expressions of natural law had led to the formulation of the laws of mechanics by Galileo and finally to the crowning achievement of the whole scientific revolution, the famous hypothesis of Sir Isaac Newton by which the relations of all bodies in the universe were explained according to three basic laws. The appearance of Newton's *Principles of Mathematics* in 1687 was the signal for a major change in the intellectual climate of western civilization, for by that time each of the great discoveries had been seemingly verified beyond question with the invention of new measuring devices and new methods of observation. The result seemed to foretell a marvelous future for the human race which, at last, appeared to possess a means of plumbing all knowledge.

B. The Enlightenment: the Intellectual Impact of the Scientific Revolution

Newton's discoveries had the effect of transforming the thinking of large numbers of Europeans. The new thinking exalted every form of scientific knowledge. Science accordingly has grown in prestige until it has come to be looked upon by many persons in the western world as the most important of all intellectual activities. But Newton's discoveries had an immediate effect which has not proved wholly good, since they convinced many persons that all the complexities of the universe, including the diverse and seemingly unpredictable vagaries of human relations, could in the same way be reduced to relatively simple mechanical laws akin to those of the physical sciences. Newton, it seemed to

(1690). Locke declared that he would "inquire into the original, certainty, and extent of human knowledge." His purpose, though seemingly at odds with the methods of Descartes, was really to preserve Cartesian rationalism. Locke believed that all knowledge derived from the senses, that the mind of man was a blank slate or *tabula rasa* which is gradually filled with sensory information drawn from experience. In short, Locke, though his writings later were seen to have opened the way for an empirical attack on rationalism, really wanted a "middle way" which would comprehend both rationalism and empiricism. In the two generations after Locke his empirical suggestions were carried to a conclusion by two other British "empirical" philosophers: (1) Bishop George Berkeley, 1685-1753, taught in his *Theory of Vision* (1709) that "all that we see is our sensation" and in his *Principles of Human Knowledge*, 1710, that "all that exists is our knowledge." Matter, as Berkeley saw it, had no existence independent of human perception. (2) David Hume, 1711-1776, carried empiricism to its extreme conclusion in his *Treatise on Human Nature* (1739) and thus prepared the way for the philosophical reconstruction of Immanuel Kant and the Romantic School of philosophers.

1.   Religion

Growth of deism or "natural religion":
Voltaire (1694-1778) spread the ideas of the English deists in his *Letters on the English* (1734) and his *Elements of the Philosophy of Newton* (1738).

David Hume (1711-1776), the Scottish philosopher, expressed religious skepticism in his *Dialogues Concerning Natural Religion* (1779).

The leading materialist (atheist) work was Baron Holbach's *System of Nature* (1770), which described the universe as a place where no divine authority exists.

Deism, which was most widely accepted in England, was represented by the following:

Anthony Collins, 1676-1729, first put forward the Deist position in his *Discourse on Free Thinking* (1713).

Matthew Tindal, 1653-1733, author of the most comprehensive treatise on Deism, *Christianity as Old as the Creation*

many in the 18th century, had provided the key that would unlock all the mysteries of the universe. Man's task was simply to determine what the underlying laws of nature were and, by use of his reason, adjust to them so that he could live in harmony with his world. The first half of the 18th century thus became a confident Age of Reason in which it was assumed that man was an "enlightened" creature (hence the term "Enlightenment" used to describe the period) whose power to perfect himself was unlimited. No longer were men to be thought of as inherently wicked beings, imperfect and infected with original sin—men, whether they were good or evil, were products of the environment in which they lived. That men were evil, if they were, was the result of evils in their surroundings, of the bad institutions or wicked superstitions inherited from their unenlightened forebears. What man needed above all to progress (and the word "progress" was one of the great watchwords of the Enlightenment) was freedom to develop his powers of reason and to reform the evils in the world about him so that as he improved materially he would also improve morally. He had to have liberty to express himself freely, to worship as he wished, and to choose those things his reason told him were good. As a consequence, the great writers of the Enlightenment, particularly in France, were not only strong social critics but also defenders of a philosophy of "enlightened individualism."

The influence of these basic ideas reached out to touch every kind of thought. Let us now look at some of the most important of their effects.

1. Religion

In the area of religious belief the most important single effect stemming from the Scientific Revolution and the Enlightenment was a weakening of faith among the intellectual classes of Europe. It had not been the intention of many of the great scientific thinkers of the 17th century to destroy Christian theology or to weaken the basis of belief. Many of them—Newton, for example—were profoundly religious men. Inevitably, however, some of the things they said, simply because their statements seemed to be at variance with teachings long accepted as orthodox, created serious tensions between themselves and churchmen of all denominations. A great part of the difficulty arose from the fact that by stressing the importance, the permanence, and the unchanging nature of the physical laws that controlled the universe, the scientific thinkers of the period appeared to imply that God was only a sort of watchmaker who, having made the universe and set it in motion, then left it to its own devices. Such an implication challenged the stories of divine intervention in human affairs as related by scripture and the Christian tradi-

(1730), sometimes called the "Bible of Deism."

William Wollaston, 1659-1724, argued in favor of the adequacy of "a religion of reason" to serve men's needs in his *The Religion of Nature Delineated* (1722).

As the century advanced, however, there was a strong reaction among many religious groups to both Deism and rationalism. Among the more important of these groups were: John Wesley, 1703-91, and his followers, later (1784) known as Methodists, who preached salvation through faith in Christ alone; Moravian Brethren in Germany who reorganized themselves in 1732; Israel B. Eliezer (Baal-Schem-Tov), 1700-60, founder of the devout pietistic Jewish group known as the Hasidim.

2. Political Theory

Just as John Locke was the leading proponent of the philosophy of the Enlightenment, so was he also in large measure the founder of its political theory. That is not to say that everyone in the 18th century accepted what Locke had to say without question. Nevertheless, Locke's *Two Treatises of Government* (1690), which were actually written to justify the English Revolution of 1688, came to be widely accepted by the European literate community during the hundred years after the *Treatises* appeared. In brief, Locke argued that government (including even kings) was responsible to the governed as a consequence of a mythical contract entered into when society was first formed. If the contract was broken by the ruler, then the community had the right to rebel. The idea was based upon a questionable historical hypothesis but, nonetheless, had a wide influence on the thought of 18th-century Europe. The notion of limited power was carried over into French thought by Montesquieu (1689-1755) in his *Spirit of Laws*, 1748. C. A. Helvetius (1715-1771) sought to give political theory a "scientific" basis by arguing that the only rational standard of conduct was one based upon the "greatest good for the greatest number;" he published *De l'esprit (Of the Spirit)* in 1758. J. J. Rousseau (1712-1778) in his *Social Contract*, 1762, put forward the idea that society as a whole is possessed of a "general will" which directs the affairs of government. Publication of the *Encyclopedia* under the edi-

tion—miracles became impossible because they were in violation of an inviolable natural law. Even more disturbing: such a mechanistic implication made men wonder about the accuracy of scripture itself. Impelled by doubts, many scholars turned to re-examine the Bible in a new critical light, and their findings inevitably raised new questions. From this dilemma of reason and faith men found various escapes. Some denied its existence and reaffirmed their traditional beliefs. Others, most notably the school of philosopher-theologians known as the Deists, sought a form of compromise in which God was deemed not a personal deity in the Christian sense but a remote, impersonal "Supreme Being." A few went the whole way to atheism and argued that the universe, which seemed on the basis of physical law to have existed through all eternity, had no creator but was a kind of timeless machine existing without a beginning or an end.

2. Political Theory

The political theory of the Enlightenment derived from the fundamental belief that man is a creature of his environment who needs only to improve his surroundings in order to progress toward earthly perfection. In those parts of Europe, England for example, where the state and society seemed conducive to a certain amount of individual freedom and where the power of rational choice appeared not to be markedly restricted by social traditions and political institutions, the ideals and aspirations of the Enlightenment strengthened the social order. In France, on the other hand, because of growing discontent with inequities in taxation, bureaucratic inefficiency, and the entrenched position of the nobility, the ideas of the Enlightenment took on a revolutionary cast. Furthermore, the arguments of the French *philosophes* (philosophers) were reinforced in popular thinking by the successive military defeats sustained by France at the hands of England during the first half of the 18th century. As a consequence of these, Frenchmen inevitably asked what it was that gave England her advantage and concluded that it lay in the superiority of England's enlightened institutions and traditions. Leading thinkers like Voltaire and Montesquieu became ardent admirers of all things English, which they held up to Frenchmen as enlightened models. From England, too, were imported certain social and political theories originally developed by Thomas Hobbes (1588-1679) and John Locke (1632-1704) which, in French hands, were to become dangerous intellectual weapons.

Basically, however, the political theory of the Enlightenment, while it varied from individual to individual, held that as a rational being man

torship of Denis Diderot (1713-1784), a work which summarized the ideals of the Enlightenment, 1751-1765. Marquis de Condorcet (1743-1794) best expressed the Enlightenment's faith in human progress in his *Progress of the Human Spirit,* 1794.

3.   Economic Theory

The belief that there were laws governing economic activity was first given coherent form in the writings of the French physiocrats whose most important writer, Dr. Francis Quesnay (1694-1774), published influential articles in the *Encyclopedia,* 1756-1757, and his major work, *Tableau économique,* in 1756. The essence of physiocratic doctrine was a belief in the "natural order" of economic activity. Quesnay and his followers argued that wealth was not gold and silver but sprang from production and flowed through the nation to replenish the whole of society. The difficulty with physiocracy, however, was that its adherents insisted that agriculture alone produced wealth and that merchants and manufacturers only manipulated it for their own ends. Under physiocratic influences A. R. J. Turgot (1727-1781), the great French finance minister, published his *Reflections on the Formation and Distribution of Wealth,* 1766. Adam Smith, 1723-1790, after a visit to France in 1764-66 incorporated a number of physiocratic ideas into his *Wealth of Nations,* 1776. Smith's great work was not just simply a statement of *laissez-faire* principles. He was concerned to show what the mechanism was by which society functions. In explanation he formulated the laws of the market. What he strove to demonstrate was the way in which all men by pursuing their own interests would seek, as if led by an "invisible hand," the end "which is most agreeable to the interest of the whole society." Thomas Malthus (1766-1834) in his *Essay on the Principle of Population,* 1798, challenged the optimism of the 18th century by arguing that population always tends to far outstrip the means of subsistence.

had the right to create his own political institutions if those already in existence did not conform to the standards of his reason. This view did not necessarily lead to democracy, since, in the opinion of many *philosophes*, not all men had reached the level of rationality needed to make democracy work. It did imply, however—though many thinkers preferred to trust an enlightened monarch—that all those possessed of reasoning power, knowledge, and education could or should have some part in governing themselves. This belief was capable of ultimate enormous expansion and could lead to revolutionary conclusions.

3. Economic Theory

Just as the physical universe had its laws, so, too, it was assumed during the Enlightenment that human social and economic relationships were also governed by laws which it was the duty of the rational man to seek out and understand. Under the influence of this kind of thinking a great deal of new attention was devoted to understanding man's relations with his material environment and his fellow humans. To this end, society was studied as never before, and, for the first time, a serious attempt was made to create what we now call the "social sciences."

The most popular and famous of these many attempts was the work of Adam Smith, whose *Wealth of Nations*, published in 1776 was to become the Bible of the new social science of "political economy" (later to be known as "economics"). Smith was not merely a theorist of the Enlightenment, however. He was also an antagonist of certain economic theories and practices, like the restrictive system of mercantilsm, which he felt were dangerously limiting the economic growth of European society. The theory of mercantilism, whose greatest exponent had been the French finance minister Colbert (1619-1683), was derived from the belief that all trade and manufacturing had to be strictly controlled in the interests of the state. Commercial activity under mercantilism was the analogue of warfare, in which a nation strove to amass wealth by accumulating bullion (gold and silver), or by exporting goods of greater money value than it imported from its neighbors. Against this view (though he did feel that the state had the right to impose some restrictions when national interests were at stake), Smith argued that the economic world was governed by a body of laws all its own which had nothing to do with politics or the policies of states. Economic systems were controlled by natural laws which could not be flouted at the whim of human beings. Men should be left free to follow their own enlightened self-interest in economic matters and, in so doing would be acting in harmony with those laws. To facilitate this freedom, every form of restriction, tariff, or other

4.   Enlightened Despotism

Frederick the Great of Prussia (1740-1786) described himself as "the first servant of the state"; worked to improve the economic conditions of Prussia; friendly with Voltaire and other philosophers of the Enlightenment; spoke French in preference to German and interested himself in philosophy and the arts.

Catherine the Great of Russia (1762-1796): patronized the French *philosophes;* codified Russian laws; interested herself in the philosophy of the Enlightenment.

Joseph II of Austria (1765-1790): one of the few rulers who really believed in enlightened despotism; tried to institute popular education; reformed the legal code; promoted religious toleration even in the face of strong opposition from his own subjects.

barrier to unfettered trade should be abolished, and men should be let alone *(laissez-faire)* to engage in economic activity. The purpose of government was to provide social stability, security of life and property, and enforcement of contracts. If it did these things and nothing more, men, left to themselves to seek their own rational economic ends, would also ultimately serve the welfare of society as a whole.

4. Enlightened Despotism: the Political Effect of the Enlightenment

With the wide dissemination of the teachings of the Enlightenment, 18th-century Europe witnessed the rise of a new phenomenon known as "enlightened despotism." To a large extent, the system of enlightened despotism was only an extension of the older forms of absolute monarchy; but it was absolute monarchy with a difference. By the middle of the 18th century it was no longer fashionable, even among kings, to insist that their rule was justified solely by inheritance or divine right. The sovereign, following the example of the kings of Prussia, was the "first servant of the state" and was obligated to provide for the general welfare of his people by giving them efficient government, reforms when needed, and equal justice. In short, the enlightened despot, by endeavoring to rule according to the dictates of reason, justified his authority on the purely secular grounds of usefulness. Furthermore, under the influence of the prevailing ideas, he often promoted reforms which were opposed by large numbers of his subjects. For this reason, the rule of the enlightened despot might be called paternal in the sense that change was accomplished for the good of the people whether they liked it or not. But the enlightened despots were not necessarily motivated by the prevailing ideas. Many of their reforms were carried out as a means of organizing the resources of their kingdoms for greater efficiency in waging war against their neighbors and not with the welfare of their subjects in mind.

EVENTS AND DEFINITIONS

A.   Influence of the American Revolution

1. *Causes of the American Revolution:* (1) divergence between American colonial society and the mother country as a result of geographic separation, differing political evolution, and influx into colonies of large numbers of persons who felt neither political nor national loyalty to the British crown; (2) the defeat of France in the Seven Years' War which removed the danger of French conquest from Canada; (3) efforts of Great Britain to raise revenues in American colonies in support of imperial defense aroused colonial ire and led to Stamp Act opposition and later to the Boston Tea Party; (4) British attempts to maintain fur trade and peaceful relations with the Indians restricted colonial expansion across the Alleghenies; (5) resentment of the dominant position of Anglican Church in many colonies; (6) and, finally, a growing sense of American identity influenced by the growth of political consciousness among the literate classes of the North Atlantic community in both Europe and North America.

CHAPTER 5

The French Revolution and the Napoleonic Era

THE ESSENTIAL MOVEMENT

The French Revolution is one of the great historical facts of modern history. Few events have been more idealized or execrated, and few have been studied with greater care or been more completely misinterpreted. The Great Revolution, for good or ill, has stood as kind of supreme legend influencing the thoughts of men and the course of events from its time to our own. Some have looked upon the revolution as the outburst of a people driven to rebellion by centuries of royal tyranny and aristocratic exploitation. To others it has represented the eruption of an irrational mob feeling which destroyed the order, stability, institutions, and cherished traditions of a long-established society. Like most major historical events, the French Revolution cannot be looked upon as something entirely good or entirely evil but rather as a complex phenomenon whose causes and effects are still the subject of disagreement among historians.

A. The Influence of the American Revolution

Without question, one of the forces that moved Frenchmen to consider a revolutionary method of political and social change was the successful example set by England's rebellious colonies in North America. The revolt of the thirteen colonies was, after all, a rising in the name of freedom

2. *Course of the Revolution:* hostilities precipitated by four Coercive Acts (as well as the Quebec Act granting religious toleration to French Canada) intended to punish the Province of Massachusetts for the Boston Tea Party, 1774. First Continental Congress assembled at Philadelphia, Sept. 5, 1774. Military conflict began at Lexington and Concord, April 1775. Declaration of Independence formally removed the colonies from British sovereignty, 1776. American victory at Saratoga assured the colonists of French help, October 1777. Articles of Confederation formally designated the new nation as the United States of America and provided for a perpetual union of the colonies, November 1777. France signed treaty of alliance with the United States, February 6, 1778. Cornwallis surrendered to Anglo-French forces at Yorktown and virtually ended the war, October 19, 1781. Treaty of peace between Great Britain and the United States signed at Paris; recognized American independence and defined boundaries of new nation, September 1783.

3. *Influence of the American Revolution on Europe.* In a century when the ideas of Locke spread rapidly, the impact of the American Revolution was enormous all over Europe but particularly in France. The famous French local courts or "parlements" even before the American War were giving vent to sentiments that were almost democratic; the whole of Europe was increasingly permeated with political ideas that tended to exalt the notion that governments should be responsible to their peoples. The triumph of the American revolutionaries, therefore, seemed to be a triumph of plain and simple men. Alliance with the Americans had made republican ideas respectable in France and throughout Europe. After 1783 the United States displaced England in the eyes of literate Europe as the "country of freedom."

B. Domestic Causes of the French Revolution

1. Growth of Long-Range Discontent

The following were the major causes of long-range discontent:

by peoples of European stock influenced by ideas imported from Europe. In that sense, the American Revolution seemed to mark the triumph of the Enlightenment's ideals—as it did in many ways. But while the language was the same, the movement and its results were very different. In North America the revolution was not intended to destroy a hated social order or to bring down ancient institutions. It was, rather, a war of secession waged by a society which, over 150 years, had created its own institutions and traditions and wished only to control its own affairs. Americans, however much they might profess the contrary, had ceased to be Englishmen by the mere fact of geographical separation, and their revolution simply made that fact plain. Thus, the American Revolution was not a radical but a conservative movement which preserved the existing social order and the rights of property. In its aftermath came not a revolutionary Napoleonic dictator but a carefully thought-out constitutional system whose stability and continuity have made it one of the longest-lived in the modern world.

To 18th-century Frenchmen, who lacked the advantage of our historical hindsight, the American Revolution seemed to set a simple, straightforward example. Americans, it seemed, had wanted a change in their relations with England, and, when they could get it in no other way, they revolted. Revolution was thereby vindicated as a useful instrument of social and political change which might as easily be employed by Frenchmen as by anyone else. When the time came, this thought loomed large in many French minds.

B. Domestic Causes of the French Revolution

Within France itself the various causes of the upheaval that began in 1789 are customarily divided into two categories. The first of them consists of the various discontents that had grown up over several generations and created an atmosphere of dissatisfaction that grew more intense on the eve of the revolution. The second category is that of the short-range or immediate causes, i.e., the events that suddenly precipitated the revolution. Historians are still at odds as to which of these kinds of causes was the more important in bringing on the great upheaval, though most would probably concede that, in the end, both categories must be taken into consideration. Let us look briefly at each of them in turn.

1.   The Growth of Long-Range Discontent

The great paradox of France under its prerevolutionary government (Old Regime) was that it was neither the poorest nor the worst-governed

(1) Discontent of the professional and mercantile classes at their failure to achieve their rightful due from French society, particularly after 1780.

(2) The "feudal reaction" by which the nobility retained all the most important and lucrative state positions for themselves.

(3) The ideas of the *philosophes* whose criticism of existing institutions aroused a consciousness of French shortcomings among literate elements in French society.

(4) Agrarian discontent: existence of feudal dues and obligations; heavy burden of taxes which weighed on the peasantry (nobles and clergy exempted except on a voluntary basis).

(5) Discontent with government: unwieldiness and inefficiency of governmental machinery; cumbersome legal system; unequal taxation; steady growth of government costs.

2.   The Attempts at Reform Under Louis XVI

During the early years of his reign Louis XVI strove to rule according to the precepts of "enlightened despotism" and seriously undertook the formidable and long delayed task of reforming the state bureaucracy and particularly the system of state finance. The first great effort in this direction was made by the physiocratic minister of marine and finance (see p. 62), Turgot, between 1774-1776. By the issuance of Six Edicts Turgot undertook to reform taxation, abolished the restrictive and archaic trade guilds, and tried in various ways to liberalize domestic trade. Turgot was succeeded by the Swiss banker Jacques Necker (1732-1804) who tried to carry on with Turgot's reforms but was forced to resign in 1781 when he revealed the extent of the royal pension system in a famous *compte-rendu*. Despite some sporadic efforts of the king's last two finance ministers (Calonne and Loménie de Brienne), the royal debt continued to rise. Nevertheless, not all of the king's efforts at reforms were failures: the army was extensively reorganized and serfs were freed on the royal estates.

3.   Immediate Causes

(1) Public debt increased enormously by participation in the War of the American Revolution; interest rose from

state in Europe. In many ways it was among the richest; and certainly in corruption and inefficiency the French government was no worse than neighboring kingdoms. The major difficulty in 18th-century France was that many persons, particularly among the educated, had become conscious of the possibility of something better and were, therefore, increasingly unwilling to tolerate state inefficiency or entrenched privilege. Moreover, the old legal division of France into three social orders or estates (the clergy made up the First Estate, the nobles were the Second Estate, while all the rest from the wealthiest merchant to the poorest laborer were lumped together in the Third Estate) no longer corresponded to the realities of wealth and ability in French society. With the increase in national wealth and the spread of education, new social groups, but particularly the middle classes or "bourgeoisie," had come into the possession of property or acquired professional skills that made them more important members of society than many a nobleman. So long as these new men had been able to rise in the social scale and had not found the highest state offices closed to them, they had accepted the existing social system and its standards without question. Early in the 18th century, however, this state of affairs began to change. By making good use of their proximity to the king and their influence at court, the nobles were able to preserve old privileges and create new ones. Theirs, for example, was the right to hold certain offices under the crown, to exemption from taxation (which all other classes paid except the clergy), and, finally, to hold commissions in the army. With each advance in the privileges of the nobility, resentment among the middle classes grew.

Nor was this resentment directed only toward the nobles. The church, too, was exempt from all but an inadequate voluntary taxation. Furthermore, the church in France, while no more lax in its spiritual duties than the church in other countries of Europe, had also been invaded by members of noble families who monopolized its highest offices to a greater extent than ever before and, as a consequence, enjoyed a lion's share of the church's revenues.

Below the middle classes the great bulk of the population, made up of peasants (small farmers) and wage earners, had not received as large a share of the expanded wealth of France as had the upper classes. To further aggravate matters, these classes paid an even larger proportion of the national taxation (including the most important direct tax known as the *taille*) than did the middle classes. In addition, since four-fifths of the kingdom was rural, many of the heaviest obligations, among which were the outmoded feudal dues owed to landlords, fell upon the peasantry.

93 million livres in 1774 to over 300 million livres in 1789; government inability to borrow money precipitated crisis.

(2) "Necklace Affair" (1785) damaged the public reputation of Queen Marie Antoinette and of the monarchy.

(3) Assembly of Notables (1787) failed to find a solution to the king's problems; dissolved without giving the government the help that was expected.

(4) Parlement of Paris abolished after refusing to register reform edicts (1788).

4.   Condition of France on the Eve of the Revolution

France, in 1789, was still by all odds the richest and most populous state in Europe as she had been during the preceding two centuries. Her population numbered 24–26 millions and was twice as large as that of either England or Spain and just about equal to that of Russia. Paris with an estimated population of 600,000 was exceeded only by London in all of Europe. Furthermore, the diversity and quantity of French resources, the extent of French territories, and the total productive capacity of the French economy were far greater than any other nation in Europe. The annual income of the French crown, though inadequate to pay off the enormous debts of the state, was nearly 500,000,000 livres. It was thus larger than the income of Great Britain, twice as large as that of the Hapsburg monarchy, over three times as large as that of Russia, Spain, or Prussia, and twenty-five times as great as the income of the infant United States. France was in so many ways the world's most advanced country that the coming of revolution there still seems a sort of paradox.

C.   Phases of the Revolution

1.   Construction of the Constitutional Monarchy, 1789-1791

Estates General convened, May 1789. Representatives of the Third Estate formed the National Assembly, June 1789. Paris populace intervened in the Revolution with the storming of the Bastille, July 1789. Nobles voluntarily surrendered their feudal privileges: Declaration of the Rights

2. The Immediate Cause: Financial Crisis

The event that precipitated the revolution was a financial crisis that had been building up throughout the 18th century. Numerous wars, the enormous costs of maintaining a permanent military establishment, and the charges on the public debt, all combined to keep the state from balancing its budget. When the government proposed new taxes which would have taken away the exemptions of the privileged classes, an impasse was reached. In the face of refusal on the part of the nobles to give up any of their privileges, King Louis XVI (1774-1792), as a last resort summoned the ancient feudal representative body of the kingdom, the Estates General, which had not met since 1614.

C. Phases of the Revolution

The representatives of the three estates who attended the opening of the Estates General in May 1789 did not intend to make a revolution that would destroy the monarchy. What most of them wanted, including the representatives of the Third Estate, was some solution to current problems. Even extremists seem to have had no desires beyond the establishing of a permanent representative body like the English parliament and the reform of administrative abuses. The tragedy for those who were reform-minded lay in the fact that, in order to accomplish their ends, they had to have the acquiescence of the king. The king, for his part, though he was anxious to find some way out of his dilemma, was unwilling to make any concessions that would infringe the privileges of the higher clergy and nobility, since he reasoned that such concessions would also weaken his own authority. In the end, it was the king's failure to accept the need for such changes that made the revolution into something the men of 1789 did not intend it to be and finally destroyed the monarchy. Moreover, once the forces of discontent were fully unleashed, the Paris mob quickly learned that it was in a position at moments of crisis to direct the course of events. When the Paris populace stormed and carried the Bastille on July 14, 1789, the revolution had really begun.

1. First Phase: the Construction of Constitutional Monarchy, 1789-1791

Despite these rumblings of violence, the representatives of the Third Estate in alliance with sympathetic members of the other two Estates pushed ahead in the years between 1789 and 1791 with the task of non-violent constitutional reform. In June 1789 they defied the king and transformed the Estates General into a National Assembly whose purpose was

of Man proclaimed, August 1789. New constitution accepted by King Louis XVI, July 1790.

2. Second Phase: the Republic, the Reign of Terror, and the Directory, 1792-1799

The king indicated his unwillingness to accept the new order of things by attempting to flee France ("flight to Varennes"), June 1791. Declaration of Pillnitz by Austria and Prussia threatened intervention in French affairs, August 1791. Legislative Assembly, provided for under the new constitution, began to meet, October 1791. France entered War of the First Coalition (1792-1797), April 1792. Threat of invasion caused rioting in Paris, August-September 1792.

France proclaimed a republic; National Convention (1792-1795) met to draw up a republican constitution for France, September 1792.

Louis XVI executed, January 1793.

Committee of Public Safety formed, April 1793. Reign of Terror, "dictatorship" of Robespierre, 1793-1794. "Thermidorean Reaction," (1794, drove Jacobins and other revolutionary extremists from power. Constitution of 1795 (August) ushered in the rule of the Directory (five-man committee), 1792-1799.

Italian campaigns of Napoleon Bonaparte (1796-1797) resulted in victorious Treaty of Campo Formio with Austrians (October 1797). Napoleon's Egyptian expedition (1798-1799). *Coup d'état* of 18 Brumaire brought Napoleon to power, November 1799.

D. The Rule of Napoleon, 1799-1815

Period of the Consulate, 1799-1804; period of the Empire, 1804-1815.

to write a constitution for the nation. During the two years that followed, the old feudal privileges of the nobility were swept away, a manifesto declaring the rights of man was issued, the church and its lands were nationalized, and a new constitution, which established a permanent system of representative government (Legislative Assembly), came into force. With these achievements, the first phase of the revolution ended in an apparent victory for the middle classes and their aristocratic allies.

2. Second Phase: the Republic, the Reign of Terror,
   and the Directory, 1792-1799

Unfortunately for the hopes of the moderates, the king quickly gave proof of his hostility to the new constitution by trying to flee the country. This hostility, along with the growth of republican sentiments among the members of the new Legislative Assembly, steadily increased the unpopularity of the monarchy. When it seemed plain that foreign powers might intervene in behalf of the king, the Assembly declared war on Austria and Prussia. Under the threat of invasion (1792), rioting broke out in Paris, a republic was proclaimed (September 1792), and a new revolutionary body, the National Convention, was summoned to draw up a republican constitution. In the Convention a new group of radical republicans, the most important of whom were the group known as Jacobins, speedily tried and executed the king and then, in February 1793, declared war on England, Holland, and Spain.

To combat the internal and external dangers of the moment, a Committee of Public Safety was established under the direction of the Jacobin leader Maximilien de Robespierre (1758-1794). This body, in an effort to protect the revolution against its enemies, resorted to the Reign of Terror (1793-1794), in which thousands of persons lost their lives, including many former leaders of the revolution. Alarmed at the spread of the Terror, the National Convention overthrew and executed Robespierre.

From 1795 to 1799 France was ruled by a Directory made up of five members who, in spite of the military successes of French armies, became increasingly unpopular because of a mounting wave of domestic problems. In November 1799 Napoleon Bonaparte, whose victories in Italy and Egypt had made him popular, turned the Directory out of office and seized political power.

D. The Rule of Napoleon: Consulate and Empire, 1799-1815

The advent of Napoleon marked the end of a period of revolutionary uncertainty and indecision. The search for a stable, workable form of gov-

1. Napoleon's Career

Born: Ajaccio, Corsica, August 15, 1769, of noble but impoverished parents. Brought to France in 1779, he studied as a military cadet at Brienne and later at the *Ecole Militaire* in Paris. Commissioned in the artillery, he early became a zealous supporter of the revolution. In 1793 he achieved reputation for his part in helping to expel British naval forces from Toulon and was promoted general of brigade. Saved the Convention from a royalist mob, Oct. 4, 1795 (13 Vendémiaire). As a reward, Napoleon was given command of the Army of Italy where his victories, particularly at Arcola and Rivoli, forced the Austrians out of the war and made him a popular hero. Seized power, November 1799. First Consul, 1799-1804. Consecrated (but not crowned) Emperor of the French by Pope Pius VII (Dec. 2, 1804) after an overwhelming popular plebiscite (3,572,329 to 2569). Revived a nobility based on merit and created an absolute monarchy more centralized and efficient than that which had been overthrown by the revolution. Established a network of client states ruled by members of his own family and close associates. After divorcing Empress Josephine married Marie Louise of Austria, April 1810, by whom he had a male heir (King of Rome). Napoleon forced to abdicate and exiled to Elba, 1814. Returned (March-June 1815) for "the Hundred Days." Exiled to St. Helena after Waterloo and died there, May 5, 1821.

2. Domestic Policy

Founding of the Bank of France, 1800. Concordat of 1801 entered into with Pope Pius VII restored the Catholic church (which had been opposed by the revolutionary governments). *Code Napoléon* drawn up, 1804-1810. Establishment of *lycées* (secondary schools), 1802. Napoleon also confirmed the land-holding rights of the French peasants; reformed local government; regularized the system of taxation.

For all of his various reforms and innovations, the rule of Napoleon cost France dearly. Not only did he enormously increase the police power of the state, but his continuous demands on French manpower and resources ultimately brought the country to the edge of exhaustion. In the end, despite the

ernment appeared to have ended in the rule of a single strong man whose military successes raised French national pride and made France the leading power of Europe as she had been in the days of Louis XIV. At first, Napoleon's popularity rested on more than just military victories. He was able to claim with some plausibility that he was the true "son of the revolution" whose purpose was to preserve and consolidate all that the revolution had accomplished for the French people. His armies were infused with revolutionary zeal and carried this spirit with them to all parts of Europe, where they were received as liberators from tyranny and feudal oppression. As it grew in power, however, the aims and purposes of Napoleonic France changed. It ceased to be the symbol of freedom for the European masses and became instead a symbol of old-fashioned conquest and repression. By the end of his life Napoleon had filled Europe with fear and disillusionment.

The significance of the Napoleonic era, apart from its overturning of the European *status quo*, lies in the fact that it produced the first great egalitarian dictatorship of modern times. Though the comparison should not be pushed too far, France in that period has sometimes been likened to the totalitarian states of the 20th century which combine mass appeal with efficient and repressive government just as the Napoleonic state did. In the light of this comparison, let us look now at the domestic and foreign policies of Napoleon.

1. Domestic Policy

At the beginning of his rule Napoleon preserved the forms of classical republicanism by establishing a Consulate (1799-1804) controlled by three elected "consuls" of whom the most important was Napoleon himself. Once entrenched in power, he began a series of internal reforms, ostensibly to improve the efficiency of government and to restore order, but actually to increase his own authority. Local government was centralized, peasant landholding rights were confirmed, a system of universal education was established (but never completed), a new law code (Code Napoléon) was drawn up, and the Catholic church was restored to its official position. Politically, however, Frenchmen gradually lost more than they gained as Napoleon steadily deprived them of elective power. By 1804, when he assumed the title of Emperor of the French, he had actually created a more efficient form of the old absolute monarchy against which Frenchmen had originally revolted. The last years of his reign saw the recurrence of continual crises as France, exhausted by protracted wars and a long-drawn-out English naval blockade, was drained of wealth and manpower.

glory and romance of the "Napoleonic Legend," the great effort of European conquest and domination had a serious effect on France's international position in Europe.

2. Foreign Policy

War of the Second Coalition (Austria, Britain, Russia), 1799-1802, terminated by the Treaty of Luneville (with Austria), 1801, which practically ended the Holy Roman Empire, and the Treaty of Amiens (with England), 1802.

War of the Third Coalition (Austria, Britain, Russia, and Sweden), 1805-1808: Nelson's victory at Trafalgar (October 1805) prevented invasion of England; Napoleon defeated Austrians and Russians at Austerlitz, December 1805; Prussians (who entered the war belatedly) defeated at Jena, October 1806; Napoleon established the Continental Blockade against Britain (Berlin Decree), November 1806; Peace of Tilsit (between Tsar Alexander I of Russia and Napoleon) divided Europe between the two, and Russia agreed to enter the blockade against Britain, 1807. This treaty marked the high point of Napoleon's success.

Peninsular War, 1808-1813: when Napoleon attempted to make his brother Joseph king of Spain, the Spaniards revolted; and the British landed troops (1808) to aid them. War with Austria, 1809, concluded by the Treaty of Schönbrunn which forced Austria to cede a large part of its territory to France and her allies.

Invasion and defeat in Russia, 1812.

The Wars of Liberation, 1813-1815: Napoleon defeated at Leipzig ("Battle of the Nations"), October 1813, by Austria, Prussia, and Russia; forced to abdicate, 1814; returned from exile on Elba ("The Hundred Days"), March-June 1815; final defeat by English and Prussian armies at Waterloo, June 1815.

2. Foreign Policy

The foreign policy of Napoleon was actually nothing more than a long series of military campaigns against various coalitions of European powers. In almost every instance down to the Russian campaign of 1812, Napoleon was brilliantly successful against continental states. The one nation which he could not subdue was England, whose seapower kept him from crossing the English Channel and laid France and the entire continent under continual siege. The high point of Napoleon's power was reached at the Peace of Tilsit in 1807 when, following victories over Austria, Prussia, and Russia, he was able to turn all Europe for a time into a French fortress by means of his Continental System. In this way he intended to force England into submission by cutting her off from European markets, but the attempt met with failure when his allies were driven by necessity to maintain trade relations with Britain in spite of his prohibitions against it. The downfall of the Napoleonic Empire and its satellite system began with the failure of French armies to conquer Spain (1808-1813) and was finally precipitated by the invasion and retreat from Russia (1812). At Leipzig (1813), and again at Waterloo (1815) after a brief period of restoration, the Napoleonic Empire was completely destroyed.

EVENTS AND DEFINITIONS

A. The Congress of Vienna and the Resettlement of Europe, 1815-1830

The major effects of the international settlement made at Vienna in 1814-1815 were as follows:

(1) Congress of Vienna, 1814-1815, restored the Austrian and Prussian monarchies; created the kingdom of the Netherlands (which included both the Netherlands and modern Belgium); organized the Germanic Confederation to replace the defunct Holy Roman Empire; recognized the reorganized kingdom of Poland under the rule of the Russian Tsar Alexander I; greatly strengthened the kingdom of Prussia as a barrier against the revival of French power.

(2) The Holy Alliance, by which rulers were asked to rule according to Christian principles, established by Tsar Alexander I, September 1815; never particularly effective.

(3) More important was the Quadruple Alliance (Austria, Britain, Prussia, Russia), organized to preserve the peace settlement, November 1815; became the Quintuple Alliance with the admission of France, 1818.

(4) Congress System: Under the influence of the Austrian

CHAPTER 6

The Interval of Reaction
and the Continuing Revolutions

THE ESSENTIAL MOVEMENT

**A. The Congress of Vienna and the Resettlement of
Europe, 1815-1830**

The representatives of the various European states who met at Vienna
to settle the affairs of Europe after the downfall of Napoleon were motivated by three desires: first, in so far as it was possible, they wished to restore the *status quo* of 1789; second, to keep the dangerous power of France
in check; and, third, to suppress the disruptive forces and ideas stirred up
by the French Revolution. In addition, most of the states represented were
anxious to improve their own power positions at the expense of their neighbors, so that though the Congress of Vienna has usually been looked upon
as the restorer of Europe, it was, in fact, the creator of a new international
system. From its deliberations emerged the tightly knit Congress System
which was intended to keep the settlement at Vienna intact. Unhappily for
its projectors, neither the system nor the settlement was to last for more
than a generation.

minister of foreign affairs, Prince Metternich, the major powers met in a series of "congresses" intended to promote co-operation in preserving the *status quo*. The most important of these were Aix-la-Chapelle (1818), Troppau (1820), Laibach (1821), and Verona (1822).

(5) The Congress System broke up when Britain refused to support intervention in Spain out of fear that it might be extended to Spain's rebellious South American colonies, 1822. The major powers were also divided over the question of intervening in the Greek War of Independence (1821-1831) against the Turks.

B. The Industrial Revolution

1.   Major Technological Advances

(1) Coal and Iron: revolution in use of coal as a fuel occurred in the 17th century; coke first used for smelting iron by Abraham Darby, *c.* 1709; "puddling" process for wrought iron developed by Henry Cort, 1783; Bessemer perfected blast furnace, 1857; S.G. Gilchrist made low-grade iron ores available for mass production by perfecting process for removing phosphorus, 1878.

(2) Textiles: Kay's flying shuttle improved the weaving process, 1733; Hargreaves' spinning jenny, 1770; Arkwright introduced machinery into textile factories, 1774-1780.

(3) Mechanical Inventions: James Watt (1736-1819) perfected first efficient steam engine, *c.* 1770; 496 of them built between 1775 and 1800. Invention of the turning lathe improved manufacture of machine tools and machinery, 1794. First transatlantic steamship crossing, 1819. World's first steam railway (Stockton and Darlington) opened, 1825; by 1850 Britain had 6600 miles of rail line. Transmission of the first telegraph message, 1844. Opening of Drake's oil well in Pennsylvania, 1859; beginning of commercial exploitation of petroleum.

2.   Economic (Financial) Innovations

Founding of the Bank of England, 1694; creation of the English (funded) national debt (early 18th century) gave financial security to the British economy. Patents, protecting the

B. The Industrial Revolution

The great problem of the statesmen who made the settlement at Vienna was to preserve it in a Europe which was rapidly being transformed by forces beyond their control. One of these forces, whose effects had already been felt decisively during the Napoleonic Wars, was the Industrial Revolution. The term itself, like the terms "Renaissance" and "Reformation," is no longer regarded as historically accurate, since the process by which industrial change came to the western world was not sudden or revolutionary but rather the result of a long period of evolution stretching far back into the European past. It is true, however, that the last half of the 18th century, particularly in England, witnessed an acceleration in the rate of invention, which is why historians have thought of the years between 1760 and 1830 as the period when the Industrial Revolution actually occurred.

Essentially, the term "Industrial Revolution" is intended to describe a time of transition when machines began significantly to displace human and animal power in the various processes of manufacture, but there is more to it than that. In its broadest sense, the Industrial Revolution was a complex movement which saw not simply the introduction of machinery into technology but also the development of a whole new set of production techniques and the utilization of a new form of energy (steam power) which substantially increased the productive capacity and the wealth of the western world. In this respect, it was not a new or unknown phenomenon but a speedup in the tempo of that economic expansion which, as we have seen, had been taking place in Europe since the middle ages. Why it should have occurred when and where it did, namely, in 18th-century England, has long been the subject of much historical speculation. In the main, however, the most important causes of this extremely complex movement fall into

rights of inventors, systematically granted in England after 1721. Founding of the London Stock Exchange, 1773. Restrictions on joint-stock-company organization removed by Parliament, 1825.

3.   Improvements in Agriculture and Food Production

As in industry, great changes in agriculture were made possible by increases in capital investment which, particularly in England, expanded the size of farms and estates, the development of larger food markets which stimulated demand, and a slow but significant improvement in the techniques of planting, harvesting, and animal husbandry. Some of the more significant innovations in technique were as follows. *England*: Charles, Viscount Townshend (1674-1738) promoted crop rotation; Jethro Tull (1674-1740) introduced Dutch planting techniques into England; Robert Bakewell (1725-1795) developed selected breeding of livestock. *Continental Europe:* the German chemist, Justus Liebig (1803-1873), published his findings on soil chemistry (1840). *U.S.A.:* patenting of Cyrus McCormick's improved reaper, 1834; invention of steel plow by John Deere, 1837.

C.   Social Effects of the Industrial Revolution

(1) Growth of a new class of industrial owners and managers; increase in the size of the industrial wage-earning class (proletariat).

(2) Growth of urbanization: Agricultural Revolution led to enclosing (fencing or hedging) of previously open land and the displacement of a large segment of the rural population.

(3) Trade fluctuations (depressions in the business cycle) created economic uncertainty.

(4) Increasing demand for extension of political power: growth of constitutional (limited) monarchy; rise of republicanism; steady extension of the franchise.

(5) Growing demand for state intervention in social and economic matters: factory legislation regulated hours and conditions of labor; English Parliament permitted trade unions to be organized, 1824-1825.

two general categories, the technological and the economic. In the technological category are two major causes of the Industrial Revolution: (1) the
growth and dissemination of technical knowledge throughout Europe at
the end of the 17th century; and (2) the presence in England of a pool of
skilled and semiskilled workers who, willingly or unwillingly, were able to
adjust themselves to the new forms of production. In the category of economic causes four seem to have been most significant: (1) the existence
by the 18th century in England and other parts of western Europe of investment capital which had been accumulated over several generations in
large enough amounts to be available to merchants and manufacturers at
relatively low rates of interest; (2) the growth of a fairly widespread bank-
ing and financial system which made capital easily available for investment
in new ventures; (3) the appearance in the 18th century of a class of managers and investors who were willing to risk capital in untried ventures and
to wait for fairly long periods before receiving a return on it; (4) the presence in England of certain important natural resources like coal and iron
in sufficiently large and easily accessible quantities to make their industrial
utilization economically feasible; and (5) the absence of internal customs
lines which made England the largest free trade area in Europe. Because
English society possessed all of the foregoing in abundance, England was
the first country to undergo the process of industrialization. England was
also the first to face up to most of the social problems that followed in its
wake.

C. Social Effects of the Industrial Revolution

Though the industrial changes that began in the 18th century were
ultimately to raise the living standards of western man to higher levels than
any previously known in history, the evils associated with the Industrial
Revolution seemed, for long, to outweigh its benefits. Institutions, social
relationships, and habits that had endured for centuries were suddenly
transformed or destroyed. In the rural areas of England the desire of the
great landowners to increase the yield of their estates led to the fencing in
of common lands (enclosure movement) on a large scale and the displacement of a large part of the rural population. In the long run, this movement
probably had the favorable effect of increasing the food supply needed to
support a growing urban population (the Agricultural Revolution). To a
lesser extent it may also have helped to create the labor supply needed for
the growing factory system, though natural population growth probably
played a larger part in providing the necessary manpower for mills and factories. But these possibilities were not in the perspective of the thousands

(6) General economic expansion of western Europe which manifested itself in many ways and had a great many varied effects. For one, the new industrialization worked very much to the advantage of Great Britain so that during the mid-years of the 19th century that nation was pre-eminently the world's greatest power. Statistics indicate how great was the wealth of the British economy during this period. In 1815 Britain produced sixteen million tons of coal; in 1835 thirty million tons; and by 1848 fifty million tons. British iron production doubled from one to two million tons between 1835 and 1848. It is estimated that British smelters supplied half the world's production of pig iron by 1850. British cotton manufacturers monopolized the world's market; and the British merchant marine comprised 60 percent of the world's tonnage.

On the Continent, Belgium's economic growth was nearly as rapid. Railway network made Belgium the center of continental economic expansion. By 1849-50 Germany had 3000 miles of railroad, France 2000 miles, and Austria 1000. The result was to enormously facilitate the growth of trade and the expansion of European industry. The first half of the 19th century thus witnessed a rapid widening in the technological and economic gap between European and non-European societies (except for the U.S.A.).

D. The Revolution in Thought: Advent of the Isms, 1815-1848

1. Romanticism, c. 1780-1830

A. ROMANTIC LITERATURE. J. J. Rousseau's *La Nouvelle Héloïse* (1760) foreshadowed the Romantic literary attitude. German poet J. W. Goethe (1749-1832) published *Die Leiden des jungen Werthers (Sorrows of Young Werther)*, 1773. Publication of William Wordsworth's *Lyrical Ballads*, 1798.

B. ROMANTIC PHILOSOPHY. Publication of the *Critique of Pure Reason* by Immanuel Kant (1724-1804), 1781. Edmund Burke's (1729-1797) *Reflections on the Revolution in*

of persons dispossessed of holdings which had often been in their families for centuries. They migrated to the expanding factory towns and thus helped to quicken the process of urbanization which has been one of the important results of the Industrial Revolution. To the man who lived through this change, particularly if he found himself driven from the countryside into crowded city slums where his life was given over to long hours of work under harrowing conditions, little if any of it could seem beneficial. Under such circumstances, few can be blamed for thinking that their lot was actually worse than it had been before, though squalor and poverty were not suddenly created by the Industrial Revolution. The concentration of human suffering in crowded cities did, however, have an important effect. Men came to be aware as never before of the social evils of their time, and this awareness led to demands for political and social reform on an unprecedented scale. By the middle of the 19th century these demands had forced the English state to intervene and pass social legislation designed to eliminate some of the worst of the evils.

With social reform came political reform, though for very different reasons. While the Industrial Revolution adversely affected many, it improved the lot of some. The wealth it created enriched the middle classes and led increasingly to demands for their enfranchisement, which finally came in the 19th century. Once the middle classes had gained political power, the way was opened for the advent of mass democracy and, presently, for the welfare state.

D. The Revolution in Thought: Advent of the Isms, 1815-1848

One of the major symptoms of change in early 19th-century Europe was the sudden appearance of a large number of new ideas which were to have an enormous influence in reshaping western civilization. Never before in history, even in the heyday of the Enlightenment, had men striven more to systematize their thoughts and beliefs than they did in the first half of the 19th century. Every form of belief, every manifestation of intellectual activity was classified, thought out, and given a definite name. Since many of them are still in common use, it is well to know something of their origins and meanings.

1. Romanticism

The most important of these new "isms" and one which comprehended the others in its intellectual scope was Romanticism. The term has so often been used in a rather vague way to characterize certain forms of literature and art that we frequently forget that it was solidly grounded in

France (1790) inaugurated the conservative attack on the revolutionary element in 18th-century rationalism. G. W. F. Hegel formulated the ideas afterwards published in his *Philosophy of History*, 1823-1827.

      c. POLITICAL AND SOCIAL EFFECTS OF ROMANTICISM. Some of the leading Romantic writers of the early 19th century were conservative in their religious and political outlooks in large measure as a result of what they regarded as the political excesses of the Revolutionary and Napoleonic periods. Men like the English Lake poets—William Wordsworth (1770-1850), Samuel Taylor Coleridge (1772-1834), and Robert Southey (1774-1843)—while they ardently supported the French Revolution in their youth, had become traditionalists and conservatives by 1815. The generation of younger Romantics, after 1820, tended to link themselves with liberal and nationalist movements. Victor Hugo (1802-1885) equated Romanticism with liberalism in literature; while the young English poets, Lord Byron (1788-1824) and Percy Bysshe Shelley (1792-1822), passionately espoused Greek independence.

2. Liberalism

      Adam Smith's *Wealth of Nations* (1776) strongly influenced the development of liberal thought. Publication of Jeremy Bentham's *Principles of Morals and Legislation*, 1789. T. R. Malthus's *Essay on Population* (population grows geometrically; subsistence resources increase arithmetically), 1798. David Ricardo's *Principles of Political Economy*, 1817. James Mill's *Elements of Political Economy*, 1821. John Stuart Mill's *Principles of Political Economy*, 1848.

      It must be understood that liberalism as it took form in England during the early 19th century was made up of two diverse streams of thought which were not entirely in intellectual harmony but which, nonetheless, had very important political and social effects. The first of these streams of thought originated in the economic theories of Adam Smith (see p. 62) who took the view that in economic matters the individual must be allowed the widest measure of freedom to pursue his own ends. Smith argued that in so doing the interests of the individual and society as a whole would coincide almost naturally and automatically. The second stream of thought that went into the composition of English liberalism came from the

philosophy. Romanticism was not a totally new and different way of looking at the world. In a sense, everybody who believes or has believed that
man is something more than a reasoning machine reflects the Romantic
attitude. For Romanticism began in the last decades of the 18th century as
a reaction to the teachings of the Enlightenment on the nature of man and
the universe. In contrast with the view that man was a creature controlled
only by his reason and that the universe was a fixed and unchanging clockwork mechanism, the Romantic philosophers asserted that man was also a
creature of his emotions and that the universe was not a static and colorless
physical system but rather a vast organism filled with an infinite variety of
things which were constantly changing and developing. It should not be
thought, however, that the Romantics were anti-intellectual (i.e., opposed
to reason). After all, the Romantic tradition did produce one of the most
important schools of modern philosophy which included the great German
thinkers, Immanuel Kant (1724-1804) and G.W.F. Hegel (1770-1831).
The Romantics paid homage to the human intellect but believed that it
represented only one part of human activity.

The coming of Romanticism was accompanied by a significant transformation in ways of human thinking. Men turned increasingly to history
and biology in an effort to find in those fields of knowledge the patterns of
change and development which were believed to control man and the universe. The result was a vast amount of social and biological theorizing
which culminated in the hypotheses of thinkers as widely separated in outlook as Karl Marx (1818-1883) and Charles Darwin (1809-1882).

2.   Liberalism

More closely tied to the Enlightenment in spirit and outlook than any
of the other "isms" of the early 19th century, liberalism came in time to
be looked upon as a belief peculiar to the middle classes. A "liberal" was
one who believed in individual freedom, both political and economic. He
wanted the power of the state curbed, believed in efficiency and economy
in government, and while he was not usually a democrat, he did have faith
in representative government (in the form either of a constitutional monarchy or a republic) and in an extended franchise. Where the early 19th-
century liberal differed from his 20th-century counterpart was in his attitude toward state power. The former would have been horrified at the 20th-
century liberal's calm acceptance of the state's right to intervene in social
and economic matters, even on the side of justice. In that respect, the 19th-
century liberal was often a doctrinaire adherent of Adam Smith's teachings,
one who believed strongly that any interference with the economic law of
supply and demand could result only in disaster.

writings of Jeremy Bentham (1748-1832) who based his philosophy on a maxim originally enunciated by Helvetius (see p.
60) that the guiding principle of society should be "the greatest good for the greatest number." Bentham realized that in
order to achieve this end it might be necessary at times to
force individuals to submit to the will of the whole of society.
In the main, however, he assumed that such occasions would
be so infrequent that his followers came to believe that they
could safely incorporate Smith's *laissez-faire* doctrines into
Benthamite thought.

3.   Nationalism

(1) French revolutionaries invoked the spirit of the "nation in arms" by mass conscription, 1793.

(2) Nationalist reaction against Napoleon in Spain (1808-
1813), Austria (1809-1810), Russia (1812), and Prussia (1813).

(3) Romantic movement, by emphasizing the history and
literature of the various European peoples, reinforced and
glorified national sentiment; for example, the German philosopher J. G. Fichte (1762-1814) stirred up feeling against Napoleon by his *Addresses to the German Nation* (1807-1808).

(4) Romantic nationalist movements often idolized the
nation as the great vehicle of folk tradition. While this kind
of adulation was to have evil effects later in the 19th century
and in the century following, in its beginnings Romantic
nationalism was often highly idealistic. Giusseppe Mazzini
(1805-1872) was a typical example of a Romantic nationalist
and idealist. He believed that in struggling for the cause of
Italian freedom he was struggling for progress and civilization everywhere, and not just for Italy alone.

4.   Socialism

A. UTOPIAN SOCIALISTS. Claude Henri de Saint Simon
published *The New Christianity*, 1825. Robert Owen's socialist colony at New Harmony, Indiana, founded, 1825. Charles
Fourier (1772-1837) hoped to found a series of rural co-oper-
ative associations *(phalanstéres)*. Louis Blanc (1811-1882) advocated the founding of "national workshops" owned and run
by the working classes but financed by the state. P. J. Proud-
hon (1809-1865) attacked the idea of private property in his

Liberalism as a social philosophy and guide to action had its greatest influence in 19th-century England, where several generations of economic and social thinkers devoted their efforts to its elaboration. In general, these fell into two groups. The "classical economists" stressed its economic side and developed the teachings of Adam Smith, often to gloomy conclusions. The most famous of these were Thomas Malthus (1766-1834), who concluded that population must always outstrip food supplies, and David Ricardo (1772-1823). A second group developed more fully the social and political aspects of liberalism. Its best known members were Jeremy Bentham (1748-1832), James Mill (1772-1836), and John Stuart Mill (1806-1873).

3. Nationalism

Nationalism, by which is meant loyalty to one's nation and people, was no new thing in European history, but, like so many other European ideas and movements, it was changed at the opening of the 19th century into something far more intense and far more demanding than it had been. This change resulted in part from antagonisms stimulated by Napoleonic conquest and in part from a growing feeling, first noticed among Frenchmen in the early days of their revolution, that worship of the national spirit was an adequate substitute for religious belief. In those areas of Europe where national independence had for long been achieved, strong national feelings were seldom manifest except during periods of crisis. Wherever national independence or unity were suppressed or held in check, there nationalism burned fiercely. Under the impact of this new spirit, folk cultures were revived as 19th-century Europe witnessed an extensive upsurge of cultural nationalism. The powerful force of national feeling created the two new nation-states of Germany and Italy and helped to becloud the international atmosphere in the years immediately preceding the First World War. In our own day we have been less enthusiastic about nationalism as a force for good than were Europeans of a century ago, for nationalism has shown the 20th century many of its seamier aspects.

4. Socialism

The last major ideological creation of the early 19th century was socialism. Though socialism in some form or other appears to have been one of the continuing aspirations of man, it was the 19th century that gave it a broader intellectual base and a greater popular support than it had ever had before. The wide appeal of socialism stemmed from the fact that it was a moral movement, a "cry of the heart," against the inequalities of wealth and the social sufferings caused by the Industrial Revolution. Through the efforts of a number of 19th-century social thinkers this sense of moral out-

What Is Property? (1839).

B. MARXIAN OR "SCIENTIFIC" SOCIALISM. Karl Marx was one of the significant figures of 19th century not only because his ideas were to become the ideological bases of Communist societies in the 20th century but because he was also in the great tradition of those 19th-century intellectual "synthesizers" twho sought to formulate a simply comprehensive and coherent theory which would explain, once and for all, the totality of man's relationship with the material world. The fact that he also had an extraordinary capacity for rapidly absorbing vast amounts of diverse knowledge and was a prolific writer made him, by all odds, the greatest scholarly figure of the 19th-century socialist movement. It is, therefore, probable that he would have been one of the major intellectual figures of recent history even if 20th-century events had not transpired to give him a political as well as an academic historical significance. *Marx's career and writings:* Born, May 5, 1818, in Treves, Germany (then Rhenish Prussia). Of Jewish parentage, he became a Christian at the time of his father's conversion to Lutheranism in 1824. Met Friedrich Engels, who became his lifelong friend and frequent collaborator, 1843. Together they wrote *The Communist Manifesto* at the end of 1847; this work remains, even today, the best epitome of classic Marxian theory. Expelled from Prussia in 1849 and refused satisfactory asylum in France, Marx went to London and remained there for the rest of his life. In 1859 he published the first part of what was intended as a full-scale treatise *(Critique of Political Economy)* covering the whole field of economics. When this failed to meet his expectations, he began again and in 1867 published the first volume of *Das Kapital (Capital)*. Throughout his later years he maintained an active interest in the European socialist movement and sought to give it direction through his writings. He died and was buried in London in March 1883. Ferdinand Lassalle (1825-1864) organized the German Social Democratic Party, 1862-64. First International Workingmen's Association (the Internationale), a body intended to comprehend all the militant socialist parties of the world, formed in 1864. Second International organized, 1889.

rage was transformed into a political program which, at least by the Marxian socialists, was also made the basis for a "scientific" interpretation of social relations. To the socialist thinker the great problem of humanity was not how to produce goods (he assumed that all of the problems of economic production had been essentially solved with the coming of the Industrial Revolution) but how to distribute them. In his eyes the enormous wealth created by the new machine power was more than sufficient to provide abundance for all. The difficulty with the existing system, as the socialist saw it, was that it permitted wealth to be concentrated in the hands of a small group of persons and thus deprived the working masses of a just share in what was rightfully theirs. It was the great socialist hope to provide a social mechanism whereby wealth might be equitably distributed to all.

The "Utopian Socialists," so-called in derision by their opponents because of the supposed impracticality of their theories, were the first to attempt a socialist solution of the problem of distributing wealth. To this end they formulated various schemes, ranging from the introduction of a new secular religious faith as advocated by the French count and philosopher Saint Simon (1760-1825) to the foundation of separate model socialist communities as undertaken by the English reformer Robert Owen (1771-1858). No one of these was ever more than temporarily successful, and the movement as a whole gained little popular support.

The most famous socialist writer of the 19th century, largely because of the success which his theories were to enjoy at a later date, was Karl Marx (1818-1883), who worked and wrote in collaboration with Frederick Engels‘(1820-1895). Marxian or "scientific" socialism has been a powerful intellectual and political force for generations since Marx's death. What Marx did, in essence, was to erect an edifice of social speculation on intellectual foundations which he believed would give it the status of a science. In so doing he made use of the philosophy of history put forward by the German philosopher Hegel, whose popularity was at its height when Marx began to write. Hegel had seen the whole of history as a series of conflicts between rival systems of thought. Marx agreed that history demonstrated a pattern of conflict—but not conflict of ideas. For Marx, history revealed the unfolding of a struggle between classes in which, as he saw it, the working class (proletariat) must ultimately emerge victorious and establish a classless society, because it was at once the largest class numerically and the class that produced everything that was economically useful in society. In this way the old problem of equitable distribution of wealth would be solved finally and permanently.

The ultimate victory of the proletariat, according to Marx, was not a

(*Essential Movement continued on p. 94*)

matter of guesswork. He saw it as the inevitable result of historical forces which he had analyzed "scientifically"; it could not fail to happen. This certainty many of his followers were to cling to even when later events had cast serious doubts on the validity of Marx's forecasts and interpretations. With the passage of time it became increasingly clear to all but the Marxian faithful that Marx had formulated not a science but a new secularized religion whose goals were in many ways as "utopian" as those of the earlier socialists whom he had derided.

CHAPTER 7

The Breakdown of the Conservative System, 1830-1848, and the Resurgence of Nationalism, 1850-1871

THE ESSENTIAL MOVEMENT

The settlement at Vienna, though seemingly guaranteed by the system of alliances established by the powers victorious over Napoleon, had begun to break up within ten years after the battle of Waterloo (1815). The various states may well have wished to follow the lead of the Austrian statesman Prince Metternich (1773-1859) in suppressing revolutions wherever they appeared, but their own interests often forced them to support revolutionary movements whether they wished to or not. Thus, in 1822, England acted with the United States (Monroe Doctrine) to prevent the conservative powers from sending troops to put down Spain's rebellious colonists in South America. In 1827, England, France, and Russia intervened in behalf of Greek revolutionaries in arms against their Turkish overlords. Furthermore, from 1830 onward all the major European states found themselves faced with serious domestic problems that gave them little opportunity to interfere in the affairs of other nations.

EVENTS AND DEFINITIONS

A. The Victory of Liberalism in Western Europe

1. France

Restoration of the monarchy, 1815-1830: Louis XVIII (1814-1824), brother of Louis XVI, came to the French throne at the overthrow of Napoleon. His successor, Charles X (1824-1830), a strong royalist, precipitated the revolution of July 1830 by promulgating the five repressive "July Ordinances."

Reign of Louis Philippe, 1830-1848: "July" or "Bourgeois" monarchy established as a result of the revolution of 1830; crown given Louis Philippe, Duke of Orleans. The new monarchy disappointed radical hopes by limiting the franchise to about two hundred thousand persons. A policy of repression under Francis Guizot, chief minister from 1840 to 1847, led to the revolution of 1848.

The Second Republic, 1848-1851: Rioting in Paris overturned the July Monarchy, February 1848. Rural France repudiated the revolution by electing a conservative, largely royalist, national assembly, April 1848. Bloody working-class riots in Paris suppressed, June 1848. Louis Napoleon Bonaparte (1808-1873), nephew of Napoleon I, elected president, December 1848. He came to power by playing up the "Na-

A. The Victory of Liberalism in Western Europe after 1830

Throughout Europe in the years after Waterloo the forces of liberalism and nationalism worked ceaselessly against the system established by the conservative powers. By 1830 these forces had become so strong that they constituted major threats to the security of many governments. In central and eastern Europe, where dynastic states still flourished, nationalism was the greater danger as men were stirred by a desire for national independence or unification. In the West, on the other hand, the demands of middle-class liberals for various political reforms grew louder about 1830 and finally led to major changes in France and England. By that time, however, it was already plain that liberal reforms would not be enough and must, in the end, be steps in the direction of mass democracy. Behind the liberals stood the newly aroused working class and its intellectual supporters, who were already asking for a democratic franchise and popularly elected parliaments. In England and France the great problem of the state was how much to concede without opening the floodgates to democracy. The different ways in which this problem was solved in the two countries led to important contrasts in their political history since that time.

1. France

The issue was settled first but with shorter-lived results in France. There the anger of the middle classes, the workingmen, and many intellectuals had increased steadily as a result of repressive policies pursued by the Bourbon monarchs who had been restored to the throne after the downfall of Napoleon. In July 1830, revolution broke out in Paris and the last Bourbon king, Charles X (1824-1830), was forced to abdicate. At the last moment, the revolutionaries were persuaded to accept a new king, Louis-Philippe(representing the Orleanist branch of the Bourbon family), in place of the republic hoped for by the political radicals of the middle and working classes. The result was the "Bourgeois Monarchy" of the period 1830-1848. While it lasted, political power, to the disgust of republican elements in France, was lodged in the hands of a small group of industrialists, bankers, and merchants. In their efforts to retain authority, the heads of the new state became nearly as repressive as their predecessors and thus set the stage for a new revolution.

In February 1848 an outburst of rioting in Paris overturned the Bourgeois Monarchy and established the short-lived Second Republic. Once the revolution occurred, however, a surprising political rift among the rural peasantry, the middle classes, and the Paris working class was discovered.

poleonic Legend" of past greatness and by promising concessions to all classes in France. Through a series of political maneuvers, Louis Napoleon overthrew the Second Republic (December 1851) and established the Second Empire (December 1852); he took the title of Napoleon III.

2. England

During the 18th century the English Parliament had developed the system of responsible or cabinet government by which the ministers of state (prime minister and others) were made responsible for their actions to the House of Commons (lower house of Parliament). However, the right to vote for members of Parliament was narrowly restricted and unrepresentative. After the Napoleonic Wars, agitation for various political and social reforms became so strong that the Tory (conservative) government finally had to make concessions to it.

Major English Reforms, 1815-1848: (1) Test Act, which kept Protestants who were not members of the Church of England from holding public office, was repealed in 1828; (2) Catholic Emancipation Bill freed Catholics of the same disability, 1829; (3) Reform Bill of 1832 gave the vote to all those who paid £10 rent a year (i.e., the middle classes) and eliminated the rotten (unrepresentative) boroughs; (4) slavery abolished throughout the British Empire, 1833; (5) first Factory Act undertook to regulate working conditions in textile factories, 1833; (6) municipal government reformed, 1835; (7) Chartist Movement (called after the "charter" outlining demands for further political reform) demanded a democratic franchise, 1839-1848; (7) Corn Laws repealed, 1846.

The peasants preferred the retention of some form of monarchy; the middle classes were divided between constitutional monarchy and a republic; while the working classes, already influenced by socialist thought, favored a democratic republic. The extent of this rift was such that it helped to destroy the republic and, in the end, became the most serious division in French politics for the rest of the 19th century. In the immediate confusion of the moment, a new political figure, Prince Louis Napoleon Bonaparte, a nephew of the first Napoleon, was able to get himself elected president of the republic. By 1852, following a political *coup d'état,* he had elevated himself to the throne of the restored Napoleonic Empire (Second Empire) as Napoleon III. For eighteen years (1852-1870) France was to be governed, once again, by an authoritarian state decked with the trappings of democracy.

2.   England

In England, where the political settlement of 1688 continued to function, the issue did not come to open revolution but approached very close to it. Despite the limitations on royal power, there had been no extension of the franchise nor any reform of political institutions. At the opening of the 19th century the country was still governed by the great landholders. The electoral system further contributed to the restriction of political authority, for no new boroughs (electoral units) had been created during the 18th century and few of the new industrial towns had any direct parliamentary representation. As opposition to this restricted system grew, so too did opposition to the privileged economic position of the landholding classes, whose income from the sale of grain was protected by Corn Laws which prohibited the import of foreign grain until the price of domestic grain had reached an abnormally high level.

The first breach in the position of the landholders was made with the passage of the Reform Bill of 1832, which extended the suffrage to the English middle classes. In 1846 the Corn Laws were repealed, and England entered upon an era of free trade and prosperity that marked the high point of Queen Victoria's reign (1837-1901) in the mid-years of the 19th century. With the repeal of the Corn Laws, England recognized officially that she was no longer an agricultural but an industrial society whose welfare depended more upon the products of her mines and factories than of her farms. Liberalism had won not a complete but a substantial victory; and an England beginning at last to feel the first real economic benefits of the Industrial Revolution was spared the revolutionary upheavals of 1848. Within a generation the first step was to be taken toward democracy with the passage in 1867 of a second major reform bill that extended the franchise to the city working classes.

B. The Failure of Nationalism in 1848:
Central and Eastern Europe

1. Austria

The repressive policies of Metternich, whose purpose was to preserve the Hapsburg dynasty by holding liberalism and nationalism in check, finally led to a nationalist reaction among the diverse peoples of the Austrian empire in 1848-1849. Revolt in Vienna (March 1848) spread to Italy, Bohemia and Hungary.

Austrian army suppressed revolt in Prague (Bohemia), June 1848.

Austrian General Radetzsky defeated Sardinia-Piedmont (July 1848 and March 1849) to destroy hopes of immediate Italian unification.

Russian armies aided the Austrians in crushing the Hungarian republic of Louis Kossuth, June-August 1849. Austrian power restored in central Europe.

2. Germany

Revolution in Berlin (Prussia); Prussian king promised to draw up a constitution, March 1848. Frankfort National Assembly convened to write a national constitution for Germany, May 1848.

King of Prussia refused to accept the crown of a united Germany from the Frankfort Assembly, April 1849.

"Humiliation of Olmütz": Austria forced Prussia to give up any immediate plans for German unification; Germanic Confederation of 1815 restored, November 1850.

B. The Failure of Nationalism in 1848: Central and Eastern Europe

In central and eastern Europe and also in Italy the conservative regimes, though shaken by the wave of revolution that spread outward from France in 1848, managed to hold their own. Excluding Italy for the moment (see pp. 102-103), let us look briefly at the reasons why these other revolutionary movements failed.

The great difficulty with the revolutions east of the Rhine in 1848-1849 was that those who supported them were frequently at cross-purposes with one another and thus succumbed easily to the armed strength of the conservative dynastic governments. This weakness stemmed from the fact that while in the West—in countries like England or France—the aims of revolution were liberal or even mildly socialist, in central and eastern Europe they were intermixed with nationalist aspirations. Thus in Germany the attempt of an elected representative assembly which met at Frankfort to draw up a liberal constitution for a united nation was frustrated because the various German states, Austria and Prussia especially, would not or could not give it their support. The new Germany, it seemed plain, could not be both a liberal and a unified national state. The same was largely true of the Austrian Empire, where the hope of German liberals to give a constitution to the empire was defeated because Slavs, Magyars, Poles, and other subject peoples did not want a liberalized Austria but their own independent states. During the ensuing chaos and indecision the king of Prussia and the Austrian emperor, by retaining the loyalty of their armies, were able to destroy all opposition and maintain the *status quo.*

C. The Resurgence of Nationalism, 1850-1871

Despite their temporary setback in the revolution of 1848, the forces of nationalism quickly revived. In the third quarter of the 19th century they broke through ancient barriers and created two great new nation-states, Germany and Italy. These new nations conformed to the 19th-century pattern of nationalism in that their unity was derived from the language, traditions, and geographical association of a single people. With the appearance of these new states, nationalism became a more powerful and, at the same time, a more dangerous force than ever before.

C. The Resurgence of Nationalism, 1850-1871

1. Italian Unification, 1848-1870

Revolt in Italy quelled by Austrian armies, 1848-1849. Count Cavour became premier of Sardinia-Piedmont (1852) and took his country into the Crimean War against Russia (1854-1856) on the side of France and Britain in order to win aid for Italian unification. Napoleon III of France fought as an ally with Sardinia against Austria; Austrians surrendered Lombardy to Sardinians, 1859. Giuseppe Garibaldi (1807-1882) and his thousand Redshirts captured Sicily and Naples, 1860. United kingdom of Italy proclaimed, 1861. Italian gained Venetia by aiding Prussia in the Seven Weeks' War against Austria (see below), 1866. Withdrawal of French garrison from Rome enabled Italian army to occupy the city, 1870.

2. German Unification, 1848-1871

Frankfort Asssembly failed to unify Germany, 1848-1849. Prussia undertook to rebuild its army and increase its military strength, 1859.

Bismarck appointed chancellor of Prussia, 1862.

War with Denmark over the provinces of Schleswig and Holstein, 1864.

Tension with Austria over the administration of the captured provinces resulted in the Seven Weeks' War between Austria and Prussia, 1866; Prussians forced Austria to withdraw from Germany; separate North German Confederation formed under the headship of Prussia, 1867.

Bismarck led the Confederation into victorious conflict with France (Franco-Prussian War), 1870-1871. German Empire proclaimed at Versailles, January 1871. Treaty of Frankfort (May 1871) forced France to pay an indemnity of five billion francs (a billion dollars) and cede the provinces of Alsace and Lorraine to Germany. New German state emerged as strongest power of continental Europe.

1.   Italian Unification, 1848-1870

Italy, for centuries only a "geographical expression" made up of various small sovereign states and dependencies, began to feel the urgings of national unity when Napoleon conquered and unified the area in the years before 1815. At the Congress of Vienna the unity imposed by Napoleon was destroyed, and Italy again became a territory divided into small states. In the face of great opposition from Austria, whose possessions and influence in Italy were extensive, and from the popes who, as temporal rulers of lands in central Italy, stood to lose a great deal by unification, popular demand for a united Italian state continued to grow. In 1848-1849 the decision of the kings of the small Italian state of Sardinia-Piedmont to lead the unification movement gave Italian patriots reason to hope that their time was at hand. When military defeats by Austria in 1848-1849 frustrated those hopes, Count Cavour (1810-1861), the Sardinian prime minister, sought by diplomatic methods to get outside help against the Austrians. In this way, Italy was able to enlist, first and temporarily, the support of France (1859) and, later, that of Prussia (1866) in driving Austria from the peninsula. With the capture of Rome by Italian troops in 1870, the new Italian state emerged as one of the major powers of Europe.

2.   German Unification, 1848-1871

On the surface, there were many similarities between the Italian and German unification movements. Both resulted from the upsurge of strong nationalist feelings, and both were directed against a single strong enemy, Austria, which resisted the two movements with military force. In Germany, as in Italy, the leadership for unification was given by a single strong state. Prussia's chief minister, Prince Bismarck (1815-1898), was, like Cavour, the architect of the new nation. There, however, the resemblance ended, for Prussia had far greater military resources than Sardinia-Piedmont and, in Bismarck, a leader who knew how to make the best use of them. Convinced by the failure of the liberal Frankfort Assembly in 1848-1849 that the only way to unify Germany was by resorting to "blood and iron," Bismarck worked industriously to build up the military power of Prussia to a point where she could safely challenge Austria. With diplomatic skill, Bismarck was able to carry his country into three successful wars, against Denmark in 1864, Austria in 1866, and France in 1870-1871. In this way, he created a new German Empire whose rulers were the former kings of Prussia. Between 1871 and 1914 this new nation was to become the strongest single power of continental Europe.

EVENTS AND DEFINITIONS

These years marked the period when the nations of Europe clearly dominated the rest of the world:

(1) Between 1800 and 1930 the number of persons of European stock in Europe and North America increased from 200,000,000 to 700,000,000.

(2) Between 1900 and 1914 four major countries (France, Germany, Great Britain, and the United States) shared among them over fifty per cent of the world's wealth.

CHAPTER 8

The Western World, 1871-1914

THE ESSENTIAL MOVEMENT

Between 1871 and 1914 western Europe became, as never before, the
center of a worldwide civilization. During that period the great overseas
migration of men and capital and the steady improvement in industrial
techniques and organization combined to give the western European masses
a higher standard of living and a greater measure of economic security than
any the world had ever known. Inevitably, these advantages also gave rise
to peculiar difficulties of their own. One important result was a rapid, almost explosive, growth of population which was more and more concentrated in large cities where men lost that sense of permanence and stability
so characteristic of agricultural societies. The growth of urbanism also made
all people more dependent upon the complex international economic system
which supplied them with subsistence; in consequence, events in remote
parts of the earth could affect their lives in unforseen ways. Furthermore,
the continually rising standard of living also raised the level of human expectation and led, in times of economic crisis, to an intensity of political discontent to which the state could not remain indifferent. And, finally, Europe, because of its overwhelming industrial and military power, was also
able to affect the lives of countless millions of non-Europeans who had come
within the orbit of its economic system and been touched by its civilization.
Colonial peoples could not remain unchanged under the impact of European ways and ideas, and, as their consciousness of things European grew,
so too did their resentments.

A. Political Reforms and the Emergence of the Mass Electorate

1. France

Third French Republic proclaimed after the defeat of the French armies at Sedan, September 1870. Revolt of the Paris Commune suppressed, 1871. Constitution of the Third Republic put in force, 1875. Third Republic weathered attempted monarchist *coup d'état* (1877) and the Boulanger crisis (1886-1889). Struggle between the Third Republic and the Catholic clerical party ended in compromise, 1890. The Dreyfus Affair (1894-1906) seriously divided the nation but finally ended in a clear-cut victory for the forces of republicanism.

2. Great Britain

Second Reform Bill extended the suffrage to the urban working class, 1867. W. E. Gladstone (1809-1898) began his attempt to solve the problem of Anglo-Irish relations by sponsoring an Irish Land Act, 1870. Benjamin Disraeli's (1804-1881) second ministry, 1874-1880. Gladstone's franchise bill granted suffrage to rural working class, 1884. First Irish Home Rule Bill defeated, 1886. Second Home Rule Bill defeated by the House of Lords, 1893. Boer War, 1899-1902. Formation of the Labor Representation Committee (later became the Labor Party), 1900. Liberal Party inaugurated new program of social legislation, 1906 (see § B.2, below). Parliament Act deprived House of Lords of all but a suspensive veto on legislation, 1911. Irish Home Rule Bill passed but suspended until after First World War, 1914.

3. Germany

Kulturkampf (battle for German culture) waged against the Catholic church by Bismarck, 1871-1883; May or Falk Laws severely limited Catholic civil rights, 1873. Antisocialist laws passed, 1878. Accession of William II (1889-1918); resignation of Bismarck as chancellor, 1890. Emperor William took

Thus a rich European society, which grew ever richer in the two generations before 1914, found also that its wealth brought new and increasingly complex problems.

A. Political Reforms and the Emergence of the Mass Electorate

One of the unhappy legacies left by the French Revolution was the problem of restoring a feeling of mutual trust and a sense of common identity between the state and the people. For centuries, consciously or unconsciously, the great mass of Europeans had thought of their own interests and those of their rulers as one and the same. That faith was dealt a serious blow when the French Revolution destroyed the Old Regime. As a consequence, the political efforts of the 19th century were directed toward somehow restoring this sense of common identity. For a time the conservative governments in the pre-1848 era tried to use force toward this end, on the theory that once men were again accustomed to the rule of state bureaucracies unchecked by representative institutions they would simply endure what they could not change. The revolutions of 1848, for all of their immediate lack of success, nonetheless had the effect of forcing the various European states—even the most despotic of them—to consider ways of winning the approval and confidence of their peoples. The commonest effort toward achieving this end was by extending the franchise and thus giving the masses a larger share in local or national government. Even before 1871 steps had been taken in this direction, but it was not until after that date that Europe as a whole underwent a fairly widespread process of democratization. By the first decade of the 20th century it appeared that almost every European state was following a common pattern of political evolution that would ultimately see the triumph of parliamentary democracy. As always, the great differences in the speed of this development were between eastern and western Europe. In general, the great western industrial states achieved democracy first, but after 1900 even countries like Russia and Austria-Hungary seemed to be moving, albeit slowly, in that direction.

How successful was the extension of political franchise in winning the loyalty of European masses for the various European states between 1870 and 1914? The answer would seem to be that it was very successful indeed, though other factors like the rise of literacy (which made men the object of mass conditioning by means of newspapers, magazines, etc.), the improvement of subsistence standards, and the introduction in at least some European societies of rudimentary welfare legislation must also have played a part. For all of the seeming social and political unrest that existed in Europe

an increasingly larger share in the direction of affairs. Socialist (Social Democratic) Party became strongest numerically in the German Reichstag (parliament), 1912.

4. Austria-Hungary

Constitutional compromise (*Ausgleich*) of 1867 created a dual monarchy of Austria-Hungary with separate governments under one sovereign for the two countries but a common administration for war, foreign affairs, and finance. Failure to include other subject peoples (apart from the Hungarians) aroused national enmity. Suicide of Archduke Rudolf, heir to the throne, 1889. Universal suffrage law passed for Austria, 1907. Assassination of Archduke Franz Ferdinand at Sarajevo (Bosnia) in 1914 was the immediate cause of the First World War.

5. Russia

See pp. 126-128 for events leading up to the Russian Revolution.

B. Social Problems and the Growth of State Responsibility

1. Rise of Trade Unionism

British parliament repealed Combination Acts prohibiting the formation of trade unions, 1825. Trade Union Congress of Great Britain formed, 1868. Austria legalized free trade-union association in 1867; the Netherlands in 1872; France in 1884; and Germany after 1890.

2. Social Legislation

Great Britain passed first successful Factory Acts (1833 and 1844), Mines Act of 1842, and Ten Hours' Law of 1847. France enacted similar legislation to curb factory abuses in 1874 and 1883. Germany under Bismarck introduced first sickness insurance (1883), the first workmen's-compensation law (1884), and the first old-age security law (1889). Great Britain followed Germany's example with a workmen's-compensation act (1906), old-age-pension law (1909), and national unemployment insurance (1911).

just before the First World War, the loyalty of the masses to the existing political order even under the most authoritarian governments was proved beyond question once fighting was joined in 1914. The First World War was so long, so bloody, so costly in manpower and resources because, among other things, the intense nationalism of the European masses was so great that peace could not be negotiated short of almost total exhaustion. If public morale had not been so high in every major European country, the war could never have dragged on as it did.

B. Social Problems and the Growth of State Responsibility

After the middle of the 19th century the growth of social consciousness stimulated by the Industrial Revolution began to have marked effects. These may have been hurried by the spread of socialist ideas and the organization of socialist parties among the European working classes. With the extension of democracy, the gradual rise in the real wages (i.e., the purchasing power) of the working classes, and the general increase in European wealth, it now seemed feasible to grant to the masses social benefits which had formerly been reserved for the privileged few. Moreover, the great increase in European population and the continued urbanization of European society forced the state to deal with a complex of problems which had not previously been regarded as part of its responsibility. Slowly, and often in a piecemeal way, the various European governments undertook to provide a number of new services for their peoples. Expanded educational opportunities, improved public health measures, even some forms of compensation and unemployment insurance (the latter particularly in Germany and England), all became a part of the accepted responsibility of the state by 1914. So complete was the transformation that in the process 19th-century liberalism ceased to be

3. Socialism as a Political Force

For all of socialism's strong appeals to the European masses, it had initial difficulties in organizing itself as a political force. In large part these difficulties arose because of very strong ideological conflicts within socialist ranks. The First International (organized in 1864), for example, foundered as a result of serious differences between anarchists and other socialists. Anarchists saw in all existing institutions of society— church, state, and all combinations of economic or industrial power—only corrupting elements which were destroying mankind. Only if these were totally eliminated from society, would it be possible to return man to a kind of primitive stateless condition in which men could live in peace and happiness as equals without need to exploit each other. Other parties of the left, including to some degree even the Marxists, while they agreed that the state was evil when controlled by the exploiting capitalist classes, nonetheless, took the view that the state should not be obliterated but that it should be seized and used as an instrument of social equalization in behalf of the working masses. The two most important leaders of late 19th-century anarchism were Prince Alexander Kropotkin (1842-1921), a Russian nobleman who came to the movement out of intense intellectual conviction, and Michael Bakunin (1814-1876), another Russian aristocrat whose fervor won him a large following among the European working classes just before his death. Bakunin's success in this respect led Karl Marx and his supporters to demand the expulsion of the anarchists from the First International in 1873. In the long run, Marx's fears proved groundless, for while the anarchists continued in existence they never achieved a position of dominance within the socialist movement.

More dangerous to Marxian socialism was the rise of socialism as a political movement, for socialist parties as they came into being throughout western Europe tended to adapt themselves to the existing political situation which proved increasingly advantageous as the franchise was gradually expanded in most countries to include the working classes. As a result, a single United Social Democratic Party for all Germany came into existence in 1875; others were formed in Italy (1891) and Great Britain (1900). The Fabian Society was founded in Brit-

a philosophy of individualism and, under the designation of the "New Liberalism," became a philosophy of state intervention in favor of social justice for those who had fallen behind in the economic struggle.

With these developments a new internal conflict arose in the minds of the masses and, in particular, among the industrial workers. Socialism, from the beginning, had always been regarded as the antithesis of nationalism. Marx and his followers, for example, had believed that the international proletariat was actually stateless and had no real loyalties beyond those of class. The state was only an instrument used by the ruling capitalist classes to exploit and oppress the workers and therefore had to be overthrown. Given this belief, then, the growth of democracy and the increase in state responsibility set up tensions within the socialist movement. A great many socialists came to believe that it was possible to achieve the goals of socialism without resorting to violent revolution or immediately destroying existing institutions. The state itself would become the instrument of transition from capitalism to socialism. As this idea spread, strong socialist parties (among which were the German Social Democrats and the British Labor Party) with an unrevolutionary, reformist outlook came into existence. Meanwhile, outside the sphere of politics, the trade-union movements in industrial countries strove with a great deal of success to win for their members a larger share of the existing wealth by way of increased wages, shorter hours, and improved working conditions. Thus the socialist movement found itself torn between national loyalty and the class struggle. When war finally came in 1914, the great majority of socialists, confronted with the necessity for choosing between the nation and international socialist solidarity, put national interests uppermost.

Nonetheless, despite these changes and the continuous rise in the standard of living, Europe, particularly in the years between 1900 and 1914, was disturbed by an increase of industrial and other kinds of violence. The economic discontents may be explained in part by a leveling off of real wages during that period. Another element contributing to economic unrest was the recurrence of cyclical depressions which became more intense as Europe's economic system grew in complexity and became more dependent on international trade. The other forms of discontent may be traced, however, to another peculiarity of modern life, namely, the rise of organized mass opinion caused by improved communications and the spread of literacy among the masses. Men were conscious of themselves, of their interests, and of their places in the political or social order as never before; and, with the growth of this consciousness, tensions of all kinds—national, international, social, and political—increased throughout the western world.

ain to promote "gradual (practical) socialism," 1883-84. By the 1890's a growing conviction that Marxian revolution was not imminent led some socialists, e.g., the German Social Democratic leader Eduard Bernstein (1850-1932) to call for a policy of "revisionism," i.e., to suggest that revolutionary goals could be attained best not by violent but by peaceful parliamentary tactics. In Russia, however, where there was no effective parliamentary system, socialist parties, on the whole, remained revolutionary in outlook. There the Social Democratic Party, founded in 1898, later (1903) split into two groups, the Bolsheviks (majority), who remained revolutionary Marxists, and the Mensheviks(minority), who were less revolutionary in outlook. Union of French Socialist Parties, 1905. The Second International, founded in 1889, disintegrated in 1914 at the outbreak of war.

Pope Leo XIII (1878-1903) issued *Rerum Novarum* (1891), encyclical applying Christian principles to relations between capital and labor.

C. Science and Thought

1. Major Scientific Achievements

The last quarter of the 19th century in both science and technology saw the beginning of that unprecedented era of scientific achievement which culminated in the major breakthroughs of the twentieth century and whose manifestations we are still witnessing in ever greater profusion. The world's railway mileage quadrupled between 1870 and 1900. The first skyscrapers appeared in Chicago and New York. Great canal-building projects at Suez, Kiel, and, after 1900, across Panama revolutionized transoceanic communication. The internal combustion engine and the first wireless transmission were accomplishments of the 1880's and 1890's. The first successful, sustained heavier than air flight took place at Kitty Hawk, North Carolina in 1903.

Physics and Mathematics. James Clerk Maxwell (1831-1879) first put forward his electro-magnetic theory of light, 1871. Wilhelm K. Röntgen (1845-1923) discovered X-rays, 1895. Pierre (1859-1906) and Marie Curié (1867-1934) isolated radium, 1898. Max Planck (1858-1947) put forward the Quantum Theory, 1900. Ernest Rutherford (1871-1937) and Fred-

C. Science and Thought: the Need to Live with Uncertainty

The 19th century is usually looked back on as an age of confidence and security when men believed, perhaps not quite so dogmatically as they had in the 18th century but nonetheless firmly, that the world was progressing in the right direction. As in every age, there were some doubters; but, on the whole, the 19th-century European had reason to be proud of his accomplishments. He had seen the death rate lowered, slums cleared, sanitation advanced, food production increased, and educational opportunity expanded, all within a relatively brief span of years. The greatest achievements of the age, however, were made in the field of science, where the results of research manifested themselves in spectacular engineering and industrial advances. The pure scientist remained a remote figure whose work was not always understood, but men were willing to agree that he must be accomplishing something important when they could see around them the practical results of his experiments and discoveries. Everywhere it seemed that science had provided a key that must finally solve all of man's problems, not easily or quickly as the 18th century had thought, but nonetheless inevitably and ultimately.

1. The Darwinian Hypothesis

To understand the dominant mood of the 19th century, a mood that lasted well beyond 1880, we must first understand that like the 18th century it was a time when men still hoped to reduce all knowledge to a single unified system of thought (synthesis). Though the major scientific thinkers of the 19th century were aware that this was not so simple a matter as it had seemed to their forebears, the great number of discoveries in all fields of human endeavor down to 1850 seemed to promise that the hoped-for goal might not be far off.

It was in this atmosphere of anticipation that Charles Darwin (1809-1882) published his *Origin of Species* in 1859. Because some such discovery had been long foretold by earlier speculations in the field of biology and because it seemed to settle so many important questions having to do with the development of living things, the book created a stir not unlike that caused by Newton's discoveries long before. Darwin, like Newton, offered what seemed to be a sound and unanswerable explanation for a natural process which many biologists had speculated about for a long time but had been unable to explain. Essentially, the problem was to account for the natural progression from simple organic forms to highly complex ones throughout geological time. All the evidence of geology and paleontology

erick Soddy (1877-1956) propounded theory of disintegration to explain radioactivity. Albert Einstein (1879-1955) first put forward his special theory of relativity, 1905. Rutherford bombarded the atom with radioactive particles, 1911. Werner Heisenberg (1901-   ) put forward the principle of indeterminacy to explain subatomic physical phenomena, 1927.

Biology and Medicine. Publication of Charles Darwin's *Origin of Species* (1859) and *The Descent of Man* (1871). Gregor Mendel (1822-1884) published the results of his experiments on plant heredity, 1865. Louis Pasteur (1822-1895) discovered the theory underlying immunization through vaccination, 1885. Sigmund Freud (1856-1939) launched his first psychoanalytic work on the subconscious, 1895. Walter Reed (1851-1902) proved that yellow fever was transmitted by a mosquito, 1900. Sir Frederick G. Hopkins (1861-1947) discovered vitamins, 1906.

2.   Philosophy

A. INFLUENCE OF SCIENCE. ■ Science of "sociology" came into existance with the writing of Auguste Comte (1798-1857). Herbert Spencer (1820-1903) applied the theory of evolution to social thought; rise of "social Darwinism." ■ Beginning of modern psychology: Wilhelm Wundt (1832-1920) in Germany and William James (1842-1910) in the United States; Ivan Pavlov (1849-1936) discovered the "conditioned reflex" by experimenting on dogs. ■ Materialism, i.e., the belief that nothing spiritual exists and that the universe consists only of matter, reached its height in the writings of the German scientist Ernst Haeckel (1834-1919).

B. REACTION TO MATERIALISM AND MECHANISM: GROWTH OF MODERN IRRATIONALISM. Like the earlier Romantic philosophers, many late 19th- and 20th-century thinkers rejected the belief that man is a reasonable being. For most of such thinkers man was, on the contrary, a creature controlled by his impulses and emotions, that is, by his will rather than his intellect. To this view the work of Freud and Pavlov contri-

(study of fossils) seemed to point toward some kind of evolutionary process extending over thousands or even millions of years, but every theory advanced until the publication of Darwin's work had failed to account satisfactorily for many of the significant facts. Darwin, after some years of careful research, advanced a theory that resolved the problem by asserting that the process of evolution was one in which organisms possessed of certain favorable heritable characteristics would survive and found species while others, less favorably endowed, would die out. Darwin referred to this process as "natural selection," which must inevitably lead to the "survival of the fittest."

Apart from its scientific plausibility, the Darwinian hypothesis had other effects on 19th-century thought that went far beyond Darwin's own intentions. It seemed, for example, to deny the whole idea of the divine creation of the world and aroused a theological controversy that lasted for two generations. Theorists of various kinds saw in its emphasis on the struggle for survival a justification for their own particular kinds of ideas: to Marxists it seemed to confirm the class struggle in history; to believers in *laissez-faire* economics it seemed to prove that life is a struggle for economic survival among individuals. Racists and nationalists used it to justify the exploitation of "inferior" races or to exalt the "superiority" of particular nations. Each of these social Darwinists, as they were called, found in the Darwinian view of evolution whatever it suited him to believe.

2.   The Changing Climate of Scientific Opinion

Darwin's achievement, while it remains even today one of the great landmarks in scientific thought, was to be the last major synthesis of the confident 19th-century world of science. After 1870 a new mood, which in one variation or another has continued to the present time, began to make itself felt. Changes in scientific thought brought on by a number of new discoveries during the last decades of the century, particularly in the fields of astronomy and physics, led men to wonder, first, whether the laws of the universe were so fixed and stable as they had seemed in the theories of Galileo and Newton and, finally, whether the formulation of a final synthesis of all scientific knowledge might not be far more remote than anyone had thought a few years before. The most important discovery in this connection was that of Albert Einstein (1879-1955) who, in 1905, propounded the theory, since confirmed in a variety of ways, that space and time were not absolute but rather were relative quantities, that matter is energy and energy is matter, and that both are subject to constant change. While Einstein's relativity theory contributed significantly to the development of modern atomic physics, it contained implications which were disconcerting and led to a revolution in scientific thinking. Men could no longer refuse to

buted (though they themselves were not irrationalists) by stressing the importance of subconscious drives and conditioned reflexes. Among the more important 19th- and 20th-century philosophers and social thinkers who emphasized the irrational nature of man were: ■ (1) The New Idealists, who carried on the philosphical traditions of Kant and Hegel and tried to preserve spiritual values in the face of materialism. The most prominent of them were the Englishman F.H. Bradley (1846-1924), the American Josiah Royce (1855-1916), and the Italian Benedetto Croce (1866-1952). ■ (2) The Anti-Rationalists who believed in the primacy of the human will and the force of myth in controlling human beliefs and actions. Among them was Friedrich Nietzsche (1844-1900), who rejected Christian teaching and the democratic ideal as weak and degrading beliefs and who exalted the virtues of the strong (supermen). Two important Italian members of this school were Gaetano Mosca (1858-1941) and Vilfredo Pareto (1858-1923).

C. MODERN FASCIST THOUGHT. One of the important intellectual by-products of the revolt against reason was to be found in modern Fascist or Nazi thought, particularly as it later developed in Italy and Germany during the 1920's and 1930's. As a doctrine, Fascism was not clearly thought out or coherent. It purpose was to refute Marxism and democratic liberalism, both of which were based on the assumption that the universe and the actions of men were capable of rational explanation.

Where Marxism and liberal democracy stressed the power of reason, Fascism stressed the power of "unreason," of the human emotions or "will."

When Marxism and liberalism argued that men were motivated by economic desires, Fascism argued that men were motivated by ideas or "myths" which drove them to act in such a way that they were no longer slaves to their material environment but masters of it. Fascism, therefore, made use of nationalism or (as in the Nazi case) of racism as myths to impel peoples to action; and both rejected the Marxian idea of a "class struggle" in favor of a social ideal of class harmony within a corporate state whose interests took precedence over everything else in society.

The state thus became all-powerful and could not be

face the possibility that scientific knowledge might not be able to arrive at absolute, final truths about the nature of the universe.

3.   The 20th-Century Scientific Breakthrough

For all of the growing doubt about man's ability to know ultimate truth about the nature of matter and the universe, there was still no letup in the dizzying pace of scientific achievement after 1900. Men possessed techniques and an ever-expanding body of knowledge which made the 20th century the most brilliant scientific era that the human race had ever known. Indeed, the measure of human accomplishment in every area of scientific activity was such that the improbable became commonplace and the impossible became probable. The very dimensions of the planet shrank with each decade, and outer space by mid-century seemed clearly within human reach. It was a cliché to say that the vast majority of the greatest scientists the world had ever known were alive in the year 1960. And yet the claim was valid. If man had doubts about what he might ultimately do, they were not sufficiently strong to dull his curiosity or to deprive him of the will to seek new answers to old questions.

resisted. Furthermore, the state was not an instrument controlled by the masses but the tool of an elite (the Nazi or Fascist leadership) whose power was an expression of the nation's or the people's will.

D. The Growth of International Tension and the Coming of the First World War

The Sources of German Strength, 1871-1914.

a) Population growth: from 40 million in 1871 to 67 million in1914 (the population of France, in contrast, increased during the same period from 36 million to 39 million). Moreover, Germany'spopulation was a youthful one; down to 1910 about 32% of the population was under 14 and only about 4% over 65. As a result, the German army's annual intake of recruits was about twice that of France.

b) Industrial strength: German iron production rose from 1½ million tons in 1871 to over 17 million tons in 1914 (France in thelatter year produced only 5 million tons). German steel production in 1900 reached 7 million tons and exceeded that of Great Britain by 1½ million tons. By 1914 Germany was the world's leader in the electrical and chemical industries. Between 1871 and 1914 the value of German exports increased fourfold, from 2½ billion marks to 10 billion marks.

c) Intellectual and scientific advances: this was also the period when German cultural achievements made that country a leading center of artistic, scientific, and academic accomplishment.

1. European Rivalries: Alliance and Entente

Formation of the Three Emperors' League (Austria, Germany, Russia), 1873. Russo-Turkish War (1877-1878) nearly led to hostilities between Russia and England; Russia forced to give up most of her gains from the victorious Treaty of San Stefano at the Congress of Berlin (1878), where Austria was also given a mandate over the Balkan provinces of Bosnia and Herzegovina.

Austria and Germany formed a military alliance (1879), which became the Triple Alliance with the addition of Italy in 1882. Bismarck negotiated the secret Reinsurance Treaty with Russia (1887), which was allowed to lapse at his retirement, forcing the Russians into alliance with France (1894).

After the Fashoda Incident in 1898 (when an Anglo-

THE ESSENTIAL MOVEMENT, *Continued*

D. The Growth of International Tension and the Coming of the First World War

In international relations, the two most important developments of the period 1871-1914 were the emergence of imperial Germany as the leading military and industrial power of Europe and the great industrial transformation and internal economic growth of the United States. Of the two, the rise of Germany was more immediately significant because the newly acquired strength of the United States was not to be felt for a number of years. What made Germany so important was the fact that it possessed several characteristics which, in combination, made the German Empire unique among European states. It had a large population imbued with a strong sense of nationality, great natural resources which were effectively utilized by an expanding industrial system, a strong army, and, during the first eighteen years of its existence, an astute international statesman in the person of Bismarck. As a consequence, the new Germany was to dominate European power politics as no other state had been able to do since the days of the first Napoleon. Furthermore, since this dominance was achieved not by open war but by diplomatic manipulation behind which there lurked the threat of war, the international atmosphere of Europe became more and more tense during the last years of the 19th century.

1. European Rivalries: Alliance and Entente

The heart of the problem of European international politics was to be found in the relations of the six leading states—Austria-Hungary, France, Germany, Great Britain, Italy, and Russia. Two of these, Austria-Hungary and Russia, were dynastic empires whose policies were, in part, shaped by their need to keep subject peoples within their own borders from becoming dangerously restive. For Germany the great European problem was to keep France from revenging herself for the disastrous defeat of 1870-1871. At the same time the picture was complicated by the fact that in southeastern Europe another great dynastic state, the Ottoman Empire (Turkey), was disintegrating and leaving behind a power vacuum in that area which the other powers strove to fill. In the midst of these mounting tensions the growing national aspirations of the Balkan peoples and the inhabitants of the old east European border lands (Poles, Czechs, Slovenes) added the

French war almost began over territory in Africa), Britain
and France settled all their major differences and formed
the Entente Cordiale (1904). Russia and Britain formed the
Anglo-Russian Entente (1907) which brought France, Great
Britain, and Russia together in the Triple Entente against
the Triple Alliance.

The formation of this system of alliances heightened tensions among the leading powers, so that each international
incident made the international atmosphere increasingly grave.
Among the most important of these crises were: first Moroccan
Crisis caused by the German emperor's visit to Tangier in de-
fiance of French interests there, 1905; Algeciras Conference
over Morocco resulted in French diplomatic triumph over Germany, 1906; annexation of Bosnia-Herzegovina by Austria
aroused Russian protests, 1909; second Moroccan Crisis, 1911;
First Balkan War (Bulgaria, Serbia, and Greece against Turkey),
Oct. 1912-May 1913; Second Balkan War (Greece, Serbia, Rumania, and Turkey against Bulgaria), June-July 1913; assassination of Archduke Francis Ferdinand at Sarajevo, June 1914;
Austrian ultimatum to Serbia (July 23) and declaration of war
on Serbia, July 28, 1914.

2.   The Revival of Imperialism

The period was marked by growing imperial rivalry intensified by a new and stronger nationalism which led to the
partition of Africa and further European expansion into Asia
and the Pacific area.

A. GREAT BRITAIN. Disraeli purchased an interest in the
Suez Canal to protect British communications with India and
the Far East, 1875. Britain moved to check Russian expansion
in central Asia (Afghan War, 1878-1879). British occupied
Egypt, 1882. Fashoda Incident almost caused war between
Britain and France, 1898. British conquered the Boer republic
in South Africa, 1899-1902. Britain and Russia divided Persia
into "spheres of influence." 1907.

B. BEGINNINGS OF THE BRITISH COMMONWEALTH. During the period 1871-1914, Britain also granted limited self-
government and later virtual independence (dominion status)
to certain parts of her empire (mainly those settled by peoples
of European stock): Canada (1867), Australia (1900), New
Zealand (1907), and the Union of South Africa (1910).

element of uncertainty to the relations of the larger powers. National minorities, seeking independence from large states, were aided and abetted
by rival large states, while numerous small states placed themselves within
the power orbit of the larger nations. In the end, however, it was the war-
like conduct of German foreign affairs after Bismarck's retirement in 1890
and the sheer increase in German military and naval strength that frightened powers like Russia and Great Britain into joining France against her.

Progressively, then, the pattern of international politics moved in the
direction of an armed-camp system in which the larger nations divided
into two major armed alliances surrounded by a cluster of smaller states
whose interests and ambitions overlapped. By 1882 the diplomatic skill of
Bismarck had brought into existence the Triple Alliance of Germany,
Austria-Hungary, and Italy. To counterbalance this group, France and
Russia first formed their Dual Alliance in 1894, to be followed ten years
later by the Entente Cordiale between France and England. In 1907 the
alignment of the powers was finally completed when England, France, and
Russia formed the Triple Entente. With this development, the stage was
set for the drama that began in 1914.

2. The Revival of Imperialism

While Europe was dividing into Alliance and Entente, other interests
outside the sphere of European internal affairs helped to intensify international distrust. Of these, the most important was a new and revitalized
imperialism which, after 1870, led to clashes among the European states in
all parts of the globe.

Imperialism (i.e., the conquest and exploitation or extermination of
one people by another) was nothing new in the history of the world. The
great empires of antiquity had flourished by this means. The term "imperialism" has come, however, to have a different meaning when applied to
European expansion since the 16th century. With some few major exceptions, as for example in North America or Australasia where European colonists have taken over the land directly and virtually eliminated the native
peoples, European imperialism has taken the form of economic penetration
by individual merchants or trading companies whose main interest was
trade rather than conquest. In the attempt to preserve trade relations and
to provide security for merchants and traders, military conquest sometimes
followed economic penetration but it was often resorted to out of necessity
when other expedients had failed. Over a period of 300 years the great
maritime powers—England, France, Holland, Portugal, and Spain—had

(Essential Movement continued on p. 122)

acquired in this way large territorial holdings in all parts of the earth. Some of these had great commercial value and supplied the controlling European power with raw materials and a ready market for its manufactured goods. Others seemed to cost more in terms of military protection and administration than they actually gave to the "mother" country.

By the middle of the 19th century a highly developed industrial state like England was actually doing more business with territories not directly under her control than she was with some that were a part of the British Empire. As a consequence, direct conquest as a means of preserving markets and gaining access to raw materials was looked upon with increasing disfavor in those parts of Europe, but particularly in Great Britain, where industry was highly developed. English manufacturers, it was argued, did not need the protection of a closed imperial market to sell their goods. They could sell them anywhere without fear or favor. Hence, rather than alienate colonial peoples who might become good customers if they were free and independent, it was best to let them go their own way. What most 19th-century businessmen wanted from their governments was not so much conquest as protection for capital investments overseas and security in the pursuit of trade. If foreign governments gave them these, the businessmen were usually content to abstain from direct intervention in the affairs of another country. If not, then they often became strong supporters of a vigorous policy of military conquest and expansion.

We now realize that the 19th-century businessman or investor who put his money into the development of trade or industry in underdeveloped parts of the earth was in a real sense doing a far greater service for colonial peoples than he is sometimes given credit for. Yet this sort of economic interpenetration or "imperialism" got a bad name because the European entrepreneur usually occupied a favored social and economic position in the underdeveloped country, and in this way aroused the resentments of native peoples who looked upon the foreigner, rightly or wrongly, as an exploiter of their natural resources and labor.

After 1870 the old form of imperialism through military conquest, which had seemed to be on the wane, was suddenly revived as most of the great powers engaged in a scramble for territories all over the world. The reasons for this development are more complex than they might seem at first glance. One of the standard explanations for the renewal of imperial ambitions is based upon the assumption that the great industrial states of Europe, faced with the glut of overproduction, were anxious to find markets for their goods. Markets may have had something to do with it, but were by no means the only motive. Colonial possessions were valued not simply as possible markets or sources of materials but as symbols of national greatness or as key positions in international politics or military strategy. In many cases, colonies were retained by a European state for prestige purposes despite high costs of administering and policing them. For the emergent new nations like Germany and Italy, whose ambitions were fed by strong national feelings, the acquisition of colonies became a symbol of great-power status. Partly in reaction to the new aggressiveness of these states and partly because of the growing uncertainty and insecurity in the last years of the century, the older imperial powers, France and England, joined in the race with enthusiasm and thus further added to the atmosphere of continual crisis that kept the world in turmoil between 1900 and 1914.

3. Europe in 1914: the Immediate Causes of War

By 1914, then, the tensions of the international scene had become almost unbearable. Neither Alliance nor Entente was any longer in a position to preserve the peace in the face of the complex problems that confronted them. Here was a major part of the difficulty, for with the growth of public awareness and the increasing influence of public opinion in public affairs, statesmen of even the most undemocratic countries felt themselves severely restricted when it came to carrying out decisions in matters of domestic or foreign policy. The very nature of modern warfare, the complicated problems arising out of the need to utilize all the resources of society as quickly as possible in the event of war, forced military leaders to risk the danger of conflict rather than permit their enemies the few hours' advantage that sudden mobilization might give. In the end, the decision for peace or war in 1914 was made not by military leaders or statesmen thinking or acting independently but rather by such men trapped in circumstances from which they could not withdraw. Thus it was that the assassination of an Austrian archduke in southeastern Europe set in motion a sequence of events which ultimately brought every major country in the civilized world to war. Once Austria-Hungary had made up her mind that she could solve the Balkan or "Eastern" problem only by force, one power after another had to enter the struggle because no one of them, under the existing alliance system, dared to withhold and see its allies destroyed one at a time. The rigidity of the great alliances had forced the leading states into an "all or nothing" situation in which war, once it came, could not remain an isolated, localized affair.

CHAPTER 9

The First World War and Its Effects

THE ESSENTIAL MOVEMENT

In many respects, the First World War is still the great turning point of the 20th century, in spite of all that has happened since. Not only did it drastically alter the relations of Europe with the rest of the world by destroying European wealth and manpower on a vast scale but it also—to a much greater extent than any of the revolutionary epochs of the past—broke the historic continuity of Europe by tearing down institutions and social structures that had lasted for centuries. In 1914, for example, France alone among the great powers of Europe had a republican form of government; all the other leading states were monarchies. Five years later only Great Britain and Italy among the major European states retained monarchical government. The First World War was revolutionary, too, in the sense that it was the first major conflict in which the populations and resources of nations were completely mobilized. As a result, the process by which the central authority of the state had increased in all countries was greatly accelerated, and various forms of what came to be known as "war socialism" were employed to regulate the lives of individuals down to the last detail of their affairs. This was also a war which employed new devices both technological and psychological on such a scale that the traditional tactics and strategy of warfare were revolutionized. No longer were admirals and generals, by manipulating military forces alone, able to direct the war to a conclusion. It was all too vast, too chaotic, for any man or group of men to comprehend

EVENTS AND DEFINITIONS

A. The Strategy of Deadlock, 1914-1918

1. Alignment of the Powers

Central Powers: Austria-Hungary, Germany, Turkey, and Bulgaria (entered in 1915).

Allied Powers: the major participants were Belgium, France, Great Britain, Russia, Serbia (all of whom entered in 1914), Italy (1915), Rumania (1916), and the United States (1917).

2. The Various Fronts, 1914-1918

A. THE WESTERN FRONT. First Battle of the Marne (September 5-12, 1914) frustrated German plans (Schlieffen Plan) for a quick victory. The western front then stabilized into a long system of entrenchments reaching from the North Sea to the Swiss border which neither side was able to break through successfully until the Western Allies did so in the summer and autumn of 1918.

B. THE EASTERN FRONT. In eastern Europe the initial Russian advance was stopped by two German victories—at Tannenberg (August 26-30, 1914) and at the Masurian Lakes (September 6-15, 1914)—which, while they kept the Germans from breaking through in the West, resulted in Russian losses so severe that they affected Russian operations for the rest of the war. Failure of the Western Allies to win through at Gallipoli (Dardanelles) in Turkey (1915) left Russia isolated. Last major Russian offensive occurred in 1916. Russian Revo-

or control. Military planning, no matter how thorough—as the Germans discovered in the opening campaign of the war—could not possibly take into consideration all the imponderables that had to be dealt with. Errors in judgment or omissions which no one could possibly foresee played a major part in determining the final outcome. The conflict was bitterly waged, in part because both sides were evenly balanced until the entry of the United States in 1917 and in part because the various nations, in an effort to get maximum support from their peoples, converted the struggle into a crusade for survival or for the preservation of a cherished ideology, e.g., democracy or German *Kultur*. In so doing, however, they committed themselves to a total war from which there was no withdrawing short of final victory or defeat. In the end, the result was complete exhaustion and a situation in which there were "neither victors nor vanquished but only common ruin."

A. The Strategy of Deadlock, 1914-1918

Unlike the Second World War, the struggle of 1914-1918 became a continuing military deadlock in which, after the first few months of conflict, both sides settled down to a struggle of attrition that devoured lives and wealth on an unbelievable scale. Only on the eastern front and in Asia Minor was large-scale tactical movement possible. Elsewhere, the fighting was soon stabilized in a vast system of entrenchments which stretched for miles along the lines of battle. This state of affairs came about because of the initial failure of the German armies to break through in the West and because the Russians, mobilizing faster than was expected, forced the Central Powers (Germany and Austria-Hungary) to wage a two-front war before they had disposed of France and England.

Once stalemate had been reached, it was only a matter of time before the greater potential resources of the Western Allies would begin to work in their favor. Even worse, from the German point of view, was the fact that as the war progressed the original Austro-German advantage of central position was soon offset because of British seapower. Britain, as in the days of Napoleon, was able to set up a gigantic blockade which cut the Central Powers off from the rest of the world and drove them to the use of unrestricted submarine warfare in an effort to break free. It was a desperate gamble that failed, for it helped to bring the United States into the conflict and thus insured the defeat of Germany and her allies.

Before the conflict was ended, however, the peoples of Europe found themselves driven to increase and extend the powers of the state as these

lution led to an armistice (November 28, 1917) and the humiliating Treaty of Brest-Litovsk with Germany, March 1918.

c. THE WAR AT SEA. By December 1914 all German surface units except isolated raiders were driven from the sea; Germany's colonies had been occupied; and Britain had established a massive North Sea blockade which cut Germany off from overseas supplies. The indecisive battle of Jutland (1916) bottled up the German fleet for the remainder of the war. Unrestricted German submarine warfare (February-March 1917) helped bring the United States into the war.

3. Nature of Wartime Political Organization

Germany: the German war effort was by far the most intensively organized and controlled. In 1916 Walter Rathenau (1867-1922), a leading German industrialist, was made a kind of economic dictator under whose direction a rigid system of war socialism came into being. All production was subordinated to wartime needs, and the minister of war was given the right to determine the work of all males between seventeen and sixty. Britain and France: the allied powers scarcely went so far as the Germans, but they did move in that direction. France set up special boards to plan production. Britain in May 1915 virtually made Lloyd George (1863-1945) the dictator of its industry.

B. The Collapse of Russia and American Intervention

1. The Russian Revolution

a. BACKGROUND. Tsar Alexander II abolished serfdom (1861); introduced the local self-government (*zemstvos*) and reformed the legal system (1864). Growth of revolutionary societies (*Narodniki* and Nihilists) after 1869. ■ Assassination of Alexander II (1881) led to a policy of repression and Russification of minorities under Alexander III (1881-1894). ■ Beginning of industrialization (particularly during period when Count Serge Witte was minister of finance), 1893-1903. ■ Russian Social Democratic (Marxist) Party founded, 1898. ■ Disastrous Russo-Japanese War (1904-1905) resulted in unsuccessful revolution (October 1905) and promises of reform by Tsar Nicholas II (1894-1917). Duma (parliament) established but not particularly effective, 1906-1916. ■ Rus-

had never before been expanded in history. The magnitude of human and material sacrifice staggered the imagination. In Great Britain, for example, it was discovered by March of 1915 that two weeks of spring offensive had used up more ammunition than had been fired away in the three years fighting of the Boer War only fifteen years before (1899-1902). The loss of human life was so great during 1915-17 that both sides virtually gave up any hope of a military breakthrough which might end the war quickly. Such massive expenditures of blood and treasure required a total reorganization of society and a reallocation of human and material resources on an unprecedented scale. Noncombatants were placed under a discipline as rigorous in its way as that of the fighting forces.

B.   The Collapse of Russia and American Intervention

Two great events in the year 1917 foreshadowed the future history of the 20th century. The first of these was the collapse and withdrawal of Russia from the war. The second was the entry of the United States on the side of the Allies. In a sense, both events marked the end of Europe's world hegemony, for though Russia and the United States owed much to European influence, one was geographically on the perimeter of Europe and the other was separated from it by 3000 miles of ocean. Each was destined to emerge within a generation as a new type of superpower, continental in extent and with resources that gave it a strength which far exceeded that of any one of the older powers of pre-1914 Europe.

1.   The Russian Revolution

One of the surprising paradoxes of the First World War was not the collapse of Russia in March 1917 but the fact that she was able to continue the struggle for so long in the face of far greater losses than those suffered by any other power. Russia, in 1914, though great industrial advances had been made, was still an undeveloped agricultural society whose standard of living was far below that of the other major states of Europe. Serfdom, which had disappeared from most parts of western Europe as early as the 16th and 17th centuries, held on in Russia until abolished by Tsar Alexander II (1855-1881) in 1861. Industrialization had been taking place very slowly during the last two decades of the 19th century, but with it came an increase in social and political unrest. By 1900 the Russian state was clearly an anomaly in contrast with the rest of Europe—a major country still ruled by an autocratic despotism

sia participated in First World War, 1914-1917, which led to political and social collapse.

B. THE REVOLUTION AND ITS RESULTS. Food riots in Petrograd (now Leningrad), March 1917. ■ Nicholas II abdicated, March 15, 1917; provisional government formed under Kerensky. Lenin arrived in Russia, April 1917. ■ Bolsheviks gained control of the workers' and soldiers' revolutionary organizations (soviets) and overturned the Kerensky government ("October Revolution"), November 6, 1917 (according to the western calendar). Elections to the constituent assembly (sometimes referred to as "the only free election in Russian history") returned 420 Social Revolutionaries as against 225 Bolsheviks, November 25, 1918. When the assembly met it was at once dissolved by Red troops (January 18, 1918) and thus the only significant opposition to the new regime was effectively disposed of. Treaty of Brest-Litovsk (March 1918) with Germany led to the loss by Russia of Poland, the Ukraine, and all the non-Russian borderlands. Promulgation of the first Soviet constitution, July 1918. The civil war, 1918-1920: a series of campaigns in European Russia and Siberia were finally consummated with the defeat of White forces under Denikin and Wrangel by the end of 1920. War with Poland (April-October 1920) ended with the Treaty of Riga (March 1921) which defined the boundaries between the two countries. The policy of "war communism," 1917-1921: during this period the revolutionaries strove to put into practice the social theories of Marx and Lenin. Land was nationalized (February 1918); food was forcibly requisitioned from the peasants (December 1920). At the coming of the Bolsheviks to power all banks were nationalized. Later, in January 1918, the national debt was repudiated. Workers were forced to join compulsory trade unions and denied the right to strike. By 1921 a combination of circumstances (allied blockade, civil war, and the revolutionary economic policy) made worse by a sharp decline of production in industry and agriculture brought about a virtual collapse of the economy. A mutiny of sailors at the Kronstadt naval base (February-March 1921) finally drove the Communist Party to consider a drastic revision of its policies. The result was the New Economic Policy (NEP) which began to be implemented during the course of 1921. In the main this new policy, which had been sponsored by Lenin himself, provided for some re-

untempered by any of the forms of western democracy or liberalism, a country without a parliament or any semblance of popular government, where final authority was vested in a single man whose power was maintained by a vast secret police. In 1905, a disastrous war with Japan led to a popular uprising which was finally suppressed with difficulty and only after a number of liberal reforms had been promised. These the state carried out with only a half-hearted effort in the years before 1914.

In spite of these difficulties and in the face of the rising strength of revolutionary groups—the most important of which were the two Social Democratic Parties, namely, the Bolsheviks (majority) and the Mensheviks (minority)— Russia like every other major power was swept by nationalist fervor on the eve of war in 1914. Except for a small body of the extreme Marxian left, the Bolsheviks headed by V. I. Lenin (1870-1924), all political groups supported the war, which Russia was thus able to enter with a large measure of popular backing. The early stages of the conflict, however, quickly revealed the weaknesses of Russian society. Russia simply did not have the industrial resources to fight a modern war, and by December 1914 a shortage of munitions forced the Russian army to give up the offensive and stand upon the defense. In a desperate effort to get help through to their beleaguered ally, France and England tried to force their way through the Straits of the Dardanelles held by the Turkish allies of Germany. When this move failed, Russia was cut off from the West, and, as her supplies of food and war materials dwindled, total collapse became inevitable.

Even with the breakdown of authority and the abdication of Tsar Nicholas II (1894-1917) in March 1917, it looked for a time as though Russia would continue the war with a liberalized, constitutional government. But the situation had become far too chaotic. The Russian masses were sick of war, and, as the peasants serving at the front heard rumors of impending land redistribution, Russian armies began to disintegrate. At this juncture, the Germans, to assist Russian collapse, allowed Lenin's Bolshevik antiwar faction, which had been exiled in Switzerland, to cross German territory and return to Russia. Using the slogan "Peace, land, bread!" this group created a situation in which the militant Bolsheviks, who actually made up a very small minority of the Russian population, were able to seize power in October and November of 1917 and take Russia out of the war.

The aims of Lenin and his Bolshevik associates were those of Marxian revolutionaries. They believed themselves to be establishing a dictatorship of the proletariat which would soon be superseded by a classless society. To this end, they proceeded ruthlessly to wipe out every form of

laxation of rigid central controls. The food levy was abolished; the peasants were permitted to dispose of their surpluses in the free market; small individual farms were allowed to exist; and entrepreneurs were permitted to maintain private commercial establishments in the cities.

2.   The United States as a World Power

American victory over Spain and acquisition of overseas positions brought the United States into the arena of world powers, 1898-1900. At the time of its emergence the United States had grown from a nation with a population of slightly less than 4 million persons inhabiting a continental land area of about 900,000 square miles in 1790 to one which in 1900 had a population of more than 75 million inhabiting a continental land area of more than 3 million square miles.

Introduction of mass-production methods into Ford factory at Detroit marked the new upsurge in American productive power, 1909. Inauguration of Woodrow Wilson, 1913. Completion of the Panama Canal under American auspices, 1914.

United States entered First World War (April 1917). Though possessed of vast wealth and enormous reserves of manpower, the utterly unprepared state of the country made it impossible to utilize either men or material quickly. The desperate plight of Britain and France in 1917 (units of the French army had mutinied in May and June) led to serious friction with their new ally over the question of whether U.S. troops should be used as replacements for British and French forces or should fight under a separate American Command. At the insistence of General John J. Pershing (1860-1948) the separate identity of the U.S. army was preserved but at some cost in time. Nevertheless, by November 1918 just under 2 million Americans had been transported to Europe where they had made their numbers felt during the last great offensive of the war at St. Mihiel (September 12-13) and the Argonne (September 26-October 15, 1918). Earlier, in January 1918, President Wilson issued his Fourteen Points as the basis for a just peace. Though Wilson had high hopes that his proposals would be embodied in the Treaty of Versailles, he was doomed to disappointment.

political opposition, whether of the right or left. By 1921, when Lenin and the Bolsheviks had consolidated their power, Russia (now known as the Union of Soviet Socialist Republics or U.S.S.R.) had become a one-party state where democracy as understood in the West was no longer practiced.

2. The United States as a World Power

When the United States entered the First World War in April 1917, an era in American and world history had come to an end. From 1865 onward the population of the United States had steadily expanded and with expansion had come industrialization and an amazing capital growth, particularly after 1890. Between the latter date and 1914, American industry by introducing the technique of mass production had prepared the way for a new phase in the Industrial Revolution which was to raise American productive capacity and the American standard of living to a level far beyond that of 19th-century Europe. This new-found industrial and economic power the United States now devoted to winning the war in Europe.

American public opinion had been brought to this decision slowly. Preoccupied as they were with their own internal expansion throughout the 19th century, most Americans had neither concern nor interest in relations with other states unless their own interests or those of the western hemisphere were directly affected. Though they had been influenced by the upsurge of the new imperialism in the 1890's, most Americans were not yet ready to participate actively in great-power politics. Moreover, their various kinds of European ancestry made them somewhat reluctant to intervene in what seemed to them to be a European war. The direct cause of their intervention was Germany's resort to unrestricted submarine warfare, which convinced President Wilson (1856-1924) and other American leaders that the Germans did not really accept the rule of law in international affairs.

With the collapse and withdrawal of Russia, whose presence on the allied side had been something of an embarrassment, the war suddenly became a great struggle for the forces of freedom and democracy. President Wilson was able to proclaim a crusade whose goals were set forth in Fourteen Points and which laid down a proposed settlement for Europe on the basis of Wilson's own assumptions as to what constituted the principles of justice and fair dealing in international affairs. The United States having taken this position, it seemed necessary for her to play a larger part in the settlement of European postwar affairs than some of her citizens wished her to play.

C. The Peace Settlements and the Postwar World, 1919-1923

1. The Treaty of Versailles, January-June 1919

Major provisions: (1) important territorial cessions by Germany, including Alsace-Lorraine to France and West Prussia to Poland; (2) Germany declared solely responsible for the war; (3) German army limited to 100,000 and navy to six warships; (4) Germans to pay for all civilian damages and the costs of Allied occupation; (5) League of Nations to be established for the prevention of future wars.

2. Treaty of St. Germain with Austria (September 1919)

Ratified the break-up of the Hapsburg empire, restricted the military power of Austria, and forced heavy reparations on her.

3. Treaty of Neuilly with Bulgaria (November 1919)

Returned the Dobrudja to Rumania, transferred western Macedonia to Yugoslavia and western Thrace to Greece.

4. Treaty of the Trianon Palace with Hungary (June 1920)

Deprived Hungary of almost three-quarters of its former territory and two-thirds of its inhabitants.

5. Treaty of Sevres with Turkey (August 1920)

Ratified the break-up of the Ottoman Empire. Turkish nationalists, under Mustapha Kemal, refused to accept it and forced the signing of a new treaty at Lausanne in 1923.

C. The Peace Settlements and the Postwar World, 1919-1923

The peace settlement, which followed the termination of hostilities in November 1918, was arrived at through a series of five treaties, the most famous of which was the Treaty of Versailles, signed on June 28, 1919, between Germany and the allied powers. Like the war itself, the period of readjustment that followed was a time of chaos and complexity when the intentions of statesmen, whether good or bad, were often defeated by conflicting interests and unforeseen events. It was Wilson's hope that peace could be concluded on the basis of the liberal-democratic principles and respect for national rights which he had put forward in his Fourteen Points. To promote this object he worked to establish the League of Nations as an instrument for the enforcement of international agreements.

Unhappily, Wilson found his plans for a just and moderate peace unacceptable to the most important of his European allies for quite understandable reasons. Most of them, and France in particular, had suffered enormous losses at German hands. They and their peoples could not conceive of any peace settlement that did not make Germany responsible for the payment of vast reparations.

Furthermore, in his desire to recognize the independence and integrity of small nations, Wilson ran head on into one of the troublesome facts of European life. Many national and ethnic groups had no true geographical homeland but were spread across the face of Europe in such a way that they could not be easily rearranged within the limits of separate states or territories. As a consequence, many of the agreements reached were completely unworkable and contributed to the ultimate weakening of the peace settlement.

The other serious weakness of the settlement was the "war-guilt clause," a statement written into the Treaty of Versailles by which the Germans were forced to acknowledge that they alone were responsible for causing the war. This ill-considered action, along with the attempt to reduce Germany to the status of a third-rate power, seriously damaged the new German (Weimar) Republic and, in later years, made it possible for German nationalist groups to charge that the Treaty of Versailles was an unjust, dictated peace.

While the settlement was being drawn up, all Europe was passing through a series of revolutions and readjustments. Many war-torn countries reacted strongly against regimes that had led them into the debacle; and since it was assumed in the public mind that some method of demo-

(Essential Movement continued on p. 136)

cratic control might have prevented the holocaust, a strong reaction in favor of democratic government took place. Ancient dynasties were overthrown, and republics were everywhere proclaimed. Significantly enough, it was plain that what many Europeans resented was not so much the fact of war itself as the humiliation of defeat, since most of the countries that overthrew their governments were on the defeated side.

Much of the unrest, however, was engendered by the economic and social dislocation brought on by the conflict itself. Europe was painfully learning that the cost of the war had to be borne by victors and defeated alike—that although a defeated country like Germany might suffer most in an immediate sense, rich "victor" countries like Great Britain had also lost more than they could ever hope to recover. Overseas investments slowly, accumulated for generations had been sold, often at a loss, to pay for supplies and munitions; and this liquidation changed many European countries from creditors to debtors, particularly to the United States, for the first time in history.

The disappearance of these sources of income was doubly disastrous because it came at a time when the obligations of the state were greater than ever before. All through the war political leaders in almost every nation had laid stress on the rewards that must follow victory. Each country, in one way or another, had promised its people some increase in political and social benefits in return for an all-out effort. These had come to be a part of popular expectation in countries like Britain and Germany even before the war, and now that peace had come, governments were expected to make good on their promises—no easy matter in nations where a large part of the national income had to be devoted to replacement of wartime losses and to payment of enormous interest charges on fantastically huge national debts. For most states the great problems of the immediate postwar era were economic survival and recovery, in the face of which increased social benefits had to wait. As a consequence, the years following the peace settlement bred a feeling of distrust and disillusionment among the masses, an attitude which was to lead in some countries to the totalitarian experiments of the twenties and thirties.

CHAPTER 10

Democracy and Dictatorship, 1923-1939

THE ESSENTIAL MOVEMENT

However much democracy may have seemed popular in the period immediately after the First World War, its vogue was brief in some countries. The continuing tribulations of many European states made it clear that the mere introduction of democratic institutions was not in itself sufficient to cure all the ills of society. Men grew impatient of delay and in many countries began to demand drastic measures or to listen to the extravagant promises of power-seeking demagogues.

In the wake of these discontents, two political systems, Fascism and Communism, both of which embodied principles of absolute authority that had seemed to be waning before 1914, contended against liberal democracy for the loyalty of Europeans. In some cases, this revival was the result of political opportunism which enabled a strong party or faction to seize control of the state. In other cases, and to some extent in all, it resulted from a growth of disillusionment, from a feeling that the existing political system had not provided enough benefits for the masses, that democratic parliamentary government could not restore damaged national prestige or that it was the tool of an exploiting class of capitalists.

Whatever the various reasons, it was clear, particularly after 1933, that the era following the First World War was a time of crisis for democracy, a time when men raised questions about its efficiency and its effectiveness in solving human problems. Some political theorists began to question its usefulness as a system of government in all but the richest

EVENTS AND DEFINITIONS

The End of Dynastic Europe After 1918.

A. Successor states carved out of former dynastic empires.

    1. Division of Austria-Hungary.

        a. Republic of Austria proclaimed (September 1919). New state had a population of about 6½ million; before 1914 it had numbered over 50 million.

        b. Hungary at first proclaimed a republic (November 1918) later after a Communist government had been overthrown the country was declared a monarchy under the regency of Admiral Miklos Horthy (1868-1957).

        c. Czechoslovakia with a population of about 15 million was the wealthiest of the Austro-Hungarian successor states. Proclaimed a republic in October 1918.

        d. Kingdom of Yugoslavia proclaimed December 4, 1918. Consisted of former independent states of Serbia and Montenegro as well as Croatia, Slovenia, and Dalmatia which had been part of Austria-Hungary.

    2. Division of Imperial Russia.

        a. Polish Republic proclaimed at Warsaw, November 3, 1918 was composed of territories held before 1914 by Russia which had possessed the largest area Austria-Hungary, and Germany.

        b. Finland: proclamation of independence, July 1917. At first a monarchy under German influence, the country later (July 1919) became a republic.

        c. Lithuania: independence proclaimed, February 1918; recognized by Soviet Union, July 1920.

        d. Latvia: independent republic established, November 1918; finally recognized by Soviet Union, August 1920.

        e. Estonia: independence proclaimed, November 1917; recognized by Soviet Union, February 1920.

B. The Irish Free State (afterward Republic of Ireland) recognized as virtually independent by Great Britain in the Treaty of London, December 1920.

societies; poorer states, they contended, needed order and discipline and could ill afford the inevitable confusions and compromises required to make democracy work. Their arguments were reinforced by a growing feeling that man was not, after all, quite so rational a creature as he had seemed to be to the enlightened philosophers and liberal reformers of the 18th and 19th centuries. Far too many human actions and judgments seemed to derive not from a reasonable, objective assessment of the world but rather from irrational, subjective emotions and desires. If man was thus irrational—and an ever larger group of thinkers agreed that he was—then liberal-democratic government was an impossibility, an unreality which had to be replaced by a controlled and directed system whose rulers had the superior wisdom to make decisions. In this respect, however, there were great differences between the ideologies, though not the practices, of various totalitarian states. The rulers of Fascist countries like Italy and Germany asserted that men were irrational beings whose ultimate purposes on earth could be achieved only if they identified themselves with a hypernational state whose unquestioning servants they must become. Under Communist totalitarianism, while it was still assumed that man was rational and that society could function democratically, there was only one set of conclusions to which human reason must automatically lead and only one party capable of wielding power. In the end, then, Communism, for all of its professions to the contrary, differed little from Fascist totalitarianism.

One other point should also be understood about modern totalitarianism. It is not just a restoration of the old forms of monarchical absolutism under another name. Even divine-right monarchs were limited to some degree by the countervailing power of a strong church or deeply ingrained social traditions. To many contemporary observers, the frightening things about the "new absolutism" of the 20th-century totalitarian state are (1) its remarkable and ruthless efficiency in marked contrast with the often bumbling inefficiency of old-fashioned tyrannies and (2) the fact that its rulers acknowledge no formal limitations to their power. Every action or decision is justified according to the political myth (usually ascribed to the 18th-century French-Swiss writer, Jean Jacques Rousseau) that the rulers are carrying out the "general will" of the people, though the people are seldom given the opportunity to do more than give perfunctory approval to actions taken in their name.

A. The United States and Western Europe

1. The United States

United States Senate rejected the Treaty of Versailles and with it the League of Nations, March 1920. Washington Naval Conference limited naval armaments among the major powers, 1922. United States adhered to the Kellogg-Briand Pact (Pact of Paris) outlawing war as an instrument of international policy, 1928. Stock-market crash and depression, 1929. Inauguration of F. D. Roosevelt, 1933; beginning of the New Deal.

Important New Deal legislation: (1) Agricultural Adjustment Act (May 1933) provided for compensated crop curtailment—later (1936) declared unconstitutional by the Supreme Court; (2) National Industrial Recovery Act (NRA) (June 1933) created a code of fair competition and guaranteed labor's right to organize and bargain collectively—declared unconstitutional in 1935; (3) several Emergency Relief Acts, passed between 1933 and 1935, authorized the government to spend over $5 billion on public works to increase employment; (4) Social Security Act (1935) provided for support of needy aged and unemployment compensation; (5) Wages and Hours Law (1938) prescribed minimum wages and maximum hours for those industries in interstate commerce—also prohibited child labor.

Beginning of rearmament in the face of Axis danger; Roosevelt asked congress for defense appropriations, January, 1939. United States' proclamation of neutrality in European war, September 5, 1939. Congress passed the Lend-Lease Act for aid to Britain, March 1941. Roosevelt and Churchill formulated the Atlantic Charter, a joint declaration of peace aims, August 1941. Roosevelt asked Japan to clarify her aims in Indo-China, December 2, 1941. Pearl Harbor attacked, December 7, 1941.

A. The United States and Western Europe

1. The United States

The major goals of the western European democracies in the period between world wars, particularly of Britain and France, were economic rehabilitation and the preservation of international security. For the United States these were not serious problems. The wartime expansion of her economic system, while checked briefly by the business depression of 1921, continued into the 1920's, which were to be remembered afterwards as one of the most prosperous periods in American history. Separated by the breadth of the Atlantic from Europe, Americans tended to forget about the problem of military security. As the years passed, American public opinion underwent a revulsion toward participation in the First World War. The removal of the German menace made wartime fears seem remote and unreal; and as they receded many Americans began to question the necessity for their country having participated in the struggle. A strong isolationist sentiment was reinforced by suspicions that American intervention had been the result of clever manipulation by great industrialists and Wall Street financiers anxious to gain wartime profits. In this overly skeptical frame of mind Americans watched the rise of European totalitarianism as something remote and inconsequential to themselves.

This complacency about international and domestic issues was suddenly shocked in 1929 with the coming of the Great Depression. Americans, who had come to believe themselves secure against the misfortunes that plagued other peoples, now found that they too were a part of the worldwide economic network and that their own economic system was also subject to fluctuations in production and consumption. Furthermore, because the level of American economic expectation was high, demands for some kind of state action to deal with unemployment and overproduction began to be heard. The answer to these demands came with the election to the presidency of Franklin D. Roosevelt in 1932 and the inauguration during the following year of his New Deal legislative program. While neither socialist nor collectivist in intent, it increased beyond precedent the range of state responsibility in American life. Though historians still argue as to the success of the New Deal in eliminating the American economic ills of the 1930's, there is no doubt that millions of Americans approved it. In a sense, all arguments as to its efficiency were finally suspended with the coming of the Second World

2　Great Britain

A. BRITISH LOSSES IN WORLD WAR I. 947,000 killed, about 2 million wounded; total British debt was increased about tenfold over that of 1914; the war alone had cost Britain about $40 billion; liquidation of large amounts of British overseas investments.

B. ECONOMIC AND SOCIAL PROBLEMS. Serious social unrest over unemployment, particularly in the coal industry, led to demands for nationalization by the miners and to severe strikes, the most serious of which—the Great General Strike of 1926—almost paralyzed the government. ■ Revolt in Ireland ("War of the Black and Tans"), 1919-1921, culminated in the Treaty of London (1921) which recognized southern Irish independence (Irish Free State); the six northern counties of Ireland (Ulster) remained within the United Kingdom. ■ Unemployment remained serious all through the 1920's and fell below the million mark only in one year—1927. Adverse trade balance (costs of imports over proceeds of exports) grew larger from year to year.

C. POLITICAL DEVELOPMENTS. Liberal Party ceased to be the second major party and was supplanted by the Labor (Socialist) Party which came to power under Ramsay Mac-Donald in 1924 and again in 1929-1931. National (coalition) Government formed to meet the international economic crisis, 1931. Britain began to rearm against growing German military power, 1936-1937. ■ Munich Agreement, 1938, revealed British weakness when Hitler was permitted to dismember Czechoslovakia. ■ Britain and France guaranteed Polish security against Germany, March 1939; Germany attacked Poland, September 1; Britain declared war on Germany, September 3, 1939.

3.　France

A. FRENCH LOSSES IN WORLD WAR I. 1,385,000 killed, over 3 million wounded; 300,000 houses and 20,000 factories and workshops destroyed; national debt increased some twelve to fourteen times that of 1914. These enormous losses

War, for the enormous wartime expansion of American industry, accompanied by a sudden upsurge of population in the forties and fifties, opened the way to an even higher level of well-being than that of the 1920's.

2. Great Britain

For Britain and France the story of the years between the wars was very different. Britain, to a greater extent than any other victorious power, had suffered from the economic effects of the war, though none of the fighting had occurred on her soil. Unlike France, where agricultural production was still sufficient to meet the needs of the French population, Britain, because she had deliberately sacrificed her agriculture in favor of industrial growth during the 19th century, had to worry about foreign-trade deficits which, in the long run, could seriously lower her standard of living. For more than a century Britain had imported more than she exported. Down to the end of the First World War this deficit had presented no serious problem because the British had been able to make it up in a variety of ways but mainly through income on overseas investments. Owing to the sale of these during the war, the British plight began to grow serious; and Britain, with an aging industrial plant, was no longer able to maintain the great economic lead she formerly held over other nations. Between the wars, then (and to an even greater extent after the Second World War), the British economic system was dependent upon the economic health of the countries with which Britain traded. For that reason the British did not look with such disfavor as did the French on the economic recovery of Germany, a circumstance which led to a fairly serious Anglo-French rift during the 1920's. Even worse for the British were the domestic effects of their international economic problems. Year after year the tide of unemployment rose until it amounted to 10% of the employable population. In the 1930's there was some recovery, but the gains were quickly dissipated as the need to rearm against Germany became acute.

3. France

In France, on the other hand, the major problems were not only economic but also political. The constitutional structure of the Third Republic (which had come into existence following the overthrow of Napoleon III during the Franco-Prussian War of 1870-1871) was such

strongly influenced French thinking on the matter of German war reparations and security between 1919 and 1939.

B. ECONOMIC AND SOCIAL PROBLEMS. The main problem was that of reconstruction, which France met by spending a large part of her income on rebuilding during the 1920's; by 1927 France was well on the road to recovery. War debts: France owed about $2¼ billion to her former allies; this was not balanced, as France had hoped, by German reparations.

C. POLITICAL DEVELOPMENTS. In her search for security against German revival, France adhered to the Locarno Treaties (1925) and the Kellogg-Briand Pact (1928). ■ Attacks on the government from the Right (Fascists and royalists) led to the formation of the Popular Front (Radical Socialists and Socialists supported by the Communists) under Leon Blum, 1936. Blum's social reform program caused discontent and forced him out of office, 1938. ■ Polish crisis of 1939 led to French declaration of war on Germany, September 3, 1939.

B. The Totalitarian States

1. Italy

A. ITALIAN LOSSES IN WORLD WAR I. 600,000 killed, and only 9,000 sq. mi. of territory gained. Though Italy's wartime costs were not as great in terms of money spent as those of some other powers, the major Italian problem even before 1914 had been a permanent annual deficit; and for that reason Italy could ill afford her wartime losses.

B. ECONOMIC AND SOCIAL PROBLEMS. Large population and low standard of living, particularly in southern Italy,

that few governments could exist for long without the support of more than one political party. Furthermore, since France, in contrast with Britain, possessed not a two-party but a multiparty system, the state of French politics was—inescapably—turbulent and uncertain. Worst of all was the fact that for much of the Third Republic's existence groups on the extreme left and right regarded it as nothing more than a temporary arrangement which would last only until they gained power and changed it into some other form of government. In this sense, every French election was a fight for the life of the republic, with the moderate parties of the center usually combining to give it their support.

In spite of this political uncertainty and the difficulty of collecting all the German war reparations allowed her by the Treaty of Versailles, France made great strides toward economic recovery in the era following the First World War. Even so, Frenchmen were still obsessed with fear of German resurgence. To meet this danger, French diplomacy built up a system of alliances with neighboring states in the 1920's; and in the 1930's France placed her reliance in a strong mass army which was intended to be used offensively in conjunction with the complex defensive network known as the Maginot Line which had been constructed at great cost along the Franco-German border. When war finally came in 1939, France, to her misfortune, was not prepared to deal with the new tactics of mobility which had been developed by the leaders of the revived German army.

B. The Totalitarian States and the Coming of the Second World War

While the democracies of the western world struggled with internal problems that sometimes seemed to threaten the existence of their democratic institutions, other countries tried to solve their problems by turning to that new 20th-century invention, the one-party totalitarian state.

1. Italy

The first major European state to move in this direction was Italy. There the disappointment at Italy's failure to win greater territorial concessions at the Paris Peace Conference and the postwar dislocation of the Italian economy gave rise to conditions that seemed very nearly revolutionary. To combat the possible danger of revolution on the left, quickly formed bands of *Fascisti*, black-shirted adherents of the former Socialist leader Benito Mussolini (1883-1945), undertook to break the power of the various revolutionary parties and to restore order. By vio-

coupled with inadequate industrial development. Industrial unrest and unemployment led to widespread strikes in Italian industry (rise of a strong Syndicalist movement), 1919. Growing economic dislocation as a result of the expenditure of limited Italian resources in World War I.

    c. POLITICAL DEVELOPMENTS. Fascists seized power, 1922. Mussolini guaranteed Fascist control of parliament by changing electoral laws, 1923. Liberals, Socialists, and Communists suppressed, 1924-1925. Universal suffrage abolished, 1928. Lateran Treaties settled long-standing differences that had lasted since 1870 with the papacy; National Council of Corporations established 1929. Economic depression caused hardship throughout Italy, 1930-1935. ■ Italians invaded Ethiopia, October 1935; League of Nations unable to apply sanctions. Italy sent troops to aid Franco in the Spanish Civil War, 1936. ■ Italy joined Axis Pact with Germany and Japan and withdrew from the League of Nations, 1937. Founding of the Chambers of Fasces and Corporations, 1938. ■ Italy invaded and conquered Albania, 1939. ■ Declaration of war against France and Britain, June 1940.

2.   Germany

    A. GERMAN LOSSES IN WORLD WAR I. In addition to heavy losses in manpower and wealth expended during the war, Germany also lost (as a result of the Treaty of Versailles) 13% of her territory, nearly 10% of her population, and all of her former colonies. Furthermore, the Germans were expected to pay reparations originally set at $33 billion; later these were scaled down, and in the end Germany paid only about $6½ billion.

    B. ECONOMIC AND SOCIAL PROBLEMS. ■ (1) German popular resentment at the Treaty of Versailles: German nationalists, who disliked the fact of defeat and the lowering of national status, soon began to claim that the German army had not been defeated but was "stabbed in the back" by disloyal persons at home; there was also serious resentment over the "war-guilt" clauses and the demand that Germany pay for all civilian losses to the allied powers. ■ (2) Between 1921 and 1923 Germany was confronted with serious inflation

lence and terror, Fascism spread across Italy until, in October 1922, the Fascist leadership was able to coerce the King into calling Mussolini to power as head of a coalition cabinet. Once in control, the latter moved quickly to overturn existing democratic-parliamentary procedures and to establish the one-party state. By 1928 the transformation was complete, and Italy was ruled by a Fascist bureaucracy. Ten years later, in 1938, after a series of changes, the Fascist conception of the "corporate state" emerged in its final form. Under this system twenty-two "corporations" were created, covering every aspect of Italian economic life. Each corporation consisted of representatives of labor, management, and the state. In theory, Fascism was thus bringing into existence a society where the corporate interests of all groups and classes would be served. Actually, this society worked to benefit the state only.

Once securely in control of the Italian domestic situation, Mussolini turned his attention to foreign affairs. His ambition was to make Italy into a major military power strong enough to win a great overseas empire. In 1935 Italian Forces invaded Ethiopia and precipitated the first major European international crisis on the road to World War II. When the League of Nations failed to deal decisively with this situation, it became plain that the League was moribund. The way was now prepared for further acts of aggression on the part of the Fascist powers, Italy, Germany, and Japan.

2. Germany

In Germany the totalitarian or Nazi (a shortening of the German word "National" which was part of the name of the National Socialist German Workers Party) state emerged more slowly than it did in Italy. Following the settlement at Versailles, the German Republic had been forced to cope with a number of serious problems that would have vexed the most stable of governments. Germany had been stripped of all overseas possessions. A large part of the national income was demanded to pay reparations. The country was torn by private warfare between various extremist groups of the left and right. Under such conditions, the republic was unable to broaden the basis of its support and maintained itself only through a coalition of moderate parties. On top of these difficulties the Great Depression of 1929 came as a crowning blow. In the disordered conditions that followed, many Germans, frightened at the rising Communist menace, came to look with favor upon the Nazi Party and its leader, Adolf Hitler (1889-1945)—or if not with entire favor, then at least as an alternative to Bolshevik revolution.

Hitler, an Austrian-German demagogue whose curious sense of

which saw the mark fall until a trillion marks were equal to one dollar. With time it also became clear that Germany simply could not pay the reparations demanded, despite the revisions downward of the Dawes Plan (1924) and the Young Plan (1929). As a result, the depression of 1929 caused international chaos because Germany had been borrowing abroad to pay the reparations bill.

c. POLITICAL DEVELOPMENTS. German Empire overthrown, November 1918. Attempted Socialist (Spartacist) revolution suppressed, January 1919. Weimar Constitution created German Republic, July 1919. German nationalists led by General Erich Ludendorff (1865-1937) and Adolf Hitler tried to overthrow the republic ("Beer Hall Putsch"), 1923. Growth of the Nazi Party, 1924-1929. ■ Failure of the Austrian Credit-Anstalt Bank precipitated financial crisis in Germany and central Europe, 1931. ■ President Hindenburg appointed Adolf Hitler chancellor of Germany, January 1933. German Reichstag passed Enabling Act establishing Nazi dictatorship, March 1933. Germany withdrew from the League of Nations, October 1933. "Blood Purge" eliminated dissidents within Nazi Party, 1934. ■ Hitler denounced the Versailles Treaty and remilitarized the Rhineland, 1936. ■ German annexation (*Anschluss*) of Austria, March 1938. ■ Munich Crisis, 1938. Germany occupied all of Czechoslovakia; annexed Memel, March 1939. ■ German-Russian Neutrality Pact concluded, August 21, 1939. ■ Germany invaded Poland, September 1; declaration of war by England and France, September 3, 1939.

3. The Soviet Union (U.S.S.R.)

a. ECONOMIC AND SOCIAL PROBLEMS. Russia (U.S.S.R.) not only had to bear an estimated loss of 1,700,000 killed and nearly 5,000,000 wounded in the First World War, but also suffered enormous losses in manpower and property during the civil wars between 1917 and 1921. It was, in part, for that reason that Lenin instituted the New Economic Policy (1921). The major problem of the Soviet Union, therefore, was to reconstruct and industrialize a poverty-ridden, largely rural society.

b. POLITICAL DEVELOPMENTS. Death of Lenin brought Joseph Stalin to power as secretary of the Communist Party,

his own destiny and strange prophesyings of German greatness had made him a power among the discontented, promised the German people security, stability, and the restoration of national pride. His opportunity came in 1933, when the aged president of the republic, the former imperial Field Marshal Paul von Hindenburg (1847-1934), called Hitler to office as chancellor (prime minister) after an election in which the Nazi leader received a plurality but not a majority of the votes. Within three years Hitler had abolished parliamentary government, outlawed any but the Nazi Party, proclaimed himself "Führer" (Leader) of the German people, and begun to revive German military power. To win the fullest support for his plans he appealed, effectively, to German national and racial sentiments. The Germans were a "master race" destined to rule the earth. All those—and particularly the Jews—whom he defined as "racially impure" were subjected to mass persecution. Thus secured against domestic discontent, Hitler, with an audacity that was successful largely because the western democracies were unprepared to deal with it, began to expand the boundaries of Germany. In the spring of 1938 he took over Austria without resistance, and without significant opposition from the democratic powers; in the fall he dictated a dismemberment of Czechoslovakia which he forced the western powers to recognize in a conference at Munich; in March, 1939, he occupied all of Czechoslovakia despite the Munich agreement. The British-French foreign policy that permitted these unresisted moves was justified or execrated, according to viewpoint, as "appeasement."

3.   The Soviet Union

The Soviet Union, because of its ideology, is in many ways the most baffling of totalitarian states. Ideologically, it is the direct opposite of the Fascist states. Its aims and purposes are not those of the national state; neither does it avow any kind of racism. It professes to stand as the leader of a worldwide movement in behalf of the international working class. In this sense, its appeal is universal rather than local or national and has given to Communism an international influence never enjoyed by Fascism.

There is, however, another side to the problem which has persistently troubled the Soviet Union since its inception. While its system of ideas is intended to have universal appeal, there is no escaping the fact that

1924. Stalin triumphed over Trotsky and the leftist opposition in the struggle for party control, 1926. ■ First Five-Year Plan ("new Socialist offensive") inaugurated in an effort to industrialize and increase the economic power of the Soviet Union; first attempt made to collectivize agriculture, 1928. Trotsky banished, 1929. Repressive measures used to force peasant landholders into collective farms led to serious famine, 1932-1933. Communist Party purged of one-third of its members, 1933. ■ U.S.S.R. supported Spanish Republic against Franco, 1936-1939. ■ Mass purges of former Bolshevik leaders for treason, 1936-1938. ■ New constitution established "democratic" forms and professed to guarantee complete civil rights, December 1936. ■ Neutrality Pact with Germany, August 1939. U.S.S.R. and Germany divided Poland between them, September 1939. U.S.S.R. invaded and conquered territory from Finland, November 1939-March 1940. ■ German armies invaded Russia, June 1941 (for events of war see p. 154). Soviet wartime losses were severe and probably exceeded those of any other belligerent by a wide margin except for Germany. According to statistics given in the official textbook history of the U.S.S.R. some of the most significant of these losses were as follows: 1710 towns and more than 70,000 villages fully or partially destroyed, 31, 850 industrial enterprises ruined, 65,000 kilometers of railway line destroyed, 98,000 collective farms devastated with a loss of 7 million horses and 17 million head of cattle. The loss of life can only be estimated, but it has been put as high as 10-12 million. For all of this and despite the restrictive nature of the regime, Soviet recovery in the 15-year period after 1945 was impressive. Two new five-year plans were introduced in 1946 and 1951. Agriculture continued to prove a weakness, though Soviet achievement in nuclear weaponry and in space science with the launching of the first sputnik in 1957 won grudging respect from the non-Communist world. Death of Joseph Stalin (1879-1953) led to a reorganization of the state under Nikita Krushchev who remained in power until October 1964.

Russia has been the center and focus of international Communism and that, as a result, Russian national feelings sometimes become mixed with Marxist doctrine. Soviet leaders have tried to explain this conflict by saying that whatever is done in the interest of the Soviet Union also serves the cause of world revolution. The U.S.S.R., they contend, must be kept strong so that it can resist the threatened assaults of capitalist countries with whom, according to Marxist theory, there must be unending enmity. This belief has made Soviet foreign policy extremely twisted and tortuous. On the one hand, there were men like Leon Trotsky (1877-1940) in the period after the revolution who insisted that everything must be sacrificed in order to foment revolution on a world-wide scale. Conversely, Joseph Stalin (1879-1953), who became head of the Communist Party and, in effect, head of the Soviet state at the death of Lenin in 1924, wished to build up the power of the U.S.S.R. first before trying to achieve the goal of world revolution. In the end, even though Stalin finally triumphed over Trotsky and undertook to "build socialism in one country" first, the ideological hope of world revolution continues to influence and shape Soviet foreign policy.

What has happened to the leaders of the Soviet Union since 1921 is that they have had continually to modify their theories in the face of shifting circumstances. Lenin was the first to do so when he discovered that his attempts to promote pure Communism were creating only chaos and disruption. To prevent collapse he instituted the New Economic Policy (NEP) which restored a certain amount of economic freedom. Stalin, after his accession to power, was realistic enough to see that there could be few economic rewards for the working classes unless something was done to increase agricultural and industrial production beyond anything Russia had ever known. The great tasks of the Soviet Union, as Stalin saw it, were to collectivize agriculture, in order to step up food production, and to establish heavy industry. Neither was easy in view of the unwillingness of the Communist regime to borrow capital from abroad in order to set the process in motion. By ruthlessly keeping the standard of living down and thus forcing the Soviet people to create the capital needed for expansion by their own efforts, Stalin was able to push through a series of five-year plans which slowly, painfully, and often inadequately, met the industrial goals set by the state. The price paid was dreadfully high in terms of human life and suffering—far higher than any democratic state could have demanded—but it served, in the end, to give the Soviet state some part of the industrial strength it needed to weather the German invasions of World War II.

(Essential Movement continued on p. 152)

Though one has to acknowledge the magnitude and effectiveness of this Russian achievement, there is no denying that, for all the enormous effort involved, the Soviet Union had and still has a long way to go before it can offer its people either the living standards or the freedoms of the West. Defenders of the Communist system continue to argue that such a time is not far off and that ultimately things will be far better in Soviet society than they are elsewhere. They may become so, but until they do, judgment will have to be suspended. Thoughtful western critics of the Soviet system are convinced that the vast apparatus of "state capitalism" is far too repressive and cumbersome ever to achieve the promised levels of abundance. Moreover, these critics also believe that it can never provide the freedoms of democratic societies no matter how much it may wish or claim to do so. As a consequence, in western eyes, the Soviet Union remains—now and for the foreseeable future—a land of harsh repression and unfulfilled promises.

CHAPTER II

The Second
World War and Its Effects

THE ESSENTIAL MOVEMENT

By the spring of 1939 it was plain that Europe had reached a position very like that of July 1914. The expansionist policies and the broken promises of Hitler introduced a mood of fatalism into international politics, and nations, once again, made ready for a conflict that seemed all but inevitable. The major uncertainty of the moment concerned the balance of power. Would the alignment of the powers be similar to that of 1914? Everything depended on Russia's decision, and the Soviet Union, which had been left out of the diplomatic negotiations of the 1930's by Germany and the western powers alike, finally declared its neutrality by signing a nonaggression pact with Hitler's Germany on August 23, 1939. Stalin assumed that this action would preserve the safety of the U.S.S.R. while the "capitalist powers" tore themselves to pieces. Afterward it was revealed that he had also secretly agreed to a partition of Poland and other parts of eastern Europe which was intended to give him a buffer against Nazi treachery. For this he paid a high price in world good will by making the Soviet Union, which had always professed to be the great enemy of Fascism and had even opposed it by active military intervention in the Spanish Civil War (1936-1939), seem hypocritical and opportunistic in its conduct of foreign policy. Worse too was the fact that this treaty gave Hitler the security he needed for the invasion of Poland and for war against Britain and France. On September 3, 1939, Europe entered again into total war.

A. The Struggle for Europe and Asia

1. Europe

Invasion and conquest of Poland by Germany, September 1939. German occupation of Denmark and Norway, April 1940. German conquest of the Netherlands, Luxemburg, and France, May 10-June 22, 1940.

Entrance of Italy as Germany's ally, June 10.

Battle of Britain: Royal Air Force kept German air power from gaining supremacy over the English Channel, August-September 1940.

German invasion of Russia, June 1941.

Japanese attacked Pearl Harbor; United States declared war on Japan; Germany and Italy declared war on the United States, December 1941.

High point of German invasion of Russia reached; Germans thrown back from Stalingrad, November 1942-January 1943.

United States forces landed in North Africa to support British offensive against Rommel, November 1942.

Allied forces invaded Italy; downfall of Mussolini, July 1943.

Western allies invaded Normandy, June 1944.

Russians (January 1945) and western allies (March 1945) invaded Germany.

Capture and execution of Mussolini, April 28; suicide of Hitler, April 30.

Unconditional surrender of the German armies, May 8, 1945.

2. Asia and the Pacific

Though the attack on Pearl Harbor in December 1941 opened hostilities between the United States and Japan, the latter had been at war *de facto* with the Republic of China since 1931 and had opened a major offensive in that country during 1937. By 1939 the Japanese had captured the Chinese capital at Hankow and forced the Chinese government to establish a new one at Chunking.

After attacking Pearl Harbor, the Japanese quickly conquered Guam, Wake, and Hongkong (December 1941); the

A. The Struggle for Europe and Asia

Though the Second World War, like the war of 1914-1918, began in Europe, it was far more world-encompassing than the earlier struggle had been. Before the conflict of 1939-1945 was finished its battles were fought across the globe from regions north of the Arctic Circle to the Tropic of Capricorn; and it was also merged into a great Asiatic-Pacific struggle between Japan and the United States. It was like the First World War in one important respect, however. Just as men were baffled by the vastness and complexity of the earlier conflict, so were they equally baffled and unable to control the movement of events in the war of 1939-1945. The common experience seemed to indicate that warfare had far outstripped man's ability to make use of it for his own ends.

Strategically, there were also great similarities between the wars. In 1939, as in 1914, Germany entered the struggle better prepared than her opponents, militarily and psychologically. As in 1914, too, the Germans gambled on a quick victory that was very nearly won. Only Britain's traditional seapower, reinforced by effective air support, kept Germany from achieving a knockout blow early in the conflict after Britain's continental allies had fallen. And again, finally, the issue was ultimately decided by the belated intervention of the United States, this time on a far greater and more decisive scale than in 1917. The war did not, however, become the stalemate of 1914-1918. The mobility of armies was much greater, and wide-ranging air armadas were able to strike farther and with more devastating effect. In this way civilian populations, as never before, were directly involved in the conflict.

Chronologically, the war was divided into two phases. Until November 1942 everything favored the Axis powers, despite the overextension of operations that saw a German invasion of Russia in June 1941 and a Japanese attack on the United States naval base at Pearl Harbor in the following December. At the peak of Axis success, Germany controlled continental Europe from the Pyrenees to the gates of Moscow, while her Asiatic ally, Japan, was unchallenged in the Far East from Burma to the Hawaiian Islands. By the spring of 1943, when the latent productive power of the United States began to make itself felt, the tide of events slowly changed in both Europe and the Pacific. A Russian land offensive in conjunction with massive western air assaults against Germany was followed by allied landings on the coast of Normandy in June 1944. Eleven months later the western allies met Russian troops amid the ruins of Berlin, where Hitler had taken his life a few days before.

In the Pacific, however, the war continued for another four months,

Philippines (January-May 1942), Dutch East Indies (January-March 1942), Singapore (February 1942), and advanced to the Solomons and New Guinea, where they threatened Australia. Battles of the Coral Sea (May 7) and of Midway (June 4-7) stopped Japanese invasion attempts on Australia and Hawaii.

Second Battle of the Philippine Sea (October 21-22, 1944) destroyed Japanese fleet as a fighting unit.

Great air offensive against Japan (May-August 1945): Atom bomb dropped on Hiroshima, August 6, 1945.

Soviet Union declared war on Japan, August 8, 1945.

Japan formally surrendered, September 2, 1945.

B. The Uneasy Peace

Wartime conferences of allied leaders at Casablanca, Cairo, and Teheran in 1943 and at Yalta (February 1945) and Potsdam (July-August 1945) determined preliminary postwar policies.

Peace treaties with Italy, Finland, Hungary, Rumania, and Bulgaria concluded at Paris, July 1946. In addition to heavy indemnities (none of which were paid to the United States or Great Britain, and the lion's share of which went to the Soviet Union), the defeated powers lost the following territories:

Italy gave up all her colonial empire and a small part of her territory in Europe; Rumania ceded territory to the Soviet Union and Bulgaria; Hungary ceded Transylvania to Rumania; Finland handed over the province of Karelia to the U.S.S.R. Earlier (1939-1940) the Soviet Union had annexed eastern Poland and the Baltic states (Estonia, Latvia, Lithuania). Germany and Austria were excluded from these pacts, because the U.S.S.R. and the western powers could not agree on the terms to be imposed on those two countries.

1. The Coming of the Cold War

A. COMMUNIST MOVES. U.S.S.R. established "people's democracies," i.e., one-party Communist governments, in Poland, Hungary, Albania, Rumania, Bulgaria, Eastern Germany, and Czechoslovakia (1944-1948), but failed in Greece. Yugoslavia became a Communist state but went its own way after 1948.

though even as Germany fell Japan was already a defeated nation. Twin offensives reaching out across the Pacific—one upward from the Solomons and New Guinea to the Philippines, the other from Pearl Harbor through the islands of the Central Pacific to Okinawa—had brought Japan to the edge of disaster. But it was still questionable in the spring of 1945 whether the fanatical Japanese leaders would surrender without facing a full assault on their homeland. In view of this contingency, President Harry S. Truman made the fateful decision which ushered in a new era and gave the beaten Japanese an excuse for surrender. On August 6, 1945, the first atomic bomb was dropped from an American plane on the city of Hiroshima. Less than a month later, on September 2, the Second World War was at an end.

B. The Uneasy Peace

Even before the end of hostilities the victorious powers had convened hopefully at San Francisco (April-June 1945) to draw up plans for an effective international machinery which would guarantee the peace of the world. The result of this conference was the United Nations Organization, whose charter came into effect on October 24,1945. Unlike the old League of Nations, this new organization was strengthened by the inclusion of the United States and Russia, the two major powers who had won the war. Within a short time, however, it became apparent that this new body also had serious weaknesses, the most important of which were (1) the rights of veto granted to the five great powers who held seats on the Security Council and (2) the fact that association and co-operation within the U.N. were, in the last analysis, voluntary. Nonetheless, for all of its shortcomings, the United Nations Organization was to function effectively during certain periods of crisis and was also to provide a means of bridging international differences that might otherwise have led to disaster.

1. The Coming of the Cold War

The great tragedy of the postwar world was the rift between East and West, between the Soviet Union and its former allies. Even as the war was being fought, there were evidences of profound distrust and disagreement among the anti-Axis powers. On one side the Soviet Union distrusted and feared the power of the West, particularly after the atom

B. WESTERN COUNTER OFFENSIVE AGAINST RUSSIAN EX-
PANSION. ■ (1) American aid to Greece (Truman Doctrine)
prevented Communist seizure of that country, 1947-1948.
■ (2) Marshall Plan advanced more than $11 billion for
European recovery after 1947. ■ (3) Britain, France, Belgium, the Netherlands, and Luxemburg set up a permanent
military organization (Brussels Treaty), 1948. ■ (4) Russians
unsuccessfully blockaded Berlin, 1948-1949. ■ (5) formation of the North Atlantic Treaty Organization (NATO)
which included Brussels Treaty signers (see above) as well
as the United States and Canada, 1949. ■ (6) United Nations' forces prevented Communist seizure of South Korea,
1950-1953. ■ (7) Formation of SEATO (South East Asia
Treaty Organization) for the defense against aggression,
1955.

2. The Awakening of Africa and Asia

Great Britain granted full independence to India and
Pakistan, 1947, and to Burma and Ceylon, 1948. Communists
won control of China, 1949. Indonesians gained independence
from the Netherlands, 1949.

Revolt of the Arab world: Revolution in Egypt overturned the monarchy, 1952, and led to the expulsion of British troops and nationalization of the Suez Canal, 1956;
France relaxed control over Tunisia and Morocco, faced civil
war in Algeria.

Independence of Ghana within British Commonwealth
proclaimed, 1957. Union of Guinea (former French colony)
with Ghana, 1958.

bomb had fallen. To protect herself against what she still believed was the inevitable hostility of the capitalist world, the U.S.S.R. either fomented revolution or seized control in countries lying along her borders in both Europe and Asia. In this way she girdled herself with satellite states nominally independent but actually under the control of Moscow. In response to these moves, the United States, as the leading western power, devised counter moves to check or prevent Communist aggression: first, the Truman Doctrine in 1947 to prevent a seizure of Greece, and then later the Marshall Plan and, finally, the North Atlantic Treaty Organization. With these innovations the era of "cold war" was inaugurated, a peculiar state of neither peace nor war in which two great agglomerations of power centering round the United States and the Soviet Union faced each other across an almost impenetrable "iron curtain" that divided them in terms of interest and ideology.

2.   The Awakening of Africa and Asia

This world polarizing of nations around the two superpowers had a number of important collateral developments. Probably the most important of these was the great Afro-Asian revolution which within slightly more than a decade saw the emergence of non-European peoples as independent and in some degree decisive forces in world politics. The outstanding example of this revolutionary change was the new Communist state of China, which within a few brief years had become the most formidable power in the Far East. Elsewhere the stirrings of a new-found nationalism overturned colonial governments that had lasted, in some cases, for centuries. This eventuality was neither unexpected nor totally new. It had begun with the First World War and continued with the gradual weakening of the European colonial powers after 1919, but the process of emancipation was accelerated by the attitudes of the two major countries whose strength was at the cores of the two great international alliances. Both the United States and the Soviet Union were opposed to colonialism and made it a part of policy to weaken colonial governments wherever they could. In playing this game the Soviet Union had a very definite advantage, since many of the most important allies of the United States were colonial powers dependent upon colonial resources and investments for their very survival. This dilemma forced the United States to supply the capital requirements of many of her allies as no nation had done before in the world's history.

3.   Postwar Europe: Decline or Survival?

United Nations Relief and Rehabilitation Administration (UNRRA), 1944-1948, worked to bring relief to war-devastated areas, Communist and non-Communist alike. Large-scale national reconstruction programs undertaken in every west European country (e.g., the Monnet Plan for the modernization of French industry); Marshall-Plan aid stimulated recovery in non-Communist countries ($4 billion spent for this purpose by 1948). Western Germany, freed of allied controls in 1948, emerged as one of the strongest economies in Europe.

Formation of the European Economic Community, 1957. Beginning of space penetration with firing of Russian Sputnik, October 1957; intensification of scientific rivalry between Russia and the West. Reorganization of France under Charles de Gaulle, 1958. Major Yuri Gagarin of the Soviet Union (April) and Commander Alan Shepard of the USA (May) became the first two humans to embark on manned space flight, 1961. International crisis over Cuban rocket emplacements, October 1962. President de Gaulle of France vetoed Britain's application for entry into European Economic Community, January 1963. Assassination of President J. F. Kennedy of USA, November 1963. Widening of breech between the Soviet Union and Red China continued into the 1960's.

3. Postwar Europe: Decline or Survival?

An intrinsic consequence of the rise of the American and Russian superpowers was the economic downgrading of Europe. Again, this was a process begun during the First World War, but by 1945 it had become so serious as to raise the question of Europe's continuance as a major force in world affairs. In the immediate postwar years, Europe, with a large part of its industry destroyed and its capital wealth dissipated to an even greater extent than in 1919, seemed doomed to a lowered standard of living and to a permanent shortage of the resources necessary for industrial strength in the modern world. Some pessimists even spoke of mass emigration as the only solution to the problem and prepared to write an end to the historic cradle of western civilization. Since that time the various western European states, though still harassed by serious difficulties, have made a remarkable recovery.

How was this accomplished? In part it was the result of the remarkable economic decision of the United States to offer financial aid without expectation of repayment in order to put war-ravaged nations back on their feet. Later this program of Marshall Aid was extended to underdeveloped countries and to nations whose help was needed in cold war diplomatic maneuverings against the Soviet Union. The result of this massive outpouring was that in those countries where the aid was used for economically productive ends, industrial and commercial recovery was very rapid indeed. Such was the case with western Europe and most other advanced industrial countries. In this respect, western Europe helped to accomplish its own recovery; for money alone, as many underdeveloped countries were painfully learning, was not sufficient to guarantee economic improvement. Western Europe still possessed the confidence, the skill, and the motivation to achieve its own economic salvation.

By the mid-1950's renewed European economic strength made it possible for a number of western countries to contemplate a new form of social and political organization within the ancient framework of Europe. As early as 1948 the Organization for European Economic Cooperation (OEEC) had come into existence for the purpose of coordinating and administering Marshall Plan Aid. Two years later, in 1950, the European Coal and Steel Community (ECSC) was created to foster a closer economic cooperation in the use of those two important commodities. Its membership consisted of France, West Germany, Italy and the Benelux countries (Belgium, Netherlands, and Luxemburg). The culmination of these early projects came in 1957 when the six members of the ECSC

(Essential Movement continued on p. 162)

agreed, under terms of what has since come to be known as the Treaty of Rome, to create an integrated European Economic Community (EEC) or Common Market. In 1959 as a kind of counter-response to the EEC Great Britain and six other European states formed a somewhat looser free trade community known as the European Free Trade Association (EFTA).

By the year 1961 it was plain that the European Economic Community was succeeding beyond the highest expectations of its original projectors. Expanded market opportunities, greater and more mobile reserves of labor, a larger pool of capital and material resources gave to the new community an economic thrust almost unparalleled in recent European history. One significant consequence of this extraordinary success was that Great Britain, whose leaders had hesitated to enter EEC out of fear that ultimately too much national sovereignty as well as close relations with the British Commonwealth countries would have to be surrendered, began to have second thoughts about participation in the new community. In July 1961 a British balance of payments crisis forced the issue and Great Britain applied for admission to the EEC.

The moment of Britain's application was not a propitious one. The British had, in effect, gambled that the new community would not be nearly so successful as it was. Moreover, they were driven to apply for membership at a moment when their own international economic position was far from strong. As a result, they were forced to ask for admission almost hat in hand into a flourishing organization whose members could not forget that Britain had turned down an opportunity of charter membership. The result was that after a period of protracted negotiation at Brussels the French government at the direction of President Charles de Gaulle vetoed Britain's entry into the European Community.

President de Gaulle's veto in January 1963 was a symbolic act which revealed to Europe and the world how much the circumstances of international politics had altered during the preceding decade. France, Germany, or Italy alone no longer had the capacities for great power status. In conjunction, however, and with the cooperation of the small but rich Benelux nations the new union was a world economic power which might in time become a major world political and military power capable of balancing and possibly even challenging the two great superpowers, the United States and the U.S.S.R. President de Gaulle's motives in keeping the British out of EEC were not those of a disinterested European internationalist. At heart he remained a Frenchman who saw in the larger framework of the European Economic Community a means of preserving the historic national entities of Europe, including that of France. Clearly, he feared that the entry of Britain into EEC would mark the beginning of what he called "Anglo-Saxon influences," by which he meant the international power combination deriving from the close Anglo-American cooperation in world affairs. The difficulty with de Gaulle's conception of the new Europe, however, was that it seemed to many observers, including some of his associates in the EEC, to be simply a return to old-fashioned nationalism or to Europe under French dominance, albeit in a slightly different guise. Moreover, there were sincere doubts in many quarters that the preservation of separate national identities was feasible in an age when the cost of military technology was beyond the capacity of any but the richest nations.

That de Gaulle was successful in his diplomatic efforts to keep Britain out of the EEC was indicative of another significant change in the power relations of post-war Europe. The French president would never have been able to do what he did, particularly in view of the strong support that Britain received from other EEC members, if France had not been so important in the functioning of the new community. Without France's central geographical position, population, and industrial resources the EEC would have been far less successful. Thus it was that one of the major events of the 1950's was the political reorganization of France in 1958 under the direction of President de Gaulle. With the transformation of the fourth into the fifth republic the political instability that had plagued France and disturbed French foreign relations for generations came to an end. While most of France's neighbors and allies were pleased at that turn of events, there were others, not the least of which was the United States, who were increasingly concerned at what seemed to be a strong resurgence of French national particularism under de Gaulle's leadership.

C.   The Course of the Cold War and Its Effect on World Affairs.

The late 1950's and the 60's witnessed a slow but perceptible change in the cold war tensions that had divided East and West since 1945. On the surface each side seemed as ideologically bellicose as ever. Russia and Red China consistently backed rebel groups and parties throughout the world whose policies were, if not openly Communist, at least anti-western. On the whole, for all of their activity, the Soviet bloc was singularly unsuccesful in adding much to the regions that had fallen into the Communist orbit at the end of the Second World War. Indeed, on at least one occasion, in Hungary during November 1956, the Soviet Union was forced to use its military might in order to prevent a satellite state from slipping away. The most notable success of Soviet policy, however, was an inadvertent one that occurred largely because of diplomatic maladroitness on the part of the United States. This was the entry of Cuba into the Communist camp following the successful revolt of Fidel Castro which reached its culmination in 1959. The Cuban Revolution led to the most serious confrontation between the Soviet Union and the United States since Korea when it was found in October 1962 that the U.S.S.R. had supplied the Cuban government with rocket weapons. The crisis was fortunately passed when the Soviet Union agreed to dismantle its Cuban rocket bases in the wake of a firm American protest that seemed to bring both powers closer to war than they had been at any time during the long period of cold war rivalry.

While American firmness undoubtedly had much to do with the Soviet Union's change of front in the Cuban crisis, other diplomatic considerations also played a part in influencing Soviet withdrawal. From the late 1950's onward it had become increasingly clear in most western capitals that all was not well with the unity of the Soviet bloc. For a complex of reasons, which seemed to be traceable to a serious ideological disagreement over the advisability of pursuing an aggressive revolutionary diplomatic policy against the West, China and the U.S.S.R. gradually split apart from 1959 onward. By the mid-1960's both of the leading Communist states had reached a point in their relations where a diplomatic rupture between them seemed quite possible. While the break stopped just short of an open breach, it was evident that relations between the two countries were more than just strained. From the western point of view this division was a mixed blessing. On the one hand, it seemed to make the Soviet Union far less belligerent than it had been a decade before and appeared to promise the possibility of some kind of rapprochement between Russia and the West. On the other hand, however, it meant that Red China, freed of Russian restraint, might pursue an independent and militant policy of its own with serious consequences not only for the peace of Asia but for the whole world.

Despite continued alarms and frictions, there seemed in the mid-60's some reason for westerners to look with a tempered optimism upon the world situation. The problems of international politics were many and seemed very far from any final solution. For all that, it was still highly significant that the two great superpowers both seemed to be aware at long last of the changes implicit in atomic warfare. For this, at least, the world community had more than small reason to be grateful.

CHAPTER 12

Europe and the Western World: Summation and Conclusion

THE ESSENTIAL MOVEMENT

What were the prospects and position of Europe in the middle of the 20th century? And what did Europeans themselves think about them? Above all else, one thing was quite clear. Many western Europeans were beginning to think of themselves within a larger context than that of the nation. For some of them the ultimate hope of preserving the integrity and identity of Europe as a whole seemed to lie in a unified or partly unified European community. For others it seemed plain that there was little hope of Europe's survival unless it functioned within the even larger context of the entire non-Communist world.

One very hard fact, unpalatable to many Europeans, was their need to depend for the present at least upon the help and co-operation of the United States if Europe was to keep its independence and identity. In the years after 1945 most western European states, either ravaged or weakened by war, were not in a position to go it alone, economically or militarily, in the face of growing Soviet power. If Europe was to be saved from Soviet domination, it was evident that western Europeans had to accept American aid which, in turn, meant that the United States, by virtue of its new position, must to some extent call the tune of western policy, particularly toward the U.S.S.R. To the peoples of long-established European states with a long history of national and international preeminence behind them, this alteration of the historic European stature was difficult to accept. Frequently, the resentments of European governments at this implicit American domination of the West, no matter how much the United States might try to avoid them, led to tensions within the partnership of the North Atlantic alliance.

Nonetheless, Europe and the various overseas communities of European stock were still members of the larger community of western civilization. The problems of European man were also the problems of western man, and it was as a westerner that the European still looked out upon the world. How then did he feel about the future, about the prospects for his civilization as it entered into the Nuclear Age?

Though there was much to make him hopeful, there was little to make him overconfident. The mood of optimism, of faith in human material and moral progress, had been tempered in the western world by the tragedy explicit in two world wars, in the rise of totalitarianism, and in the atom bomb. And these were only symptoms of even deeper-seated difficulties; it was evident that men, however hopeful they might be, had to think realistically about themselves and the world in which they lived.

What had become increasingly clear as the century advanced was that man, while he had perfected the techniques of science and technology to a point where he was able to manipulate his environment and, in some parts of the world, to raise his standard of living to undreamt-of levels of abundance, had still to worry about himself. Man's greatest problem was still man. He could invent, improvise, and improve, but, in the end, it was up to him to decide how he would make use of his creations. Moreover, the problem was complicated by the fact that for more than two centuries western civilization had been expanding throughout the earth until it had reached a point where no human activities could any longer be isolated culturally or geographically.

This expansion, along with his high level of scientific attainment, seemed to imply a dreadful possibility that man might injure himself so seriously as to prevent the further development of civilization. The atom bomb, which usually comes to mind first in this connection, was actually a tangible object whose use he might hope to control, but there was another problem which might yet defeat him. This was the problem—or problems—created by the sheer weight of human numbers, the complexity of human relationships, and the often unpredictable effect man himself had upon his material environment. In brief, the question turned on whether man was capable of understanding the consequences of his own actions. And, if he were capable, whether he could do anything to control the actions or their consequences.

Let us now try to summarize the major achievements and dilemmas of western man since 1500 by looking once again at the four main themes of this book.

1. Human Control over the World of Nature (the Material Environment)

From about the middle of the 18th century western man had pressed forward with astonishing success in his effort to control the world of nature. The movement we know as the Industrial Revolution, though its immediate effects did not always seem beneficial, brought about a happy paradox which had never before been possible in human history. While the population of the West increased, so too did its general standard of living. Western man for the first time found himself in a position where an increase in human numbers did not have the effect of creating material shortages.

Startling and even dramatic as the results of the Industrial Revolution have been in the last two centuries, they should not be thought of as something explosively unique that happened almost overnight in a historical sense. The process by which industrialization came to the western world stretched far back into the European past and was part of that intermittent general expansion which had been going forward even during the middle ages. The industrial developments of more recent times must be looked upon as a kind of technological "break through" for which centuries of previous effort and invention prepared the way.

The beginnings of this expansive movement which culminated in the Industrial Revolution reach back well before 1500. Whatever the reasons for its inception, since they are still not entirely clear to us, there began sometime toward the end of the 10th or beginning of the 11th century a series of movements which reinvigorated and expanded the life of the West. Population growth may have played some part in it, but this we cannot know with certainty because we lack statistics. Furthermore, the mere growth of human numbers has never been a guarantee of resultant intellectual or technical expansion but in many societies has forced down living standards and caused intellectual stagnation. Undoubtedly, the internal reforms of the medieval church, which reached their highest achievement in the pontificate of Gregory VII (1073-1085), played a part in this change by revitalizing that greatest of medieval institutions, the church, which in turn spread the leaven through medieval society. This effect may best be seen in the founding of new monastic orders and the growth of universities. As important as any of these was an economic and technological expansion marked, on the one hand, by the founding of new cities and the growth of old ones and, on the other, by an apparent increase in agricultural and other productivity. In this area, too, we are at loss to explain all the reasons for sudden vitality. It may be that the 11th century was simply a time when a great many developments reaching far back into earlier periods and not easily identified by historians began to have a cumulative effect. Some historians now believe that the most important cause of this great economic change was the growth of the early feudal state which, though relatively weak and ineffective in many ways, provided the degree of security and political stability needed to stimulate economic activity.

Still we must not exaggerate the effects of this expansion by assuming that it led at once to a broad extension of human control over the material environment. Western technology, until about the 15th century, lagged behind that of some Middle Eastern and oriental societies; and western man, like everyone else, could and did suffer horribly from natural catastrophes over which he had little or no control and whose consequences often altered his way of life in curiously unpredictable ways. Year in and year out, with fearsome regularity, he was visited by plagues and pests. Men sometimes died in such numbers—as in the Black Death of 1348-1349—that the very structure of society was altered and the course of human history undoubtedly changed. Famines were a common part of the human lot, and even the richest societies were seldom far removed from the danger of harvest failure and the horrors of mass starvation. In most European cities such elemental methods of disease prevention as drainage, sewerage, and pure water supply, which had been known to the ancients, were not used extensively until well along in the 18th and 19th centuries.

Nevertheless, the upward curve of scientific and technological achievement in the period between the 11th and the 18th century was impressive. New methods of navigation and ship construction made possible longer and safer voyages. The development of military technology, while it enabled Europeans to kill one another in larger numbers, also put an end to the danger, ever present until the end of the middle ages, of outside conquest by Turks or Mongols who might have destroyed western civilization. Extensive engineering projects like the canals and dikes of Holland and the great swamp-drainage undertakings of England and France brought large areas of previously unused land under cultivation. In medicine, advances in the study of anatomy and bodily functions prepared the way for even greater successes in the future. But it was in the growth of scientific thought that the greatest potential for the future was achieved, for the

17th century was one of genius which saw the formulation of those basic scientific hypotheses which were to transform the western world during the next 250 years and make its achievements unique and greater than any in previous history. By 1700 men already knew that science might well be the means of extending the "empire of man over nature" as never before.

The unique state of affairs which, from the 18th century onward, permitted population to increase in many western lands without lowering the standard of living was caused by a massive improvement in technology which not only increased total production but also, by utilizing new forms of energy like steam power and electricity, put at man's disposal resources that had never been available to him before. This technological transformation was accompanied by a vast improvement in the efficiency of production techniques which permitted western societies to produce more in specific areas of economic activity without at the same time increasing the need for additional manpower. In agriculture, for example, new methods of planting and fertilizing, of cattle breeding, and of farm organization greatly expanded food supplies (even before the introduction of modern fuel-powered farm machinery) so that a much smaller farm population could produce more than had been produced by a much larger one.

Once efficiency and machinery were combined during the course of the 19th century, however, the results were even more spectacular, as the history of American agriculture strikingly illustrates. In the year 1790, 90% of the population of the United States lived in rural areas and produced food for the other 10%. By 1950 these percentages were almost exactly reversed: about 10% of the population not only fed the other 90% but produced an unmanageable and embarrassing surplus.

Thus freed from the necessity to devote the bulk of their manpower to the primary production of food, the industrialized societies of the West were further able to diversify their productive capacities. In England, which felt the growing pains of the Industrial Revolution first and most severely, the rise of industry during the 19th century transformed the whole country—as it later transformed most of western Europe and large parts of North America—into an area of technological specialization. No longer was it necessary for Englishmen to grow all their own food. By selling their manufactured goods in an international market they were able to purchase from foreign sources both the raw materials needed to keep their gigantic industrial complex going and much of the food they needed to keep alive. Thus to a very large degree all the industrialized nations of the West, but particularly Great Britain and western Europe, traded their superior technological skills for raw materials and subsistence.

In North America where indigenous (native) natural resources were greater and food did not have to be imported, the story was very different. Neither Canada nor the United States, once they began to industrialize, was quite so dependent upon external markets for the sale of their goods or upon external sources of supply for raw materials and food. For that reason the technological supremacy of Britain and western Europe (though 19th-century Europeans did not realize it) was relatively precarious and began to be challenged in the last decades of the 19th century when non-European societies undertook to build industrial systems of their own.

Nevertheless, the early technological lead of western European nations gave them enormous advantages in wealth and power down to 1914 and even, to some extent, thereafter. Year after year capital wealth and production grew; and as they grew, the economic benefits of this growth were diffused widely among the masses. Real wages (i.e., the actual purchasing power of earnings) rose steadily with very little interruption down to the First World War. As a consequence, items like tea and meat which had been regarded as luxuries in the 18th century became a staple part of human diet in industrialized nations. As the rich agricultural areas of Australia, Canada, and the United States were brought into production, man's most ancient staple, bread, cost him a smaller and smaller fraction of his earnings.

This fortunate situation had dynamic effects both psychological and political. With the rise of wealth and of general well-being the level of mass expectations also rose. No longer were the masses content to live precariously in the midst of apparent plenty. They demanded to have the abundance shared out more widely and not restricted to the privileged few. As a result, socialist parties gained in strength during the course of the 19th century until in time all other parties were, to a greater or lesser extent, influenced by their point of view. Once this influence had become almost irresistible, its effects began to be seen in the sphere of practical politics. The wealth of the West made it possible for political leaders like Bismarck in Germany or the Liberals in England to undertake extensive welfare programs which helped to alleviate the most serious economic distress. It is important to remember, however, that this welfare legislation could not have worked out in practice if the wealth and productive capacity of the countries in which it was introduced had not been sufficient to pay its cost. The welfare functions undertaken by the late 19th- and 20th-century state were thus another evidence of the higher standard of living enjoyed by the richer industrial societies of the western world.

The striking success of the West in raising the mass standard of living was only one aspect of the process by which western man extended his sway over nature. While life for the average man was made somewhat easier, it was also lengthened. On every side there were major improvements that tended to increase human longevity. In medicine and experimental biology the 250 years after 1700 were filled with victories over one disease after another, often as a result of curative discoveries but mainly as a consequence of public-health programs and preventive medicine. Better and more plentiful food was partly responsible, but so too were sewage-disposal systems, pure water supplies, and a growing public consciousness that cleanliness was not only next to godliness but also a sure way to stave off disease. Thus while expanded medical knowledge worked to restore the health of the stricken, the chances of catching a fatal malady in the first place were very much reduced. It is significant in this connection that after about the middle of the 19th century the great plagues—which had visited western Europe with death on a mass scale at regular intervals for centuries—gradually declined both in intensity and in frequency of recurrence.

Apart from the improved standards and health conditions, benefits which most people experienced without being aware of them, the 19th century also witnessed a considerable visible betterment in the conditions of human life. Communications, transportation, and the spread of popular education helped to enrich human experience. Living, even for the masses, became something more than just a dreary succession of events between birth and death. In alleviating the humdrum of everyday life, science and technology probably had their greatest immediate impact on human consciousness. Men could see and feel the things by which these helped to make life easier or pleasanter: the gas lights and electricity that brightened homes and communities; or the newspapers, telegraph systems, and telephones that gave information about the world almost instantaneously. As a result, science, though its laws and procedures were mysterious as always to ordinary men, came to be known and respected for its practical effects. Because these were so far-reaching and extensive, men soon accepted them as an essential part of the human scene without realizing how curiously unique they were in the history of the world. Nonetheless, a consciousness of the widespread achievements of science gave to western societies a widely diffused sense of confident optimism which generally characterized the outlook of most Europeans down to 1914.

The two World Wars and the events that followed in their wake did much to tone down the 19th-century confidence of the West. Twice within a generation Europeans were ravaged by great struggles that ultimately determined the fate not of Europe alone but of the world. The lesson implicit in these two great holocausts seemed to be that man, no matter how much he might improve his science and technology, could not survive just by mastering his material environment. He must also learn to master himself; and the hope that he might learn, in view of the lingering tensions between East and West that followed the Second World War, seemed remote despite the efforts of international bodies like the United Nations.

Furthermore, the growth of world population and the continuous drive for additional resources to supply an ever-expanding global industrial network began to raise other doubts about the future of civilization. By 1964 the earth's population was estimated to be almost 3,500,000,000 and was expanding at an ever increasing rate of about 2.1% annually or approximately 63 million persons. In the light of these towering statistics did the earth have enough raw materials to give all mankind the level of well-being formerly enjoyed only by the more fortunate industrial societies of the West?

Some said that man's domain over nature would finally end when he had used up the last of his fuels and minerals or when the weight of human numbers exceeded the capacity of world agriculture to produce enough food for subsistence. Here and there voices were raised to assert that the earth's raw materials were not sufficient to give everyone everywhere the high standards of living previously enjoyed only by the western world. In the past, they contended, the richer countries had been fortunate not simply in their technological skills but in their access to the world's resources. The United States alone, they went on to argue, had used up irreplaceable raw materials like iron ore at a greater rate since 1900 than all the rest of the world put together had used before that date. Such a dizzy rate of consumption could not last. Man must retrench or face not a happy future of abundance but a grim gray world poised forever on the edge of starvation and poverty.

Others, with more hopefulness, refused to accept this dread prognosis. Human skill and brainpower, said they, must and would find a solution. New reserves of energy and food supplies would yet be found, perhaps by plumbing the depths of the sea or by moving outward to the planets. Whichever side was correct in its forecast, it was plain by mid-20th century that man's survival and his hopes of future abundance would depend largely upon his willingness to save himself, and plain also that he could not do so if he were paralyzed by despair or blinded by overconfidence.

2. Belief in an Ordered, Purposeful Universe and Historical Progress

By the middle of the 20th century western man's faith that the universe was both orderly and beneficently purposeful had undergone a number of changes and modifications.

In the heyday of Newton's discoveries, that is, about 1700, it had seemed that all the great fundamental questions about the natural world and man's place therein would soon be answered, that Newtonian physics would provide the key to unlock nature's secrets. All that remained for man to do was to fill in his knowledge of details.

Secure in this confidence, the thinkers of the 18th century saw the earth and heavens as a gigantic clockwork mechanism amenable to law and ultimately knowable in all of its aspects. Though not all the philosophers of the Enlightenment were atheistic, many of them tended to relegate divinity to a subordinate role in the world of nature. God was transformed into a divine clockmaker who, having set the universal machinery in motion at the beginning of time, sat back and let it tick along without interference.

Partly as a cause and partly as a result of the growth of this belief, the traditional religious interpretation of the universe gradually lost ground among the intellectual elites of western Europe. In this way faith in reason gradually supplanted faith in divine authority. Philosophers no longer tried to explain natural phenomena as divine manifestations but rather as manifestations of natural or scientific laws. As this way of looking at things spread, human confidence increased. The unknown was no longer unknowable, no longer beyond the power of human comprehension. All that men required in order to achieve complete knowledge was sufficient time for human reason to acquire it. Now it seemed that man could do or learn for himself what he had formerly thought only God could do or reveal.

This faith in an ordered universe and the power of the mind, though very much intensified as a result of the scientific achievements of the 17th century, was no new thing in the history of western civilization. Its beginnings went back to the earliest Greek thinkers who assumed the existence of order beneath all the shifting, diverse phenomena of the everyday world. In large measure this belief was responsible for the development of Greek mathematics and the Greek attempt, best exemplified in the thought of Plato, to explain the cosmos and the relationships of the world of matter to the world of Ideas. Indeed, it is the persistence of this Greek view of things, later carried over into Christian thought, that has come to be looked upon as one of the unique and significant elements in western civilization. Without such a faith western man might not have attempted to formulate the laws of modern science. Here, as in a number of other things, the West owes much to the middle ages, the period that was for long assumed by historians to have been one of darkness and ignorance. For the medieval philosophers, though they worked within the restrictive framework of Christian belief, helped to preserve the tradition that the universe was ordered and rational by incorporating much of Greek philosophy, and particularly the writings of Aristotle, into Christian thought. In so doing they performed an important service for the West, even while they tended to hold too slavishly to the letters of Aristotle's teachings and thus, in some respects, held up the development of scientific thought during the 15th and 16th centuries: they kept alive the basic Greek way of looking at the world.

For long the significance of this service was overlooked by historians and scientists who thought of the Scientific Revolution as a complete reaction against the medieval way of looking at things. The middle ages, said they, accepted truth on the basis of revealed authority, while science is based solely upon observation and experiment; therefore, the modern scientific method as it has evolved since the 17th century is the very antithesis of medieval thought. But it is not antithesis, for the scientific method is made up of *two* important elements: one is empiricism (i.e., observation and experiment), which scientists have regarded as absolutely essential since the days of Galileo; the other is rationalism (i.e., the assumption that nature is governed by laws). Without this rational element which was preserved from the western past by the medieval philosophers the scientific method and the scientific way of looking at the world could not have come into being.

With the great victories of 17th-century science and the exaltation of human reason as never before, men altered their view of history. Because the intellectual successes and the material accomplishments of their own time seemed superior to those of preceding generations, it appeared to follow logically that the achievements of one's descendants would be superior to one's own. History was thus the story of continual human improvement or "progress" from one generation to the next. This idea, though different from the traditional Christian view of man's movement through time, was, to some extent, an analogue of the earlier Christian view of history. For the Christian, too, history progressed, but it was not progress toward a better world in the here and now. It was, rather, a movement toward a final rendezvous—a last judgment—when the temporal world would come to its end. The Christian had always believed that man's ultimate goal was otherworldly and that while things of this world were important they were less important than the salvation of the soul and life beyond the grave. The 18th-century philosophers secularized this view by thinking of progress as a material rather than a spiritual advance. Furthermore, they did not look upon history as something that would end with a last judgment but rather as a continuous development toward secular perfection. In other words, as the power of reason dispelled ignorance and as man improved his material environment, he would re-move all those things—poverty, intolerance, tyranny—that had formerly caused evil and crime. Thus with material advancement, i.e., with im-provement in wealth and well-being, the human race would also progress morally until such time as the perfect environment would create the perfect man.

As a corollary to the above beliefs, the philosophers of the Enlighten-ment also assumed that since man was a reasonable (rational) creature his intelligence needed only to be freed from the restrictions of tyranny and superstition in order to permit him to act according to the laws of nature and thus in his own best interst. Men liberated from these restrictions would almost automatically choose the rational and the good and in this way progressively eliminate those things which were regarded as irrational and evil in the world. Furthermore, since the universe was governed by natural law, with which rational men always tried to live in harmony, men, once they had achieved a requisite amount of education, would no longer be governed by their emotions or selfish whims. They would be-come rationally objective in all their beliefs even where their own interests were concerned. Truth could always be arrived at simply by letting reason play upon the facts. Whenever issues divided human beings, they, as reasonable men, would determine what was right in terms of natural law and in that way eliminate all discords—political, religious, or otherwise.

Such an optimistic view of history and of human nature was not with-out its critics even when it was most strongly held. During the last decades of the 18th century, however, a stronger reaction against this faith in man's rationality set in when the Romantic philosophers and writers began to attack the Enlightenment's view of man and the universe as shallow and unrealistic. Man, they charged, was not always nor even usually a creature of reason but one of emotion instead. To them, the world was no clockwork mechanism governed by rigid unchanging laws but rather a complex place filled with diverse phenomena that made it something more than a colorless, lifeless machine—a complex and highly diverse organism subject to continual development and change. In so arguing, many members of the Romantic school were not attacking science or reason. They were attacking only the assumption that everything—ideas, esthetic values, human feelings—could be explained in purely scientific or rational terms. Man, they said, is also a creature of his habits, passions, traditions. To expect him to subordinate these to pure reason under all circumstances is to expect the impossible.

In shifting over from a mechanistic to an organic view of the universe and to the belief that man was something more than a reasoning machine the Romantics did not entirely reject all the ideas of the Enlightenment. Most Romantic thinkers still believed in the idea of progress in varying degrees. They assumed that reason, though not the sole governor of human thoughts and actions, still played a large part in directing them. Many Romantics also had faith that a scientific explanation of the universe was possible, but in biological or anthropological rather than physical or mathematical terms.

One thing grew clear as the 19th century advanced and the Romantic view of the world began, in its turn, to wane: *Men, however much they might react against certain scientific presuppositions and conclusions, were still convinced that the law of progress was at work and that science would ultimately solve all human problems.* This faith was greatly strengthened by the utilitarian effects of science, by technology and preventive medicine, and by the apparently steady advance toward broader syntheses of scientific knowledge, the most spectacular of which was the Darwinian theory of evolution. As a consequence, about the middle of the 19th century a new and more intense scientific materialism came into being. Important thinkers, many of whom were either scientists or people very much under the influence of scientific ideas, restated the old faith of the Enlightenment that men and everything in the universe were ultimately subject to scientific law. The universe, they asserted, consisted only of material things. The world of spirit had no objective, tangible existence. Accordingly, man himself was matter like all the other stuff of the universe; and though he had sensations and seemed to possess something called reason that made him appear superficially different from all other organic or inorganic forms, he too must be explicable in material terms. The trick was to find the link between man and the atoms of which he was composed. Once it had been found, the last great synthesis would be achieved.

For many scientists and scientific philosophers that time seemed imminent. And then occurred that great modern revolution in physics which culminated in Einstein's theory of relativity. Within a space of about twenty-five years—from 1880 to 1905—Newtonian science was reduced in status from being *the* synthesis to being a limited and special statement, and the great hope of an ultimate synthesis became, if not impossible, certainly far more remote than it had seemed fifty years before.

While the intellectual foundations of the physical sciences were shifting, western man's confidence was shaken in another significant way. The last third of the 19th century also saw the rise of a new and intensified nationalism, of a growing international insecurity, and of a challenge to Europe's long-accepted world hegemony with the industrialization of non-European powers like the United States and Japan. All three of these developments aggravated a growing sense of uncertainty that had been augmented by the loss of philosophical assurance when the absolute nature of Newtonian physics was overturned. Now there seemed further reason to doubt both human rationality and the permanence of European civilization. The ultimate testimony for this irrationality and insecurity seemed explicit in the vast tragedy that began in 1914.

The experience of two world wars, atomic destruction, and totalitarian brutality, and threats of a third holocaust hanging over their heads, made it scarcely surprising that many in the West at mid-20th century should have felt a sense of uncertainty or pessimism about the future. It was difficult to accept with any conviction the idea that the world was inevitably "progressing" toward a happier material and moral state. Indeed, to many observers, it seemed that the orderly optimistic purposes of history had reversed themselves and that western civilization, whose foundations had seemed impregnable in the 19th century, might, like earlier civilizations, be overwhelmed by misery and chaos.

Many, of course, did not share this pessimistic view of things. In some societies—most notably the United States and Canada—the rapid expansion of industrial wealth from 1945 onward allayed doubts both in the booming countries and in hard-pressed Europe by bringing about unparalleled material prosperity. Many newly independent Asian and African countries looked with confidence toward a future that seemed bright if only because they now felt that they controlled their own destinies. The Soviet Communists, firm in their belief that history was on their side and that Communism was the goal toward which all the world was inevitably moving, held fast to the philosophical optimism of Communism's founder, Karl Marx.

In the eyes of their opponents, however, Communist dreams of worldwide revolution and the establishment of a universal proletarian society were not happy things to contemplate. To most westerners it seemed that these dreams must only eventuate in a vast totalitarian network whose massive state apparatus and deadening ideology would stifle civilization under a new kind of barbarism. Some contended that Communism must be resisted on the ground that it was dangerous to all forms of human freedom. Others argued, more pragmatically, that the superimposition of a totalitarian Communist structure on the richer societies of the West would inevitably lower the western standard of living and eliminate all those amenities which western man had taken for granted in the past.

The difficulty for non-Communists, however, was that they did not have any single dominant coherent theory of man, the universe, and history to set against Communism. The West had only a variety of beliefs and theories, all of which created a state of ideological diversity (pluralism). Some said that western man could not hope to restore his confidence until he, in turn, evolved an ideology with an appeal as universal as that of Communism. Some contended that what the West had to do was to restore its traditional Christian beliefs and values, for only in these was there any hope of overcoming the widespread ideological appeal of Communist doctrine.

Though this lack of agreement in the western world was regarded by many as a weakness, others saw in it the West's greatest strength. Pluralism, said they, had been the secret of the West's success in the past and would be again in the future. Only by permitting the widest kind of intellectual freedom could the West hope to continue the civilizing process which had made western culture the most widely copied on earth. If western—and human—survival depended upon skill and brainpower, only the diversity of western civilization, which permitted men to think and act in freedom, could find a way to solve the problems of the human race. They believed that if this way of approaching human problems were strangled, western civilization and, in the end, world civilization might perish in an intellectual *rigor mortis* more paralyzing than any known before in human history.

3. The Expansion of Europe

At the end of the 17th century the process of European expansion had already reached a stage where it was no longer a development of merely European but of worldwide significance. Between 1500 and 1700 thousands of Europeans ceased to be inhabitants of Europe and took up permanent residence overseas. In some cases this residence, by the beginning of the 18th century, had extended over so many generations that Europe was a remote ancestral homeland far removed from the immediate concerns and interests of many overseas colonists. As yet no area of European settlement was politically or culturally independent of Europe, but the time of political separation for some of them was not far off. Furthermore, the European economy was already tied into a large global system of economic relations upon which Europe depended for a significant part of its commerce and for some of its material resources.

During the 18th and 19th centuries the process which saw Europe expand both internally and externally continued apace. With the great industrial transformation that began in the last half of the 18th century, wealth increased and the standard of living improved somewhat more slowly. Along with this internal expansion, there was a growth of military and political power which gave to western Europe a world hegemony that lasted for more than 200 years. In every quarter of the globe relatively small numbers of Europeans armed with superior weapons and technical skills were able to displace or bring under their control native populations who had not the means to resist their advance. Small states like England, France, Holland, and Belgium became the centers of great empires many times the size of the countries that administered them.

Through conquest and expansion Europe became with each passing generation more deeply enmeshed in a world-wide economic system whose structure already existed in 1700. The nature of this system is not always clearly understood. It was not solely and simply a crude imperialism as has been charged; for the methods of direct or open exploitation and plunder of native peoples and their resources were seldom employed. True, this kind of thing had been done and continued to be done by some unscrupulous Europeans. In the main, however, the international economic system functioned through an exchange of commodities, i.e., by means of buying and selling. The industrial states of Europe bought raw materials—cotton from India or the southern United States, tea from Ceylon, dyes and spices from the East Indies—which they processed into finished manufactured products and sold wherever they could. Nor were they entirely dependent on outside resources to keep their industries going. Countries like England, France, or Germany possessed indigenous supplies of coal and iron which went into the manufacture of goods sold in the international market.

Nevertheless, it was plain toward the end of the 19th century that Europe's reliance on a world market, though it had made many countries rich, also had serious shortcomings. The economic health of one country could affect for good or ill all others with whom it stood in relations of trade. Great depressions like that of 1873, for example, had serious international consequences. Moreover, as we have seen, once western Europe's unique industrial supremacy began to be challenged by non-European societies, the economy of Europe became a delicately balanced mechanism which could be seriously upset by a sudden shift in world market conditions. The culmination of this process by which western Europe became ever more delicately balanced in its economic relations with the rest of the world may be seen in the need for many highly industrialized 20th-century states to "export or die"—Great Britain offers one example.

Part of 20th-century Europe's problem in its relations with the rest of the world stemmed from the fact that European expansion stimulated both a hostility toward the West and a desire to emulate it in many ways. Asian and African peoples were introduced to European ideas like liberalism, democracy, nationalism, even communism, which had the effect of undermining Europe's control over many regions. Perhaps more importantly, non-Europeans learned the advantages of science and technology which not only gave Europeans a higher standard of living than that enjoyed by peoples elsewhere but also made possible European domination of vast areas outside Europe. Here was something peculiarly European that might be used against the conquering westerners. As a result, though many Asian and African leaders have rejected or say they want to reject western ideas and cultural forms, all of them, with few exceptions, have been anxious to achieve the advantages conferred by western industry and technology. Whether they can accept the material benefits without accepting the ideas and traditions in which western science and technology grew up is a moot question. Be that as it may, there was no doubt but that through a process of imitation and emulation western civilization in some or all of its aspects had reached a point by mid-20th century where it seemed well on its way to becoming the first worldwide civilization in human history.

The spread of European civilization with its scientific and industrial techniques did not mean, however, that every underdeveloped society was able to make successful use of them at once. Indeed, there was a new and perhaps alarming portent in the inability of nonindustrial societies to rapidly close the economic gap between themselves and wealthier countries. By the 1960's it seemed that any immediate improvement must be put off not for just a few years but perhaps for generations. If this was the case—and the fierce race between rising numbers and technological advance in underdeveloped countries seemed to indicate that it might be—then the West had an even greater dilemma to deal with. Clearly, an expanding and ever more sophisticated technology in the developed nations was bound to make the rich richer and the poor desperate. Could the world live divided between such extremes of have and havenot? Might not the future of man eventuate in a massive struggle between the richer and poorer nations of the earth? To thoughtful men in all countries it seemed plain that the result of such a conflict would not only be disastrous for mankind as a whole but would serve no useful end. The human race could ill afford any more struggles that would dissipate its accumulated wealth and destroy a large part of its repository of skill. No matter who was victorious in such a struggle, a war of world-wide expropriation might well destroy all future hope of human economic advance. Furthermore, even if the poorer nations could conceivably conquer the technologically advanced nations, the poor countries would not better their condition unless the conquerors could find a way of utilizing the techniques and skills of the conquered. In the end, then difficult though the idea might be for hungry peoples to accept, there was no solution to the problem of human well-being except that of having the underdeveloped peoples work out their own economic salvation by expanding their productive capacities. To prevent international tragedy the richer countries could and did offer substantial amounts of monetary and educational aid to less advantaged societies. It was doubtful, however, that such grants could be maintained as permanent subsidies if the populations of the underdeveloped countries continued to soar.

This state of affairs was the result of five different but closely related developments, each of which we must now examine briefly.

a.   Growth of Population

Since most European states had no regular census-taking procedures until the 19th century, historians and demographers (population experts) have had to rely on other, somewhat indirect evidence for their estimates of population change or growth before the year 1800. The informed consensus, however, is that the population of Europe down to about 1650 was increasing but that its growth was slow in contrast to its enormous increase after that date.

Nevertheless, all our evidence indicates that most countries had much larger populations in the year 1700 than they had in the year 1000. England, for example, is estimated to have had a population of slightly more than 1 million persons near the end of the 11th century (1086). By 1700 the estimated figure had grown to about 6 million. While these figures are small in modern terms, the rate of growth is fairly substantial. Even more important, however, was the enormous growth which most demographers believe began about the year 1650. Since that time there has taken place, quite literally, not an expansion but an explosion of Europeans. For while it is true that today the populations of Asia and parts of Africa are numerically larger than those of Europe or of areas settled by Europeans overseas, their historic rate of increase does not appear to have been nearly so high. Again, if we look at England, the most striking example of this increase, we can see how almost unbelievably high the rate of growth has been. In 1700 there were probably fewer than 10 million English-speaking persons in all the world. By 1950 that number had grown to more than 250 million.

For both the earlier and the later rates of growth there have been a number of explanations. Very probably one reason why European population grew even before 1650 was an increase in food supply. Another was the greater security provided by the expanded police power of the centralized state. Preventive medicine and extensive improvements in technology, though by no means negligible factors, were not yet developed enough to have the effects they were to have at a later date. In both periods —before and after 1650—the factor of living space may also have to be taken into account. The European continent, with some few excepted areas, had an abundance of land which could be made to produce sufficient food for its people with the agricultural techniques available. Moreover, Europeans were also moving into sparsely settled regions overseas where their skills could be utilized for the production of wealth and subsistence even more successfully.

By the middle of the 20th century the population of Europe and the western world had reached a figure which would have been inconceivable in earlier periods. At the earlier date the existing methods of agriculture and technology could not have supported anything near the number of persons alive in 1950, even at the very lowest level of subsistence. What was all the more startling about this vast growth, as we have already noticed, was not simply the increase of human numbers but the fact that this increase had not forced western man's subsistence level downward but had come about as his standard of living mounted upward toward greater material abundance.

Furthermore, though the population of Europe and of the overseas communities of European origin had not outstripped the population of the rest of the world in absolute numbers, its growth had been so great and so rapid as to make the number of Europeans and persons of European stock proportionately much larger in relation to the rest of the world than it had been 250 years before. While this growth of numbers in the West seemed to belie the Malthusian theory that men might increase beyond the capacity of their resources to support them, there were those who saw a potential danger in the continuation of this increase. These people argued that the West, fortunate in its natural resources as well as its science and technology, had been able to expand its production at rates equal to or greater than its rate of population increase. In other regions of the world, they pointed out—in parts of Asia, Africa, and Latin America—where western science and technology had made slower headway in exploiting resources and the rate of production was therefore much less, the subsistence level had risen slowly if at all. In those areas the ancient scourges of malnutrition and famine plagued men as they had for centuries.

Despite these pessimistic reservations, many westerners were convinced that scientific and technological advances would solve the problem of material shortages if it should become serious. In at least one respect, too, the ever-expanding population of the West had had obviously beneficent effects which could not be denied. Population growth in the richer societies had acted as a stimulus to economic expansion by continually increasing the demand for material goods. In a number of countries a steady rise in human numbers was regarded as a positive good without which the economic system might stagnate. For this reason, it was argued, whatever the cost in human effort or material resources, mankind could not stand at a population equilibrium.

No matter who might be proved right in this argument, it was evident by the 1960's that the increase in human mass was creating a vast number of problems, not all of which were economic. More people require more living space, more services from the state, more regulation of their activities; for human numbers contribute to the complexity of human problems. A country whose population in 1500 was anywhere from three to ten millions had many more social and political dilemmas to resolve when its population had increased ten, twenty, or even thirty times by 1965. As a result, to the fear of material shortages was added a fear that human problems might in time become so complex as to defy solution.

b.   Rise of Cities and Towns (Increasing Urbanization)

The effects of urban growth on western civilization have been so many and so diverse that it is difficult to summarize them. Some historians have gone so far as to suggest that the influence of urbanization has been more important than any other. Though the point may be argued, there is no doubt that the spread of vast centers of urban population has changed the living habits and even the ideas of modern man in many significant ways.

In 1500 the European way of life was still overwhelmingly rural and would remain so for at least another 250 years. This did not mean, however, that society had not changed radically in the centuries since 1000. The rise of towns had transformed the economic and social relations of European society in many ways. Since the very existence of populated centers requires that the agricultural system produce a surplus which can be used to feed those elements in the urban population who do not produce food for themselves, market areas were created throughout western Europe where the rural inhabitants had changed their agricultural techniques to conform to the needs of the towns. In changing them, the rural producer also changed the system of feudal-manorial relations. Serfs, as they accumulated a surplus of money, were able to transform (commute) their manorial obligations into money payments and often to purchase their freedom from serfdom. Though the process by which this change took place differed in rate from country to country (in some parts of Europe it was not completed until the 19th century), by the year 1500 the restrictive system of manorial relations had markedly declined.

The growth of cities also had important general effects. The commercial activities of the townsmen forced them to live outside the customary arrangements of feudal society. Trade required freedom of movement, a different conception of property rights, and a system of law opposed to that of the manor. By striving to win these, the town-dweller broadened the area of individual action and thus, indirectly, helped to expand intellectual and political freedom. And, finally, the new wealth of the towns eased the rigidity of the feudal class structure and created a new social mobility by making it possible for men to rise more easily in the social scale.

This last development brought into existence a new group within the European social order, sometimes called the burgesses, bourgeoisie, or, more loosely, "the middle classes." The immediate political importance of this new social element has often been exaggerated by historians, but there is no doubt that these men and the commercial form of wealth they represented did have significant long-range effects on European historical development.

To illustrate the profound nature of this continuing urban change, let us look at a few comparative figures for 1500 and 1960. At the earlier date there were no cities in all Europe whose populations equaled or exceeded a million. Only Paris with a population of perhaps 200,000 came close to the great modern cities in either numbers or the complexity of their problems. By 1960 Europe, including countries on both sides of the Iron Curtain, had more than a dozen cities with populations of a million or more. Among these were vast metropolitan areas (conurbations) like London and Paris, whose inhabitants numbered many millions. In some European countries urbanization was so continuously dense in certain areas that entire nations seemed to have taken on the characteristics of sprawling city-states.

With the spread of urbanization western man's outlook toward life changed. Since most men now lived in cities or metropolitan areas, the interests and problems of city dwellers had from the 19th century onward come to have decisive influence on the social and political development of most western societies. Into the cities in ever larger numbers had poured the working masses of the industrial era, and it was around them that the forces of democracy and later of socialism tended to cluster. Because the city industrial workers generally felt the effects of economic distress more quickly and often more severely than the rural population, the tendency of the former was to support political parties who promised them a measure of economic relief and welfare security in times of stress. Thus with the enfranchisement of the urban working class the centers of political power slowly shifted from the countryside to the city. Once the city workingman had the ballot, political parties had to reshape their policies in order to remain in power. No matter how much a politican might publicly denounce or privately hate state intervention or socialism, he had to win votes to stay in office. As a consequence, in every country of the western world the traditional liberal and conservative parties of the 19th century gradually transformed themselves until by the mid-20th century many of them resembled their 19th century counterparts in name only. Moreover, the city voting blocs had equally important local effects. The city political machine, for example, though far more powerful and significant in American life, became a fairly widespread phenomenon even in Europe.

The problems of cities were also complicated by the anonymity of their millions of inhabitants, among whom crime and immorality might be more easily hidden than in the villages or rural communities of bygone days. More difficult to deal with, however, was the peculiarly 20th-century problem of rapid urban decay, that is, the growth of slum areas and population with all their attendant problems of juvenile delinquency and education. The vast financial outlay required to solve this problem seemed, in many cases, to be beyond the capacity of all but the very wealthiest cities without some kind of subsidy from the rest of society.

Here, as elsewhere, there were pessimists and optimists. There were some who felt that unless a solution could be found for the complex problems of city life, the city must one day strangle civilization. In answer to this fear the defenders of urban life pointed to the cultural and economic importance of cities, to the fact that they, in the past, had been important links in the expansion of civilization. In a sense, the argument was irrelevant because cities existed and would continue to exist. There was no possibility of western man's retreating backward into his agrarian past. What he had to do was to find a way whereby urbanism did not become an incubus on the back of civilization.

c.   Colonization in Europe and Overseas

Though we usually associate migration and colonization with European overseas expansion, Europeans had actually been migrating and colonizing within Europe itself long before Columbus's discovery. From the 10th through the 16th centuries there was a steady movement outward from the more heavily populated regions of Europe into sparsely settled underdeveloped border regions or into areas occupied by non-Christians. Far more important and of more obvious significance in terms of world history was the expansion of Europe overseas. Never again until—and if—space travel becomes possible will men have the same experience that Europeans, beginning with Columbus, had in the 200 years after the discovery of the western hemisphere. Even more remarkable than the fact of discovery, however, were the mass migrations that led to permanent settlement and the transference of European ways and traditions to regions far removed from Europe itself. No movement on such a scale had ever been undertaken in all the world's history. Some notion of the magnitude of this migration may be had if we remember that in the period between 1607, when the first permanent English settlement in North America was made at Jamestown, and 1776, when the American Revolution began, the population of British North America increased, largely by immigration, from about 100 persons to an estimated 2.5 million. What was true of England's colonies was also true, though to a lesser extent, of the colonies of other European powers.

From the beginning of the 18th century until 1914 the great European overseas emigration became a roaring flood. Although this outward movement flowed to all parts of the earth, some figures for the United States will suffice to suggest the extent and significance of this vast phenomenon. In 1820, population statistics for the United States show, about 8000 persons entered the country as immigrants. Twenty years later the annual number of new entries approached 100,000. After the Civil War it rose well above that figure until it reached a peak of about 1¼ million in 1914. Between 1820 and 1955 it is estimated that the United States received something over 40 million immigrants, the vast majority of whom were European in origin. Large as it was, the number of transplanted Europeans received by the United States was still only one of the many streams of emigration. Never in all history was there such a movement of human beings over such distances. Though many of the emigrants traveled with severest thrift, the total money outlay involved in this gigantic transplantation staggers the imagination.

What made all the emigration possible was not only the pressure of numbers in Europe. After all, other societies in Africa and Asia had population pressures as great or greater. Europe possessed the wealth needed to develop overseas communities, and its emigrants had the skill to make the untapped resources of overseas frontiers expansively fruitful. Again, North America is the classic example, for, as men moved out of Europe, investment followed, particularly in the 19th century.

It is well to remember, of course, that this great movement was not solely the result of economic motivation. Men emigrated from Europe for a variety of religious, political, and social reasons. Usually, however, it was the young, the able, or the skilled, particularly in the latter phases of the movement, who emigrated in larger numbers because they were better able to bear the rigors of new life and the psychological shock of an unfamiliar environment. With such people economic desire—the urge "to better one's self"—probably had a large though not always a decisive influence. Emigration statistics for some countries—e.g. 19th-century Germany—seem to indicate that when economic opportunity was good at home and there were no political or social upheavals, Europeans stayed where they were. Another important fact to bear in mind in this connection is that while the opportunities in half-settled or frontier regions overseas tempted many, Europe itself was opening up new industrial frontiers that absorbed the energies of its peoples and offered substantial material rewards which did not require the cutting of familiar ties in order to win them.

Nevertheless, the existence of untilled lands and unused resources must be taken into account in any explanation of the great European emigration. Some people have perhaps exaggerated the influence of the overseas frontier in the history of western civilization, but it did act as a safety valve for population pressures and for the politically, socially, or religiously discontented. Now that the earth's last great underpopulated fertile areas have virtually disappeared, it remains to be seen what effect this change will have on societies whose members have no choice but to remain where they are.

d.   The Revolution in the Techniques of Production
     and Transportation

While it is true that the most spectacular industrial advances of modern times were made from the latter part of the 18th century onward, we now know that for some centuries before that time numerous changes had been taking place in European economic life which made the later development far less revolutionary than has sometimes been thought. England, for example, as well as other parts of northern Europe, underwent a series of important internal changes during the 16th and 17th centuries that have led some historians to refer to this period as an earlier "industrial revolution." Between 1540 and 1640 the English—followed by the Dutch and Swedes—enormously increased their production of textiles by expanding the "putting out" or domestic system of household manufacture and at the same time accomplished a revolution in the use of coal and iron. There is also evidence which indicates that by the middle of the 17th century England and Sweden between them produced nearly as much iron as all the rest of Europe together despite the fact that the combined population of the two countries was only about 8 million.

The most obvious and dramatic industrial transformation came with the great breakthrough at the end of the 18th century commonly known as the Industrial Revolution. Its two major effects were to be seen in the increased production of goods and in the methods by which these goods were transferred from manufacturer to consumer. Each of the two effects depended upon the other. Without greater production the improvement in transport and communication, though desirable, would not have become an absolute necessity. At the same time, if the methods of transport and communication had not been improved, the market for manufactured goods could not have been expanded in such a way as to make the increase in industrial production economically feasible.

In both of those areas (production and transport) the major long-run innovation, apart from improvements in industrial organization and efficiency, was steam power. Steam represented a new level of energy not ordinarily utilizable in a natural form, which man had to create from resources like wood and coal. Once the steam engine began to be used effectively both for propulsion and manufacture, it tended to heighten western production capacities, which had earlier been improved by concentrating manpower in the centralized factory.

The stages by which this changeover from wind, water, or animal power was effected took longer than we sometimes realize. The steam engine was not universally applied to the processes of manufacture the instant it was invented. Not until about the middle of the 19th century did steam begin significantly to replace other kinds of power in the more important industries. In transport, the steamship, as an economically practicable method of haulage and conveyance, did not supplant the sailing vessel until after 1870. Indeed, it was not until steam-powered engines had clearly demonstrated their advantages not only in terms of greater production and transport speed but also in terms of cost that they finally came into their own. At each stage of energy development, that is, with the utilization of electricity, petroleum, and even of atomic energy, this pattern was to be repeated.

In spite of the relatively slow diffusion of steam technology, its effects and the effects of other major technological discoveries made western Europe in the 19th century stronger and richer than ever before. The British, in particular, since they were the first to feel these effects, enjoyed such industrial and economic advantages from them that the 19th century has sometimes been called the "Age of Great Britain." During the hundred years between 1815 and 1914 Britain was the world's major manufacturer, middleman, and banker. Until the last quarter of the 19th century the British position was so strong that British industry had a virtual monopoly of the international market and a commanding lead in world maritime transport. After 1880 this situation began to change. The emergence of France and Germany as major industrial powers within Europe and the rapid industrial growth of the United States and then of Japan outside Europe challenged Britain's world industrial hegemony. By 1914 Great Britain, though she still had the lion's share of world commerce, had already fallen behind some of her rivals in important areas of production. The two world wars in the 20th century further tipped the world's industrial balance against Britain (and western Europe) until by the middle of the century the United States, actually, and the Soviet Union, potentially, had greater industrial strength than any one or two of the old pre-1914 states of Europe.

A part of Europe's relative decline was caused by the shift in sources of fuel energy. About the time of the First World War a technological changeover from coal to petroleum made western Europe, which lacked extensive oil deposits, more dependent than ever on the outside world. For the United States and Canada, however, the shift was advantageous, since both of those countries were rich in petroleum resources.

At mid-20th century, while it was evident that western Europe no longer had the clear industrial monopoly it had enjoyed in the 19th century, it was also plain that Europe, considered as a whole, was still one of the most highly and extensively developed industrial complexes on earth. If it was to remain so it could no longer rest easily on the assumption that its technological triumphs of the past would guarantee similar successes in the future. Continued technological advance depended as never before upon an even more extensive and intense cultivation of skills and research. So long as the tempo of these was not slowed, there was hope that western man might continue to open up new scientific and industrial frontiers to replace the old geographical frontiers that had almost disappeared throughout the earth.

Nevertheless, by the 1960's it was also plain that western man in his continuous effort to increase productive capacities might be creating a new sort of problem for himself. As he searched for improved efficiency he made greater use of machine power which, while it stepped up levels of production, threatened to eliminate the need for human workers on a massive scale. Would western man as a result of his own industrial ingenuity deprive large numbers of his fellow humans of economic usefulness in the social order? If so, how could those left behind in the advance of automation hope to survive? Those who regarded the process of automation as necessary and inevitable tended to argue that technological advance had always created new job opportunities in the past and would continue to do so in the future, so long as no attempts were made to impede human inventiveness. Others, alarmed at the possibility of a major displacement of men by machines, demanded that the state intervene in some effective way to prevent social disaster. Here, again, was one of those areas of human dilemma which would require a maximum of wisdom and understanding if the problems raised by increasing technological complexity were to be resolved.

e.   The Growth of Capital Wealth

The expansion of Europe—and the West—did not, however, depend upon technological improvement alone. It also depended upon an economic process without which technological and industrial growth would have been impossible. To those unfamiliar with the ways by which societies expand industrially it often seems that all men need for building an industrial system is skills and machines. Unfortunately, neither of these very valuable and necessary elements can be created overnight simply by desiring to have them. The experiences of 20th-century Asian and African societies have made that fact abundantly clear.

In any society, economic expansion (i.e., the growth of total economic production which alone can raise living standards), while it depends upon a number of factors, cannot occur unless that society possesses two fundamental things. First, it must have a large body of skilled manpower. And, second, it must have an accumulation of what we call "capital." The word "capital" has been given many meanings, but in precise economic terms it is commonly defined as "produced wealth used productively for gain." In this sense, capital is always distinguished from commodities like food, clothes, automobiles, or houses, which, though they have an economic value and may be necessary for an individual's well-being, are not always used directly to produce more wealth. Capital in its simplest form is thus an accumulation of what we call "savings," which are left over from income after all other needs have been satisfied and which may be employed for gainful purposes. For most people the easiest and most obvious way of employing such capital savings is to put them in a bank where they will draw interest. Before savings can earn interest, however, the bank's directors must make use of them in productive ways by investing them in business enterprises or in loans. In this respect, the banker acts as a manager of his depositors' money; and the individual saver is freed of the responsibility for looking after his capital himself. Since banks, in most cases, are fairly safe places to put capital, the interest rate on that capital in return for safety is always relatively low. For those who hope for a larger return, which often calls for a certain amount of speculative risk, the stock market offers another area of capital investment. There individuals keep a somewhat more direct control over their savings by purchasing stocks (capital shares which entitle those who buy them to shares of a company's earnings if profits permit) or bonds (certificates of indebtedness on which interest is paid and which are secured by a company's tangible assets). And, finally, there is a third and much more direct way of employing capital savings. That is by using them to start a business venture of one's own.

All of these methods—and many more—are so much a part of western man's economic experience that he seldom thinks about their historic significance. Often he simply assumes that they are a result of the natural order of things and that they must inevitably appear in any society where wealth has increased to a certain point. Unfortunately, as the experience of many 20th-century underdeveloped societies indicates, such an evolution is by no means automatic. In many instances it is the result of a complex of social factors that almost no societies outside the area of western civilization have possessed to a significant degree.

The first of these factors is surplus product: the accumulation of capital savings, whether undertaken by individuals as it is in western democratic countries or by the state as it is in countries like the Soviet Union, requires that a society not use all of its income for immediate consumption. In other words, its people cannot be living at a level of bare subsistence but must produce a surplus over and above their ordinary needs. Where the level of productive techniques is too low or where natural resources are insufficient, the lack of surplus becomes a difficult problem which can be solved only by borrowing capital from some outside source or by further depressing the living standards of society until a surplus is created.

The accumulation of surplus, however, is only the first step in the process of economic expansion. Opportunity to use the surplus productively is a second social factor. A method or methods for deciding what use is a third. In collectivist societies where the state, in effect, controls all economic surplus it also determines how that surplus will be used. Throughout most of the western world, however, the decision as to how savings will be employed has been left up to the individual. Wherever this latter course has been followed certain other things then have to happen if the productive capacity of society is to be expanded by capital investment. Of primary importance to the individual investor is the security of his savings—a fourth social factor. Even when he speculates by putting his money into a new venture he likes to feel that his chances of getting a return on it are at least reasonably good, apart from ordinary economic mischance. He must accordingly have faith in the political and social stability of the society in which he lives—or invests. If the state is in danger of overthrow or if external invasion threatens or if the head of state can seize his money for capricious reasons, then he is likely to keep his money at home in a strong box under the bed. Furthermore, there must also exist a means whereby investor and entrepreneur can be brought together. In the western world this means has been supplied by banks, brokerage houses, and stock exchanges, all of which are devices evolved over a long period of time for the easier circulation of capital. And, finally one other thing is also needed. Not only must speculative investors have a sense of confidence in their society, but they must be willing to forego immediate economic gains in the expectation of greater ones at some future time.

By the beginning of the 18th century most of these conditions existed in a number of western European states but particularly in England and Holland. To a large extent these conditions were the culmination of a process commonly described as the "commercial revolution" by which the capital wealth of Europeans had greatly increased from the 12th century onward. This "revolution" was the result of several causes. One was improvement in agricultural techniques coupled with the rise of towns (whose needs had prompted the rural areas to increase food production above the level of subsistence), which had helped to create productive surpluses in agriculture. Second, the growing power of the state, especially in the national monarchies, provided a stable social and political setting in which men could have confidence that their economic plans had a reasonable chance of coming to fruition. And, third, the development of improved business practices and organization as well as the growth of banks and stock exchanges had a twofold effect. On the one hand, an organizational innovation like the limited-liability joint-stock company, by sharing out the risk of loss among many stockholders, greatly reduced the danger of sudden bankruptcy and thus made a greater number of people more willing to participate in large-scale ventures. At the same time, the rise of banks and exchanges made it easier to mobilize large amounts of capital at lower rates of interest which, in turn, made possible the expansion of mercantile and industrial operations. So significant was this last development that some economic historians now believe it to have been almost as important a factor in causing the later industrial revolution as the invention of the steam engine.

In most European countries from the 18th century onward the decision as to how capital should be employed or invested was left to individual entrepreneurs. The state, particularly after the rise of *laissez-faire* economic theory in the 18th century, generally let capital flow freely into those activities where its owners could get the best return on it. The assumption behind this nonintervention policy was that of the classical school of political economy, of which Adam Smith was the first major exponent. The classical liberal argument was that men in pursuing their own ends, i.e., in their desire to get the biggest profits from their investments, would in the long run serve society by increasing its wealth and productivity. The difficulty with this point of view, as later social critics of 19th- and 20th-century capitalism pointed out, was that an individual's pursuit of profits did not always lead to the general well-being of society as a whole. A factory owner who had to worry about gaining a financial profit could not always take into consideration the economic welfare of his employees, particularly during the early days of the Industrial Revolution. Nor did financiers and investors always think in terms of improving the economic conditions of everyone. In answer to these charges, many 20th-century economists now point out that the process of capital investment during the early stages of any country's industrialization must always cost something in terms of human sacrifice. Even a state like the Soviet Union, which permits no freedom of investment choice to individuals and keeps the right to make all capital allocations completely under state control, must depress the living standards of its people until and if such time as the capital invested in various industries begins to pay off productively.

For all the seeming selfishness of their motives, the investment bankers and industrial entrepreneurs of western Europe over several generations did increase both capital wealth and production. Their success in so doing, it is now believed, was far more responsible than social legislation passed by the state for the growth of economic benefits and for the steady rise in European living standards throughout the 19th century. This point is rather complicated and needs to be made clearly. Those who feel that increased production was the significant element in European economic growth argue that if there had not been an enormous increase in goods and wealth no amount of state intervention for the purpose of distributing incomes or equalizing economic benefits would have done much good. Where the level of production is low a division of goods can lead only to a sharing out of poverty. Production has first to be raised to a point where social leglislation can make some meaningful adjustment of wealth. For that reason, at the present moment, many underdeveloped societies who publicly profess socialist policies have not been able to raise the living standards of their peoples very appreciably. They are learning the hard but elemental economic truth that production must always precede distribution and consumption.

Even so, many financiers and industrialists did not themselves always understand the process by which they had helped to create a greater abundance. Continuous capital growth is an economic chain reaction. Unless a certain proportion of profits is continually plowed back into industry for plant modernization, replacement, expansion, or (more recently) for research, a particular industry or even an entire society may find itself stagnating or outstripped in industrial competition by its rivals. For example, in their desire to maintain a high dividend rate (often as much as 10%), many British industries during the 19th century did not allocate a large enough share of receipts for replacement and modernization. Suddenly, about 1880, they discovered that industrial parvenus, like France, Germany, and the United States, were not only competing with them industrially but actually surpassing them, partly because French, German, and American industies were newer and more efficient.

As the 20th century advanced, however, men became more aware of the importance of capital growth for continued human well-being. Economists even attempted to calculate how much of its surplus an expanding economic system should reinvest in order to assure its continued growth. Not only did the profits of investors depend upon the proper redeployment of capital but so did the income and standard of living of everyone. Here another great question had to be answered. Should decision touching capital investment remain in the hands of individuals and private businesses or should it be taken over completely by the state? In Communist societies the state had won out completely. In most non-Communist societies the area of private control of capital was still a large one, though there were certain kinds of investments, e.g., the initial research and development of atomic energy or space travel, where the state alone seemed to have the capital resources necessary to undertake them. Moreover, there was a strong feeling in many western countries that complete state control would inhibit further economic growth and might, as in Communist lands, actually lower rather than raise the scale of living. This fear was by no means the result of prejudice. After all, those westerners who believed in a wide measure of economic freedom had one incontrovertible argument on their side. Up to this moment in history the Soviet Union and other Communist states, for all of their protestations of concern over the welfare of the masses, had yet to bring about a general standard of living that came close to equaling that of the West. In addition, there were those who saw in the state's complete control of all economic activity a totalitarian weapon more effectively powerful than any other in existence.

4. The Problem of Power: the Emergence of the Mass-Oriented State as the Political Form of Western Civilization

In many ways the problem of the state and its authority is the most difficult and permanent with which man has to deal. Despite the confident claims of liberalism, democracy, socialism, fascism, or communism, it seems doubtful that any perfect state, i.e., one that perfectly satisfies all of its citizens, will ever be created. As human circumstances alter, so too must the goals and functions of the state, with consequences that are seldom happy for all groups and conditions of men.

In a general way it may be said that the functions of the state depend upon two things: first, whether it exists to serve the welfare of the few or that of the many; and, second, whether it shall be controlled—even when it attempts to serve the interests of most of its citizens—by the few or by the many. For well over a century western man has tended to assume—though there is still some disagreement on the subject—that the state must serve the interests of all or of a majority of its citizens and that they, in the ultimate, must have a final control over its decisions. The matter cannot rest, however, upon these assumptions and practices of representative democracy, for they are not of themselves sufficient to solve the problems of the state. Even in democratic societies there must remain—and this fact becomes more evident as human problems grow more complex—a distinction between governors and governed, between those who actually run the state and make its decisions and those who only approve or disapprove of that which has been done or decided.

Moreover, the state has always been confronted with a seldom resolved dilemma. The act of governing frequently requires an expert knowledge beyond that usually possessed by ordinary men and a willingness on the part of rulers to make decisions that are necessary for the welfare of all but are extremely unpalatable to an important minority or sometimes even a majority of those who compose the political community. Implicit in this dilemma is the problem of power:

1. In whose interests is the power of the state exercised?
2. By whom is the power of the state exercised?
3. Are there limits, or no limits, to the power of the state? What limits, if there are any, are formed out of ethics? Out of expediency?

By the year 1700 this problem had been temporarily resolved in most western European states with the triumph of the highly centralized absolute monarchy over most other forms of government. England and Holland, however, were two important exceptions. In both of those countries political authority, though far from democratized, was not concentrated in the hands of a king or a royal bureaucracy but was more broadly diffused among the politically significant propertied groups represented in the legislative bodies of those two states. In spite of these exceptions, monarchy was the commonly accepted European form of government and would remain so for more than 200 years. Even in England, where the right of parliament to limit the king's powers in certain areas had been established by the "Glorious Revolution" of 1688, the king still wielded very broad powers and possessed an influence that made him a great deal more than a figurehead.

At this point it is well for us to remember an important historical fact about monarchical government. For centuries it was not only the most widely accepted but the most durable European method of rule. Now that it has almost disappeared we often tend to think of it as having always been arbitrary or unpopular and to assume that those who lived under it were only waiting for an opportune moment to revolt against its authority. Such a belief, while true to some degree of European political attitudes during the last few generations, is not valid as it applies to long periods of earlier history. For the fact is that monarchs and monarchy were not always unpopular. The strong monarchies that came into existence during the 15th and 16th centuries gave to many European societies a security and stability unknown during the middle ages. The king's law and the king's justice, though often imperfectly executed, still provided a greater measure of equality before the law than did feudal courts or customs. The kingly office, too, was a tangible symbol of national power and prestige to an extent seldom achieved by less glamorous elective parliaments or heads of state. But above all else the national monarchies of the early modern period established the practices and patterns of government organization that are still used in democratic states. Modern democracy has retained these while taking over the state and broadening its functions. The state itself, as an institution with clearly defined functions and obligations, was created long before.

Indeed, if we ponder the matter carefully, we can see that without the preparatory spadework of western European kings from the 15th through the 18th centuries, the modern mass-oriented state could never have come into existence at all. What these kings did over several centuries was to institutionalize their office until it became the vast public corporation we now know as the "state." The process by which they attained this end was often slow and twisted; and they themselves had no clear idea of the goal toward which they were working. If they had, they might have rejected it. In most instances, though they had a vague sense of public responsibility, European kings from the late middle ages onward strove toward immediate day-to-day objectives; that is, they were trying to expand their authority at the expense of church and nobles or to convert the uncertain irregular revenues that came to them as feudal overlords of the realm into the regular stipulated payments that we know as taxes. The best evidence of their success may be seen in the gradual transformation of the royal household into a kind of crude state bureaucracy or civil service. At first, most feudal kings were, in theory at least, simply the chief landlords of the realm, though, in practice, they were more or less than that depending on circumstances and the personal abilities of the individual ruler. As they began slowly to expand their powers they also necessarily expanded the functions of their personal servants who made up the royal household. Men who had been the king's personal retainers in time found their responsibilities and obligations enlarged as the king extended his authority over feudal society. As the obligations of his servants increased, the king created other offices and institutions to handle the greater volume of royal business. Inevitably, out of this pragmatic growth there developed a body of institutions with their own customs and procedures. Once this stage was reached—and it was attained at different times in different countries—the king no longer ruled his kingdom as a person but as a kind of corporate entity. He had become a symbol of the state.

Even as the national monarchy reached the height of its power during the 17th century, however, the very proliferation of its services and obligations created new and more complicated problems. With the growth of wealth and social mobility men were less willing to submit to the complete regulation by the state of all standards, beliefs, or social practices. And while many enjoyed the benefits conferred by a strong central authority, they looked upon it with some suspicion and not infrequently resisted its decrees. Furthermore, the property-owning classes often had a strong aversion to meeting the state's demands for the additional revenues needed to keep the state functioning properly. Here we must not forget that most kings did not themselves understand how to resolve this difficulty. Taxation as we know it had not yet come into existence, and most European monarchs even so late as the 17th century still had to depend on their own private estates for a substantial but often hopelessly inadequate part of the income needed to keep the machinery of government in working order. Nor was there anything like a modern funded or national debt which, by providing for regular repayment of loans made to the state, would have kept the state's credit clean. Most monarchs, therefore, lived a hand-to-mouth existence, always on the verge of bankruptcy and often without money for the most necessary purposes. In their struggle to keep solvent, western European kings were caught in a double squeeze. Not only had the costs of government risen as a result of expanded state functions, but they had also been driven upward by a long process of inflation known as the "price revolution" which had been going on since the 16th century. Lacking a modern system of finance, the state staggered from crisis to crisis until some adequate means was found to make up its deficits or, as with England in the 17th and France in the 18th century, the disaster of revolution overtook it.

Between 1700 and the middle of the 20th century most western governments were transformed in a fashion which was also unique to the western world. For the first time in history the state passed under the sway of mass influences and became an instrument of human welfare. Not that every western government became what we now call a "democracy," namely, a state where the ultimate political authority remained in the hands of a broad electorate possessed of complete freedom to choose its leaders. Some regimes of a totalitarian nature masked the rule of a powerful political elite behind a democratic façade by permitting only the supporters of one party or one political belief to hold office. Almost without exception, however, every western state—and many more besides—justified its existence on the grounds that it worked for the welfare of the masses and thus, by inference, had the support of its people. In this respect it mattered little whether a state was truly democratic or not. What did matter was the fact that most governments felt constrained to pay lip service at the very least to the ideal of mass democracy even when some of them denied it in practice.

The beginnings of the modern mass state reached far back into the European past, but the 18th century—and particularly the era of the French Revolution (1789-1799)—marked an important turn in its development. By that time the monarchs of western Europe had brought into being the modern state with its large professional bureaucracy and its many institutional forms. This new state was not created for the welfare of the masses. Nor did its existence depend directly upon the support of a mass electorate. The monarchs who brought it into being used it to serve their own ends, i.e., to increase their military and economic power. Nevertheless, as the ideas of the Enlightenment gained ground in 18th-century Europe, the theory of kingship began to change. Many monarchs—among whom were Frederick the Great, Catherine of Russia, Joseph II of Austria, and even Louis XVI—came to think of themselves as "enlightened despots" whose authority no longer derived simply from inheritance or divine right but from their effectiveness as rulers. No more was the king a mystical figure surrounded by divine authority but rather the "first servant of the state." Though the idea sounded perfectly reasonable and was very much in accord with the prevailing philosophy, it was actually a dangerous thing for kings to put forward. What it implied was that the monarch's rule was justified only so long as he governed effectively and well.

This shift in the political theory of kingship was accompanied by certain other changes in the intellectual climate of Europe that also boded ill for the future of absolute monarchy. Philosophers and social critics increasingly attacked the arbitrariness and inefficiency of many existing institutions. At the same time the spread of literacy and a growing consciousness of the possibility of material and moral improvement gave rise to discontent with things as they were, particularly among those classes and groups throughout Europe whose wealth and education made them aware of political and social problems as never before. Since these classes and groups were generally made up of business, professional, and literary people usually designated as the "middle classes," it has been customary to refer to the movement by which they made known their criticisms and their claims to political power as the "rise of the middle classes." This movement, however, was not simply a class movement. It was, rather, a kind of by-product of the Enlightenment, since many of the intellectual leaders of this movement thought of themselves as apologists not for a single class but for all of mankind. As they saw it, men were reasonable and rational. It followed, in their view, that each individual should be allowed freedom to follow the dictates of his reason. This view was the essence of the doctrine of "enlightened individualism" which became the basis of later liberalism.

On the assumption that man was a rational being who needed a wider measure of freedom, the philosophers of the Enlightenment went further and argued that this freedom included man's right to determine his own political and economic ends. He should be allowed freedom of speech and action (so long as these did not positively harm others), which meant freedom from the traditional restrictions of church and state. As a consequence, the state's power had to be curtailed: its sole function was to provide police protection and other essential services which would permit the widest exercise of individual freedom. It should be understood that these views did not necessarily imply the destruction of monarchy; nor did they call for the establishment of democracy. During the 18th century many *philo-*

sophes were willing to accept enlightened despotism so long as it expanded the sphere of individual freedom and reformed the institutions of society along efficient and rational lines. Above all, the state had to be truly and effectively impartial: merit and ability rather than birth or social status had to become the criteria by which the state conferred its honors and rewards. In brief, what the *philosophes* wanted was a social system in which those who possessed intelligence and ambition could rise freely in the social scale. A good education or wealth acquired as a result of one's own efforts was regarded as the best evidence of fitness for society's highest rewards. When these were not recognized by the state, the response was discontent among the middle classes.

Given this point of view, it is easy to see why enlightened individualism, and the liberalism into which it later evolved, came to be looked upon as a middle-class philosophy. Traditionally, the middle classes have been economically and socially ambitious. A philosophy of individual freedom which permits men to achieve the most to which their ability and education entitle them is, therefore, peculiarly suited to active and ambitious human beings.

In a society like that of 18th-century England, where the machinery of state was less cumbersome and enjoyed a greater measure of public confidence than in France and where the man of ambition and ability could hope to rise to the top of the social order, the pressure for reform did not become violently revolutionary. In France, on the other hand, the able and ambitious often found themselves cut off from the highest social rewards. When the resentment thus created came to be linked with the dissatisfaction of other social groups like the peasants, and when the crown failed to solve its financial problems, the result was revolution.

The significance of the French Revolution was that it made the continuation of unlimited monarchical authority virtually impossible in most European states from 1789 onward. During the 19th century the European masses ceased to identify their interests with those of centralized monarchy—which they thought of as an institution run for the benefit of a small privileged elite—and increasingly demanded a larger share in the making of government decisions. The leaders in this movement down to about 1850 were the liberal middle classes of western Europe, who strove to supplant the unchecked power of monarchy with some form of parliamentary constitutional government. Their aims were not extreme. They, like the earlier *philosophes*, did not necessarily wish to overturn monarchical government, though some of them, as in France for example, did become republicans. What they wanted was a representative parliamentary system and a franchise based upon property. Some few of them were willing to grant universal manhood suffrage, but they were a minority until the century was well advanced. In the main, most liberals desired a government that would allow wide economic and political freedom. They also wanted the state to be limited in power, economical in cost, and efficient in function.

In the long run the liberal drive for reform paved the way for mass democracy. Once European liberals had successfully won political concessions for themselves, it was difficult to withhold them from the great mass of human beings. In almost every western European country the political triumph of liberalism was, therefore, shortly followed (usually within a generation) by broad extensions of the franchise which transformed most of the traditional European monarchies into parliamentary democracies by 1914.

While the transition from centralized monarchy to parliamentary democracy was taking place, the political outlook of most Europeans and particularly that of the masses came under the influence of two important movements. The first of these was that process of industrialization which we have already noticed. The second was a movement which saw the state transformed into a social-welfare institution. Let us look at the effects of each in turn.

In its earliest stages the Industrial Revolution did not seem to confer any great benefits upon mankind. Human beings were crowded into the slums of great cities where they worked long hours under confining factory discipline. Furthermore, the mass of industrial workers depended upon their jobs for subsistence and these, in turn, depended upon the uncertainties of economic supply and demand. When periods of overproduction or underconsumption occurred, the working man found himself unemployed and often reduced to near starvation. Under these conditions it was extremely difficult for most workers to accumulate anything in the way of savings or to raise themselves in the social scale. For them the arguments of liberalism in favor of individual freedom and limited state power seemed meaningless. What good was freedom if it was in the end a freedom to starve?

As the 19th century advanced, however, two experiences occurred to alter this state of things. First of all, the working masses came to see in political democracy a possible means of alleviating their lot. If they could control the government, it might be possible to improve conditions by legislation. At the same time, their economic circumstances actually did begin to improve even without state intervention largely as a consequence of increased industrial production and the rise of real wages during the latter half of the 19th century.

The combination of this drive for democracy and the rising level of well-being had important historical effects. For one, it meant that the legislation for increased economic and social benefits, which resulted from the influence of mass democracy on the state, was assured of success because many industrial societies were now rich enough to afford the additional cost of such benefits. Here we must remember what has been said before, namely, that neither socialism nor social legislation which has as its purpose the equalization or redistribution of wealth can be successful unless there is a measure of wealth to be equalized or redistributed. In the 19th and 20th centuries, therefore, the success of democracy in forcing the state to act as instrument of social and economic welfare has been due mainly to the rising level of production and increasing capital wealth. The best illustration of this fact may be seen in the Soviet Union where, in spite of the state's avowed socialist goals, the standard of living has remained below that of most western countries because the U.S.S.R. has not yet produced enough goods to fulfill its promise of social abundance.

Another important effect of this combination of democracy and industrial wealth was to be seen in the changed attitude of the masses toward the state. In those societies where democracy was long established and worked effectively, the machinery of government came to be looked upon not as an instrument of repression or exploitation in the hands of the few but as a vast social-welfare apparatus in the service of the many. By the middle of the 20th century it was a commonplace of politics that the state —to the extent of its resources and capacities—was ultimately responsible for the economic and social well-being of the masses.

As the democratic state gradually evolved into the welfare state, western man was confronted with a new body of problems which few people had foreseen when the process of democratization began in the 19th century. The long historical augmentation of the state's powers and functions, which had begun under European kings in the late middle ages, was intensified and accelerated with the advent of democracy. Men expected more of the state and in order to meet their expectations the state had, of necessity, to expand its bureaucracy and increase its power. As these grew they complicated the problem of the state's relations with its citizens in new and strange ways.

The proliferation of state services called for the special skills and knowledge of the expert to deal with matters as diverse as public finance, old-age assistance, and atomic energy. Though the expert was a necessary part of modern state administration, his special knowledge tended to give him special powers that were almost unchallengeable. It was he who made many of the most important decisions of society, with effects that sometimes touched the lives of thousands or even millions of persons. Moreover, his combination of skill and authority often placed the expert beyond the control of the elected amateurs to whom he was legally responsible, for how could a legislator or an elected head of government (who might be a lawyer, business man, or professional politican) know enough about atomic energy, let us say, to control the work of an atomic physicist? And how could democracy function effectively in the future if its elected leadership had no choice but to defer to the rule of experts?

The other great unforeseen problem of the 20th-century state stemmed from its attempt to meet the economic and social expectations of its citizens. In the wealthier industrial societies of the West, men came to think of a steady increase in their level of well-being as a kind of birthright. So ingrained had this expectation become that, barring wars or natural disasters, it was generally assumed that each passing year must see a continuous improvement in the standard of living and a wider sharing in this standard by the masses. The assumption that such a process was not only probable but almost inevitable was, as we have seen, the basis of a great deal of political and social theory (socialism, for one example) and helps to account for the rise of the modern welfare state. Society was thought of as a kind of great economic machine which automatically produced an ever-growing abundance to satisfy the ever-growing desires of men. When, for one reason or another, it failed to do so, even briefly, there were many who saw in this failure not a natural or unavoidable limitation but only human selfishness or inefficiency. Men expected the state to protect them against such a contingency, and woe to the political leader or party in democratic societies whose term of office happened to coincide with a time of economic crisis or hardship. In totalitarian states this difficulty was met by repression and promises of something better in the future, but even there no one thought to deny the ultimate responsibility of the state to provide the highest possible living standards for its people.

With the rise of human economic expectations and the assumption that these could and should be met by the state, democratic societies faced a new kind of dilemma. At best, the distributive machinery of even the richest economic systems could not hope to supply *every* individual with all that he might expect as his just due. Furthermore, there was a danger that the state, in an effort to satisfy the ever-expanding economic demands of its citizens, might overstrain its natural and financial resources to the point of economic disaster. In areas like western Europe, where many industrial countries depended upon outside resources and markets over which their governments had no direct control, there was always the possibility, however remote, that the state—if confronted with a serious international economic crisis—might not be able to secure to its people their accustomed standard of living.

In the face of these possible contingencies there were those who asked whether democracy could possibly survive without continuous and massive economic expansion. Some pessimistic persons even went so far as to suggest that democracy was actually a political luxury which could be afforded only by the very richest societies. Whether these doubts were justified only time could tell. It seemed clear, however, that if western man was to preserve his democratic political tradition and his way of living he would have to recognize that there might at times be a gap between his expectations and the economic realities of life. He would also have to learn that the disparity between his wants and their fulfillment could be overcome only through increased human effort and the development of new knowledge and skills. In the past no civilization, however great its cultural achievements, had equaled the civilization of the West in providing the stimuli needed for the human mind to extend its conquest over the realm of nature. These stimuli, which were the result of centuries-long fusion of Judaic, Greek, Roman, and Christian traditions, still seemed to offer the best hope for democracy's survival—and humanity's.